THE LITERARY AND EDUCATIONAL EFFECTS

OF THE THOUGHT OF JOHN HENRY NEWMAN

Edited by

Michael Sundermeier

and

Robert Churchill

Roman Catholic Studies
Volume 7

The Edwin Mellen Press
Lewiston/Queenston/Lampeter

Library of Congress Cataloging-in-Publication Data

The literary and educational effects of the thought of John Henry
  Newman / edited by Michael Sundermeier and Robert Churchill.
      p.   cm. -- (Roman Catholic studies ; v. 7)
  Includes bibliographical references and index.
  ISBN 0-7734-8984-3
  1. Newman, John Henry, 1801-1890--Influence. 2. Education,
Higher--19th century. 3. Education, Higher--20th century.
I. Sundermeier, Michael W. II. Churchill, Robert. III. Series.
BX4705.N5L57 1995
282'.092--dc20   94-38965
                                                                CIP

This is volume 7 in the continuing series
Roman Catholic Studies
Volume 7 ISBN 0-7734-8984-3
RCS Series ISBN 0-88946-240-2

A CIP catalog record for this book is available from the British Library.

The Edwin Mellen Press   The Edwin Mellen Press
        Box 450   Box 67
   Lewiston, New York   Queenston, Ontario
   USA 14092-0450   CANADA L0S 1L0

               The Edwin Mellen Press, Ltd.
                 Lampeter, Dyfed, Wales
               UNITED KINGDOM SA48 7DY

           Printed in the United States of America

Contents

Introduction

"You must be above your knowledge . . . not under it, or it will oppress you; and the more you have of it the greater will be the load." This quotation from John Henry Newman, drawn from Harvey Kerpneck's essay, describes the collective intention of the authors of the following essays. Each, in its own way, attempts to engage Newman's work from the perspective afforded by our time in order to see how Newman's thought can help us understand the educational upheavals through which we presently move. Newman was reacting to a utilitarian view of education prevalent in his own time to which we are not entirely strangers today. On the one hand, state legislatures and those who think America's problems are rooted in her lack of economic competitiveness demand that universities be even more service oriented than they already are; on the other, accrediting agencies and various social and political interest groups compel those same universities to address each of *their* agendas, making the world a sweeter, better, more racially harmonious and gender-neutral place. As a consequence, the modern university is hard pressed to move above the current fray and examine what it is doing, especially when it is expected at the same time to be a place in which each group is represented by its own department, or at least program, charged with disseminating and aggressively defending against all comers a newly defined body of knowledge, and in which each such group ideally is ensconced in its own separate living, working, sleeping, and eating quarters.

1

Having participated in their own university's recent attempt to recast the curriculum, the editors realize the difficulty of achieving a comprehensive view of the proper order of things as department clashes with department and division with division, each hoping to see its dish placed more prominently on what Kerpneck calls the educational "smorgasbord." Even Newman, as is well known, was unable to execute his own plan in a satisfactory manner as the various interest groups, most prominently the Irish Catholic hierarchy, maneuvered to achieve their own, distinctly different purposes. Even when one is able to achieve apparent agreement on the broad principles which should underlie our educational efforts, all is not won. University College Dublin, the secular historical successor to Newman's Catholic University of Ireland (and to the intevening Jesuit-operated University College), may not be precisely what Newman had in mind. As modern American politicians are fond of saying, "the devil is in the details."

John Ford's essay deals with an aspect of Newman's thought likely to make many modern American academics exceedingly uncomfortable: the principle behind his attitude toward his students. It is a given in American education that universities are vendors of educational opportunities; that they are, in general, obligated to educate in as painless a manner as possible all who present themselves. Like the child-centered American family, the student-centered American university has become exceedingly indulgent of those entrusted to its care. Grade inflation, campus sit-ins, a vast proliferation of courses only distantly related to any legitimate educational endeavor, a staggering expansion of that aspect of University life known as "student services"—all are undoubted consequences of this presumption. Retention rates are monitored anxiously, and the ability to retain students until they have accumulated sufficient hours to collect a diploma is a principal measure of institutional success. Newman, however, regarded his task as a young tutor of Oriel College, Oxford, in a different light. He and several others of like mind determined, among other things, to get rid of the weaker students and to concentrate their efforts on those who worked hard and displayed the greatest potential. Then, as now, this attitude led to conflicts with less energetic and less gifted students and, most importantly, with the Administration in the person of the Provost of the college. This principle, that the University should concentrate its efforts on those most likely to profit from them, is roundly condemned today as "elitist," but nevertheless, was, as Ford observes, an element of Newman's "educational ideals," later expressed in *The Idea of a University*.

Among other things, Newman and his associates attempted to shape their students morally and spiritually. How they set about doing so is the subject of Clifford Stevens' article. Newman and the others realized that moral character cannot be taught in the same fashion as Latin, Greek, or history. Newman believed, rather, that it "is the result of personal association and influence; it is the conjunction of person with person, mind with mind, soul with soul." This, according to Stevens, resulted finally in Newman's extremely ambitious plans for the Catholic University of Ireland.

Frank Fennell addresses the question of just how much of Newman's thought *can* be tolerated by contemporary academe, and concludes that a great deal of it will no longer do: his "applied theology no longer has relevance"; his notion that teaching and research are two distinct functions is generally not accepted; and the utilitarians have carried the day regarding "the purpose of education and . . . the nature of educational institutions." However, he believes that Newman's "premises about universal truth and universal knowledge," while under strong attack, still carry "immense weight and suggestive power"; that Newman's belief that the task of the faculty is to sweeten and sanctify the lives of their students is still a goal worth pursuing; and that education is an exciting process with moral implications. In the modern university with its vast enrollments much of this affective work of education seems to have been ceded to the student-life director and the counseling center, in accordance with our penchant for specialization.

David Stephenson takes up the teaching vs research question. Stephenson interprets it as essentially an issue in the sciences rather than the humanities, and speculates that Newman's desire to keep scientific research at bay in the university was motivated by a desire to avoid the sort of clash between the scientific and religious viewpoints so common in 19th century intellectual circles. It was a desire, Stephenson contends, that flowed not from Newman's fear of objective truth, i.e., science, clashing with subjective truth, i.e., religion, but rather from Newman's "constructivist" thought, which, in line with 19th century psychology, held that "objective reality" has its origins in the "subjective reality" of the thinker. Consequently, Newman was a teacher rather than a researcher because his interest lay in "the student as learner instead of as a receptacle of objective knowledge."

Philip Rule in his essay also considers the "student as learner," particularly in reference to the notion of development, both personally and doctrinally, which played such a part in Newman's understanding both of himself and of religion. The unfolding of doctrine in religion is paralleled by the unfolding of understanding in the individual. While not concerned with teaching vs research, Rule too notes how Newman stressed the necessity of dealing with the "subjective reality" which exists within the student's mind, wherein the connections are made which give meaningful shape to the objective world without.

While Mary Ellen Jordan's essay does not address the question of education, it is included here because it offers a different perspective on the notion of development, one suggesting that Newman's development involved growth not only within the masculine paradigm but also included the acceptance of a feminine paradigm. It is significant for those interested in education in that it sets up an alternative to the masculine notion of development as a process of separation and individuation; that is, it invites one to consider the feminine model of making and maintaining affiliation and relationships. It is interesting to look at this as a gloss on Stephenson's notions regarding the cultivation of the "subjective reality" within the student's mind.

Julia Smith, like Stephenson, considers what Newman saw as the proper relationship between religion and science in the university and notes that Newman addresses the problem by requiring that each should "observe its proper limits." A necessary condition of science observing its proper limit is that theology occupy a share of the curriculum, for if it is not present, science will naturally flow into its place.

Newman, in drawing our attention to the means whereby our thought is shaped in the educational process, implicitly invites us to examine the ways in which his thought was shaped by those who came before him and the ways in which he shapes by means of his rhetoric the thoughts of his readers. One of the details of Newman's thought which interests Jude Nixon is the manner in which he was influenced by Romanticism. While it is customarily asserted that Newman is a Neoclassicist when it comes to moral and religious matters, Nixon argues that the Romanticism underpinning Newman's aesthetic attitudes and practices is not easily separated from his moral and religious thought. The powers of the mind are construed by Newman in Romantic terms, and the inspiration so central to a Romantic theory of knowledge is seen by Newman in orthodox Christian terms as divine in origin. Reason comes into play in the process of composition not as the sole source of knowledge but as a means of refining and controlling the product of a moment of inspiration—which Newman refers to as a "gestation and childbirth." The implications of such a perspective are obvious for those interested in the process of education.

John Britt discusses what he calls the "rhetoric of apologetic-autobiography" and its significance in Newman's lecture on "Literature" in *The Idea*. Here again we see a curricular consequence of Newman's interest in the process of learning as distinct from the material learned.

David Whalen addresses a rhetorical problem which is felt most acutely in literature, but which undermines our grasp of all the humanistic studies, from law to philosophy: the indeterminacy of language. Whalen asserts that Newman, while well aware of this difficulty, attributed it not to the nature of language itself but to the disintegration of man and the rest of reality; thus man's use of language is often "unreal." The proper response to the problem, therefore, is not despair or skepticism but a determined effort to reintegrate oneself with the rest of reality. This effort can be construed in many ways: it is both religious and a necessary part of the educational process—which once again points to the essentially subjective nature of university education as envisioned by Newman.

The connection between Whalen's observations regarding real and unreal language and Newman's discussion of notional and real assent is perhaps obvious. In any case, Joseph Wessling discusses how this insight of Newman's has affected the work of one of twentieth-century America's finest writers, Flannery O'Connor. This essay is a fitting close to the collection because it carries the ideas of the earlier essays to their logical conclusion: the effects that Newman's perception of reality and of the educational process are likely to have upon the receptive human being. That the happy result in one instance was a decisive shaping of Flannery O'Connor's thought suggests to the editors that the work of Newman indeed has importance for those of us engaged in education today.

Michael Sundermeier
Robert Churchill
Creighton University
Omaha, Nebraska

"A Smattering of a Hundred Things"

Harvey Kerpneck

In my copy of Newman's *Idea of a University*, many pages are separated from one another by identical small leaves from a notepad a student once gave me. The legend on each reads: "When all else fails, lower your standards." Accordingly, when I decided that I would talk to you about Newman's witty condemnation of the notion of smorgasbord education, as we have come to call it, I went at once to the University of Toronto Faculty of Arts Calendar for 1990-91, and specifically to the section devoted to English.

No such luck! We do not offer 100 courses in English—only 74. On the other hand, some of them are courses which *might* have raised a smile in Newman: English 236, Detective Fiction; English 214, The Short Story Collection; English 237, Science Fiction and Fantasy, etc. And then I realized that the cause was far from lost: not only does English offer 74 courses but our first year, introductory course, English 102, Introduction to English Studies, is really a loose, baggy monster (as Henry James called Trollope's fiction, unfairly). In 102 each of the 35 sections is taught according to each instructor's fancy; the Course Committee Chairman does not intervene to direct the selection or the arrangement of texts, there are few texts in common and the only requirement seems to be that all students taking the course should be able to pass the common examination the students sit in May—which of course makes that examination so amorphous and vague that even students who have *not* taken the course should be able to pass it. Success, then! We had passed Newman's test with flying—or should that be dragging?—colours. We not only *did*, in fact, offer "a smattering of a hundred things" (*Idea* 164), but we over-fulflled Newman's requirement by 14!

Perhaps I should remind you where my title comes from. Those leaves from the note pad are thickly clustered together in Discourse V, "Liberal Knowledge Viewed in Relation to Learning," and after he has reminded his audience of the foundation he laid in the previous discourse, that he believes that the university must educate "the intellect to reason well in all matters, to reach out towards truth, and to grasp it" (*Idea* 149), Newman goes on to talk at some length about knowledge and the new thirst in his age for knowledge. He remarks that many seem to believe that the university "is nothing more or less than a place for acquiring a great deal of knowledge on a great many subjects" (*Idea* 150-1). And he then states:

> As to that superficial acquaintance with chemistry and geology, and astronomy, and political economy, and modern history, and biography, and other branches of knowledge, which periodical literature and occasional lectures and scientific institutions diffuse through the community, I think it a graceful accomplishment, and a suitable, nay, in this day a necessary accomplishment, in the case of educated men. Nor, lastly, am I disparaging or discouraging the thorough acquisition of any one of these studies, or denying that, as far as it goes, such thorough acquisition is a real education of the mind. All I say is, call things by their real names, and do not confuse together ideas which are essentially different. A thorough knowledge of one science and a superficial acquaintance with many are not the same thing; a smattering of a hundred things or a memory for detail is

not a philosophical or comprehensive view. Recreations are not education; accomplishments are not education. Do not say the people must be educated,when after all you only mean amused, refreshed, soothed, put into good spirits and good humour, or kept from vicious excesses. You may as well call drawing and fencing education, as a general knowledge of botany or conchology. Stuffing birds or playing stringed instruments is an elegant pastime, and a resource to the idle, but it is not education; it does not form or cultivate the intellect. Education is a high word; it is the preparation for knowledge, and it is the imparting of knowledge in proportion to that preparation.

(Idea 164)

There is much here that could be misunderstood and I will try to clarify some of it as I go on. But I suspect that as I read that passage, some spines somewhere in this audience stiffened and some jaws tightened—which perhaps only *means* that not merely at Toronto have we in the university forged bravely ahead into the darkening gloom behind the great slogan I began by citing: "When all else fails, lower your standards."

In part Newman is returning in the passage I quoted to the theme he had explored in *The Tamworth Reading Room*, of February 1841, his series of letters to the *Times* about an address delivered by Sir Robert Peel at the opening of the Tamworth Reading Room. In that series of letters, Newman has many complaints about Sir Robert Peel's naive view of education but one of the most serious is that Peel sees education as an effort to stave off despair, to provide comfort in the face of the multifariousness of the world. For Peel, Newman complains, education seems in fact to have no higher object than to make one happy.

Education as Peel conceives of it, Newman complains, is an extension of Bentham's felicific calculus: if properly applied, it enables the pleasures in one's life to outweigh the pains!

Newman scoffs: "In all cases, *curiosity* is the means, *diversion* of the mind the highest end" (*ES* 188).

In fact, Newman deals with Bentham, the father of English Utilitarianism, at some length in the Tamworth Reading Room letters, and while he generally concedes the Peelite view of education to be superior to that of Benthamism, he coins a word "Broughamism" (referring to Lord Brougham) to signify that while Peel's views may be better than Bentham's, they are not much superior to those of Lord Brougham, who twenty years before had said more or less the same thing; if I could paraphrase it, the people need to be happy; make them happy through education.

Newman mocks that Peel:

> frankly offers us a philosophy of expedients: he shows us how to live by medicine. Digestive pills half an hour before dinner, and a posset at bedtime at the best; and at the worst,dram-drinking and opium,—the very remedy against broken hearts, or remorse of conscience, which is in request among the many.
>
> (*ES* 183).

Using the phrase in which George Eliot would two years later condemn empty fiction in her review "Silly novels by lady novelists," Newman summarizes his contempt for Peel's and Brougham's views as a belief in "intellectual . . . gin-palaces" (*ES* 183).

So when in *The Idea of a University* Newman scoffs at a smattering of a hundred things as (a) not having much to do with education and (b) positively counter-educational, he does so in the context of the earlier controversy with Sir Robert Peel and like-minded persons who seem to Newman to grossly undervalue education and to conceive of it in his word as a mere "diversion." In the words I quoted, for Newman "education is a high word" and it does not mean merely the elevation of one's spirit or an addition to one's happiness or the sort of refuge from the turmoil of life on the darkling plain which Matthew Arnold mocks in the final stanza of "Dover Beach."

But he is, on the other hand, very much concerned with the present condition of education, with the educational theories of the day, and that means that in part the spectre of Bentham which is raised in the Tamworth Reading Room is also a spectre which looms over Discourse V. We all remember Dickens's inimitable indictment of Benthamite, Utilitarian theories of education in the opening of what F.R. Leavis considers his greatest novel, *Hard Times*:

> "Now, what I want is, Facts. Teach these boys and girls nothing but Facts. Facts alone are wanted in life. Plant nothing else, and root out everything else. You can only form the minds of reasoning animals upon Facts: nothing else will ever be of any service to them. This is the principle on which I bring up my own children, and this is the principle on which I bring up these children. Stick to Facts, Sir!"
>
> The scene was a plain, bare, monotonous vault of a schoolroom, and the speaker's square forefinger emphasized his observations by underscoring every sentence with a line on the schoolmaster's sleeve. The emphasis was helped by the speaker's square wall of a forehead, which had his eyebrows for its base, while his eyes found commodious cellarage in two dark caves, overshadowed by the wall. The emphasis was helped by the speaker's mouth, which was wide, thin, and hard set. The emphasis was helped by the speaker's voice, which was inflexible, dry, and dictatorial. The emphasis was helped by the speaker's hair, which bristled on the skirts of his bald head, a plantation of firs to keep the wind from its shining surface, all covered with knobs, like the crust of a plum pie, as if the head had scarcely warehouse-room for the hard facts stored inside.

> The speaker's obstinate carriage, square coat, square legs, square shoulders,—nay, his very neckcloth, trained to take him by the throat with an unaccommodating grasp, like a stubborn fact, as it was,—all helped the emphasis.
>
> "In this life, we want nothing but Facts, Sir; nothing but Facts!"
>
> The speaker, and the schoolmaster, and the third grown person present, all backed a little, and swept with their eyes the inclined plane of little vessels then and there arranged in order, ready to have imperial gallons of facts poured into them until they were full to the brim.
>
> (7-8)

Hard Times, which appeared almost immediately after the publication of Newman's discourses, puts Newman's indictment of Benthamite views of education as well as even he could do. Dickens adds to the complaint that education is coming to be viewed as an application of the pleasure principle (or what, in jargon, some in our day would call "positive reinforcement") that the new theories regard those who are to be educated as empty vessels to be filled, or as Newman puts it in Discourse V as persons who can be made to "devour premiss and conclusion together with indiscriminate greediness, . . . hold sciences on faith, and commit demonstrations to memory." Newman scoffs that in practical terms this often means that they become "ill-used persons who are forced to load their minds with a score of subjects against an examination" (*Idea* 168). And he insists that even mere knowledge itself is "something more than a sort of passive reception of scraps and details" (*Idea* 167).

Couched in untechnical language though it is, and personal and idiosyncratic as it is, Newman's hostility to a smattering of a hundred different things being mistaken for education has its roots in contemporary educational controversy and thought and is part of a response which he makes jointly with others to what are coming to be the dominant philosophies of education. It has to do with his idea that the precious resource of education should not be diluted and with the opposing idea that when it is disseminated to large numbers, as it is coming to be, all that needs to be done is to transmit shows and faint shadows of knowledge. Newman's animus against a smattering of a hundred different things is not, then, a conservative animus at all but deeply connected with his idea of the importance in education of what he calls in the next Discourse "the formation of the citizen" (*Idea* 183). He objects to smatterings because they are based on false premises—like the premise that the end of education is diversion or happiness, a Benthamite or Peelite notion—because they view education as passive, but also because they do nothing to assist society—to quote Matthew Arnold again—"On to the bound of the waste / On to the City of God" ("Rugby Chapel," *Works* 292).

But this again is only part of the truth about Newman's objection to the smattering, or as we call it, smorgasbord, school of educational thought and practice. We are all familiar with Newman's many writings on Wisdom—his sermons on wisdom, his comments on wisdom in essays, his discussions of wisdom in *Loss and Gain*, etc. But we must recognize that one of the important relationships Discourse V and its animadversions against smatterings has is with the whole controversy (which transcended while including educational theory), about wisdom and knowledge that the age was also engaged in.

Matthew Arnold gives us the controversy from an educational aspect in Letter VI of *Friendship's Garland*, when he quotes his fictional middle-class manufacturer, Bottles, in praise of *his* teacher:

> Original man, Silverpump! fine mind! fine system! None of your antiquated rubbish—all practical work—latest discoveries in science—mind constantly kept excited—lots of

> interesting experiments—lights of all colours—fizz! fizz!
> bang! bang! That's what I call forming a man .
>   (71)

But Wisdom for Newman of course brings into any discussion ideas of the Church, of religion, of Revelation, of the Divine Nature itself. This is clear enough when, for example, he says of the Divine Nature in Sermon XI of *Sermons Preached on Various Occasions*: "He is an infinite law, as well as an infinite power, wisdom, and love" (185). Hence this aspect of his objections to smatterings is perhaps better represented than in the quotation from Arnold by the use to which Tennyson put the dispute between wisdom and knowledge in his great poem *In Memoriam*, which was of course published in 1850, or in other words, is not much further off on the one side of Newman's *Idea of a University* than Dickens's novel is on the other. *In Memoriam*, which is superficially a tribute to Tennyson's dead friend, Arthur Henry Hallam, is in fact a great meditation upon man and God, on "nature red in tooth and claw" (to excerpt one of the phrases from it that *everyone* knows), on the Faith that lives in honest doubt (to pick another well-known line) on a subject of great concern to Newman—the difference between proof and persuasiveness, on the disbelief of the age and a dozen other important contemporary topics (and *still* contemporary topics). It culminates, for *me* at least, in the great New Year's song, poem 106, one of the greatest of all great Victorian poems, in which Tennyson beseeches the symbolic New Year to bring about the necessary changes in the times. Here is part of poem 106:

> Ring out, wild bells, to the wild sky,
>   The flying cloud, the frosty light;
>   The year is dying in the night;
> Ring out, wild bells, and let him die.
> Ring out the old, ring in the new,

> Ring, happy bells, across the snow:
>   The year is going, let him go;
>   Ring out the false, ring in the true.
> Ring out the grief that saps the mind,
>   For those that here we see no more;
>   Ring out the feud of rich and poor,
> Ring in redress to all mankind.
> Ring out a slowly dying cause,
>   And ancient forms of party strife;
>   Ring in the nobler modes of life,
> With sweeter manners, purer laws.
> Ring out the want, the care, the sin,
>   The faithless coldness of the times;
>   Ring out, ring out my mournful rhymes,
> But ring the fuller minstrel in.
> Ring out false pride in place and blood,
>   The civic slander and the spite;
>   Ring in the love of truth and right,
> Ring in the common love of good.
> Ring out old shapes of full disease;
>   Ring out the narrowing lust of gold;
>   Ring out the thousand wars of old,
> Ring in the thousand years of peace.
> Ring in the valiant man and free,
>   The larger heart, the kindlier hand;
>   Ring out the darkness of the land,
> Ring in the Christ that is to be.
>   (958-9)

To yoke this firmly to my topic: in the introductory poem to *In Memoriam*, the invocation to "Strong Son of God, immortal Love," Tennyson prays:

> We have but faith: we cannot know,
>   For knowledge is of things we see;
>   And yet we trust it comes from thee,

> A beam in darkness: let it grow.
> Let knowledge grow from more to more,
>   But more of reverence in us dwell;
>   That mind and soul, according well,
> May make one music as before,
> But vaster. We are fools and slight;
>   We mock thee when we do not fear:
>   But help thy foolish ones to bear;
> Help thy vain worlds to bear thy light.
>   (863)

Here he contrasts Knowledge, which he insists is weak (more of that when I return to Newman again) with "reverence," and, very much in Newman's manner, opposes the present dissolution of things to his hope that society can regain its earlier condition, of "*one* music as before." In many other places in the poem the confrontation is more directly between Wisdom and Knowledge. For example, in poem 112 Tennyson takes up the question—if I can apply Newman's word—of how "high" our ideals need to be. Very much in Newman's manner he reprimands what Newman sometimes calls "false wisdom" for condemning his poems because they exalt the highest ideals, such an ideal as he associates with his dead friend Hallam and then, again very much in Newman's manner, he represents the consequence of high wisdom through evolutionary language:

> High wisdom holds my wisdom less,
>   That I, who gaze with temperate eyes
>   On glorious insufficiencies,
> Set light by narrower perfectness.
> But thou, that fillest all the room
>   Of all my love, art reason why
>   I seem to cast a careless eye
> On souls, the lesser lords of doom.
> For what wert thou? some novel power

> Sprang up for ever at a touch,
> And hope could never hope too much,
> In watching thee from hour to hour,
> Large elements in order brought,
> And tracts of calm from tempest made,
> And world-wide fluctuation sway'd
> In vassal tides that follow'd thought.
> (964-5)

After dealing in poem 113 with another false wisdom, the truism that "sorrow makes us wise," he presents in 114 a great culminating tribute to Hallam and at the same time develops fully the controversy between Knowledge and Wisdom in a very contemporary way:

> Who loves not Knowledge? Who shall rail
> Against her beauty? May she mix
> With men and prosper! Who shall fix
> Her pillars? Let her work prevail.
> But on her forehead sits a fire;
> She sets her forward countenance
> And leaps into the future chance,
> Submitting all things to desire.
> Half-grown as yet, a child, and vain—
> She cannot fight the fear of death.
> What is she, cut from love and faith,
> But some wild Pallas from the brain
> Of demons? Fiery-hot to burst
> All barriers in her onward race
> For power. Let her know her place;
> She is the second, not the first.
> A higher hand must make her mild,
> If all be not in vain, and guide
> Her footsteps moving side by side
> With Wisdom, like the younger child;
> For she is earthly of the mind,

> But Wisdom heavenly of the soul.
> O friend, who camest to thy goal
> So early, leaving me behind,
> I would the great world grew like thee,
> Who grewest not alone in power
> And knowledge, but by year and hour
> In reverence and in charity.
> (966)

My reason for quoting from this poem is that it offers such an excellent gloss to the whole controversy into which Newman enters in Discourse 5 when he asserts that an educated mind not merely knows but "thinks while it knows." Tennyson puts the controversy in a very Newmanian way in saying that one of the dangers of Knowledge is that she "leaps into the future chance"; Newman in Discourse V points out that one of the many advantages of true education, that education which is *not* a mere smattering, is that "it puts the mind above the influences of chance and necessity" (*Idea* 159). Tennyson asserts that mere Knowledge is impetuous, races ahead to possibly untenable conclusions; Newman puts this graphically in a metaphor that all travellers will immediately, (as the students say, "identify with"!):

> If we would improve the intellect, first of all we must ascend: we cannot gain real knowledge on a level; we must generalize, we must reduce to method, we must have a grasp of principles, and group and shape our acquisitions by them. It matters not whether our field of operation be wide or limited; in every case, to command it is to mount above it. Who has not felt the irritation of mind and impatience created by a deep, rich country, visited for the first time, with winding lanes, and high hedges, and green steeps, and tangled woods, and everything smiling indeed, but in a maze? The same feeling comes upon us in a strange city,

when we have no map of its streets. Hence you hear of
practised travellers, when they first come into a place,
mounting some high hill or church tower, by way of recon-
noitring its neighbourhood. In like manner you must be
above your knowledge, gentlemen, not under it, or it will
oppress you; and the more you have of it the greater will be
the load

(Idea 160-1).

In his final lines in the poem Tennyson, in an image of
Hallam perfecting himself in God, conveys poetically the idea of
Wisdom's effects; Newman describes them when he speaks of
what a smattering of a hundred things *cannot* confer on anyone:
"the clear, calm, accurate vision and comprehension of all things,
as far as the finite mind can embrace them, each in its place,
and with its own characteristics upon it" (*Idea* 160).

Here, by what Tennyson in another of his poems, *The
Princess*, calls "a strange diagonal," I have come to what my
students would *certainly* call the "positive" side of the case
Newman makes against the smattering school. For the most
part I have dealt with the negative: the Benthamite theory
underlying or supporting the smatterings ideas, the elitist view
of education implicit (and usually concealed deeply) in it, the
preference for passivity over activity, the idea of education as
quantitative, not qualitative, the idea of diverting the multitude
instead of training the mind, forming the citizen and empower-
ing the intellect. But there is another side to this discussion and
it is important too for Newman.

The smorgasbord theory is founded on the *preference* for
Knowledge. Newman has no quarrel with Knowledge, though he
refuses to equate it with Wisdom; he prefers "reason exercised
upon knowledge" (*Idea* 137), as he puts it in Discourse V, to
mere "acquirement." But he does recognize that "acquirement"
is necessary; it is simply that the smorgasbord theory knows

nothing of, or disdains, the idea of "reducing to order and meaning the *matter* of our acquirements." Still, he, acknowledges, "philosophy"—a code term he often uses to stand for the whole of education—"presupposes knowledge" (*Idea* 152). Knowledge is not wisdom: wisdom, for example, *connects* knowledge to "conduct and human life," whereas knowledge in itself is not "a state of the intellect" but "one of its circumstances . . . a possession" of it (*Idea* 150). Still, "It requires a great deal of reading, or a wide range of information, to warrant us in putting forth our opinions on any serious subject; and without such learning the most original mind may be able indeed to dazzle, to amuse, to refute, to perplex, but not to come to any useful result or any trustworthy conclusion" (*Idea* 152).

Carefully considered, knowledge is not negligible but essential, although it is only what Newman calls "the matter" of education. Without it education is impossible; yet if we place too high a premium on it—and, for example, in the way that Dickens mocks, exalt it as the be-all and end-all of learning—education becomes impossible.

With this balanced view of Knowledge as one of the positive poles of his case, Newman adds that the other pole is imperative or the world of learning—my metaphor—has no axis to move upon. The other positive pole, the *sine qua non*, is Order. I said when discussing Wisdom that we were all familiar with it from Newman's theological writings, where his stress on it arises directly from his perception of wisdom as an attribute of the Divine Nature. This is true of Order as well. For example, in that same sermon from which I quoted before, Newman asserts, "He is not a God of confusion, of discordance, of accidental, random, private courses in the execution of His will, but of determinate, regulated, prescribed action." He adds, "He is emphatically One; . . . it follows that order and harmony must be of His very essence" (*Sermons* 184). Later, he also adds, "The God of order has set up all creation upon unity, and therefore upon law" (*Sermons* 188). Later still, in contrasting the physical world with its Maker, he asserts, "But one attribute it has of God, without exception or defect, and that is the attribute of order" (188).

The concept of order is, then, like the concept of wisdom, central to Newman's whole vision of reality, of the nature of the world man is circumstanced in and in which he is to do his duty. It is for that reason that in Discourse V Newman stresses that a central inutility in smatterings or smorgasbords in education is that they *cannot* provide order. Wherever Newman looks he finds order since order is of the Divine Nature. Where order is absent it is to be desired. Where it is absent its absence can only be ascribed to what Newman calls human "fault and imperfection." Even the modern secularist and the modern scientist, Newman points out, have now simply "despised and abandoned" the view that there is no "evidence of the existence of any systematic plan" or order in the world, though they will not call it Divine.

So when Newman comes to make his counter-case against the smorgasbord theory, he points out that university education is merely a facade if it leads only to Knowledge and not to "enlargement and enlightenment" (*Idea* 153), two terms he uses as synonyms. He points out that education results only when the *matter* acquired is subjected to "the mind's energetic and simultaneous action upon and towards and among those new ideas which are rushing in upon it" (*Idea* 156). The result, according to a quotation I used before, is "order and meaning"—signifying that *without* order there can *be* no meaning.

A smattering of a hundred things cannot yield order; it can provide no means of deciding between or among the materials, the Knowledge, it purveys. It offers no principle of discrimination, no "symmetrical and consistent picture" (*Idea* 157) of the visible and invisible worlds. At one point, Newman uses another metaphor, that of "seafaring men." No matter how far they wander, as he argues, they are only passive attenders at a phantasmagoria of things. "Nothing has a drift or relation, nothing has a history or a promise." To the seaman, as Newman paints him, "one thing is much the same . . . as another, or, if he is perplexed, it is as not knowing what to say, whether it is right to admire, or to ridicule, or to disapprove, while conscious that some expression of opinion is expected of him" (*Idea* 157-8). Behind his seafaring men, it is hard not to hear the undiscerning gossip of the Senior Common Room, what we would call the Faculty Lounge, and, if we extend his metaphor further, of T.S. Eliot's 20th century room, in which "the women come and go / Talking of Michelangelo" (Eliot 3). Furthermore, as Newman adds, the mind lacking the ability to pursue Order through its Knowledge is really in what he calls a "deranged" condition; essentially, it resembles the mind of the madman:

> No one who has had experience of men of studious habits but must recognize the existence of a parallel phenomenon in the case of those who have over-stimulated the memory. In such persons reason acts almost as feebly and as impotently as in the madman; once fairly started on any subject whatever, they have no power of self-control; they passively endure the succession of impulses which are evolved out of the original exciting cause; they are passed on from one idea to another and go steadily forward, plodding along one line of thought in spite of the amplest concessions of the hearer, or wandering from it in endless digression in spite of his remonstrances
>
> (*Idea* 162).

But before closing, let me—to cite Eliot once again—remark that in my beginning is my ending. What we have now at Toronto, I suggested to you when I began, is probably a paradigm of what Newman condemns when he condemns smatterings, but it is *not* found at St. Michael's College, in *our*

English offerings but in the larger *University* English Department. Those familiar with his educational writings know how carefully Newman distinguishes between the strengths of the University and the virtues of the College—and in the College *we* have order. The larger Department offers 74 courses, of which one, English 102, is the sort of thing Newman calls a "babel"—35 courses pretending to be one, a snare to the feet and a trap to the unwary. At St. Michael's, when I set up the programme last year, I took care to see that we offered only the best 29 of these. Four are creative or other writing courses—at three separate levels. Three are introductory courses. Only one is the required motorbike tour through an art gallery—English 202, Major British Writers—but I could not avoid that. Four are year-length surveys of the different periods of English and Canadian and American literature. (Nearly *all* our courses are a year long.) Five are single-author special advanced courses in the 4th year—on Jonson, on Marlowe, on Herbert, on Hopkins, and my own course on Matthew Arnold. Most of the remainder are what used to be called at Toronto Honours courses: a year in length, dealing with single major figures, like Shakespeare, where this is warranted, or groups of major authors, like Dryden, Swift, Pope and Johnson, or highlights of a genre, like the course, English 324, in Victorian Fiction, or 328, Fiction 1900-1960, or 338, Modern Drama. I pride myself that we have Knowledge here but that *we* also have Order. And whatever may be true in the larger English Department beyond our walls, *we* are not "here as on a darkling plain / Where ignorant armies clash by night" ("Dover Beach," *Works* 212).

Works Cited

Arnold, Matthew. *The Poetical Works of Matthew Arnold.* Eds. C. B. Tinker and H. F. Lowry. London: Oxford UP, 1949.

—. *Friendship's Garland* in *The Complete Prose Works of Matthew Arnold.* Ed. R. H. Super. Ann Arbor: University of Michigan Press, 1965. 11 vols. (1960-77).

Dickens, Charles. *Hard Times.* Ed. George Ford and Sylvere Monod. 2nd ed. New York: Norton, 1990.

Eliot, T. S. *Collected Poems: 1909-1962.* New York: Harcourt Brace and World, 1970.

Newman, John Henry. *The Idea of a University.* Ed. George N. Shuster. New York: Doubleday, 1959.

—. "Order, The Witness and Instrument of Unity." Sermon XI *Sermons Preached on Various Occasions.* 6th edn. London: Burns and Oates, 1887. pp. 183-98.

—. "The Tamworth Reading Room." *Essays and Sketches.* Vol. 2. Ed. C. F. Harrold. New York: Longmans, 1948.

Tennyson, Alfred Lord. *The Poems of Tennyson.* Ed. Christopher Ricks. London: Longmans, Green, 1969.

Newman's View of Education: *The Oxford Background*

John T. Ford

Newman seems to have fallen in love with Oxford, from the day he "came into residence," Sunday, June 8, 1817, not quite four months after his sixteenth birthday (*LD* 1:34). Three days later, in a letter to his father, he described his experience of dining in hall:

> At dinner I was much entertained with the novelty of the thing. Fish, flesh and fowl, beautiful salmon, haunches of mutton, lamb etc and fine, very fine (to my taste) strong beer, served up on old pewter plates, and mis-shapen earthenware jugs. Tell Mama there are gooseberry, raspberry, and apricot pies.
>
> (*LD* 1:35)

His parents presumably could rest assured that he was well fed; whether he was also well-fitted in academic costume was a matter of opinion: Newman apparently felt that his academic gown was too long, though his tailor insisted that Newman "might grow etc etc" *LD* 1:34).

After describing this encounter with his tailor, Newman made a telling remark: "I then went HOME" (*LD* 1:34). Perhaps Newman's characterization of his lodgings at Trinity as "HOME"—in capital letters—was accidental; in any case, his

27

description of Trinity, almost a half-century later in his *Apologia Pro Vita Sua*, leaves little doubt of his enduring love for his "home" at Oxford: "There used to be much snap-dragon growing on the walls opposite my freshman's rooms there, and I had for years taken it as the emblem of my own perpetual residence even unto death in my University" (*Apo* 183).

However, after his "below the line" performance in his baccalaureate examinations, Newman's desire to remain a permanent resident of Oxford seemed crushed, only to be unexpectedly resurrected by his successful performance in the competition for an Oriel fellowship; in memorable terms intended for his future biographer, Newman insisted that he "never wished any thing better or higher than, in the words of the epitaph, 'to live and die a fellow of Oriel'" (*AW* 63).

Such was not to be the case; one of the most painful consequences of his entrance into the Roman Catholic Church was the inevitable separation not only from his former students and colleagues but also from his beloved Oxford; as the *Apologia* states succinctly and sorrowfully: "I left Oxford for good on Monday, February 23, 1846" (*Apo* 182). (This statement not only records Newman's sorrow at leaving Oxford after his admission into the Roman Catholic Church, but also hints at his anguish as a Roman Catholic in being prevented by his superiors from returning to Oxford to establish an Oratory there.) His long-desired return to Oxford did not come until thirty-two years later, when he was named an honorary fellow by Trinity College in 1878. The snap-dragon was gone. Alfred Plummer (1841-1926), a Fellow of Trinity, had previously written Newman that the building were he had lived as a freshman had been remodelled so that " . . . not only is there no snapdragon on the wall there, (perhaps the ivy has strangled it or driven it out,) but the point of view whence you saw it is gone . . ." (*LD* 25:107, n.2).

The ivy's strangulation or displacement of the snap-dragon seems symbolic. The snap-dragon might be taken to represent the values that prompted Newman's life-long love of learning: the achievement of intellectual excellence and a commitment to the highest moral ideals; the ivy might be considered to represent a utilitarian education: career preparation that is pragmatic in content and morally neutralist in orientation. Such a contrast was more than symbolic; it was at the heart of a dispute at Oriel College, when Newman was tutor and Edward Hawkins (1789-1882) the Provost.

AN EMBARRASSING EPISODE

Newman's tutorship is one of the least discussed episodes of his life; indeed, an account of his tutorship seems to have been deliberately by-passed in the *Apologia*. In treating the events of 1826, Newman mentioned in passing: "I became one of the tutors of my College" (*Apo* 26); then describing events a half-dozen years later, Newman tersely remarked: "At this time I was disengaged from College duties" (*Apo* 38)—a comment which even granted the British penchant for understatment is a remarkably oblique way of stating that he had been maneuvered into resigning as tutor.

The most revealing hint that one gets in the *Apologia* that something was amiss during his tutorship can be detected in Newman's description of the Provost of Oriel, Edward Hawkins:

> I can say with a full heart that I love him, and have never ceased to love him; and I thus preface what otherwise might sound rude, that in the course of the many years in which we were together afterwards, he provoked me very much from time to time, though I am perfectly certain that I have provoked him a great deal more.
>
> (*Apo* 19)

What was this provocation that Newman still recalled so gingerly even after a third of a century?

Some of Newman's biographers have seemingly displayed a "principle of reserve" in discussing the tutorship-dispute.[1]For example, Meriol Trevor, who on other occasions has eloquently dramatized incidents in Newman's life, has expressed some perplexity about this particular event: "In writing of these early battles, whether in the *Apologia* or in his memoir, Newman's tone is so detached, his criticism of his opponents so light and of himself so severe, that it is sometimes quite difficult to recapture the atmosphere of the actual situation" (T 1:83).

Like Trevor, other readers of Newman's "Autobiographical Memoir" which was written in 1874, not for publication, but for the use of his future biographer—can sense how deeply the incident still pained Newman, some four decades after the event. At length the cause of quarrel came, and, when it came, it was so mixed up with both academical and ecclesiastical differences between the two parties, differences which it would involve much time and trouble as well as pain to bring out intelligibly now, that a compromise was hopeless (AW 92).

For Newman, the pain was intense and long-lasting; as Louis Bouyer has perceptively observed: "Numerous subsequent allusions, very long after the event, make it abundantly clear that Newman could not get the affair out of his mind, and that it was always haunting his recollection" (B 91).

THE DISPUTE

In some respects, the tutorship-dispute was the most prosaic of conflicts: the scheduling of classes, the assigning of lecturers, and the advising of students. As Newman privately acknowledged: "It [the dispute] was immediately occasioned by a claim of the Tutors to use their own discretion in their mode of arranging their ordinary terminal Lecture Table . . . "(AW 92).

Superficially at least, the dispute was the type of problem which the registrar's computer in modern American universities might have resolved before it happened. However, as is the case in many academic controversies, the real issues were below the surface. The tutorship dispute was a conflict of personalities, of procedures, and of principles, all tightly woven together into a sort of seamless garment.

First of all there was a conflict of personalities, indeed a dispute between persons who had formerly been on the best of terms. As a senior colleague, Edward Hawkins had gone out of his way to help the talented but shy Newman, when he was first elected fellow of Oriel. As Newman later acknowledged in his *Apologia*, Hawkins had taught him to weigh his words and to be cautious in controversy; Hawkins even read and provided a critique of Newman's first sermons and other compositions (20).

A few years later, Newman had an opportunity to repay his mentor. When the Provost of Oriel, Edward Coppleston (1776-1849), was named Bishop of Llandaff, Newman supported the candidacy of Hawkins to be the new Provost. Prior to the election, Newman's closest friend among the Oriel fellows, Hurrell Froude (1803-36), tried unsuccessfully to persuade that John Keble (1792-1866) would be a better choice. Newman discounted Froude's efforts to get him to change his mind "with a laugh, that if an Angel's place was vacant, he should look toward Keble, but that they were only electing a Provost" (*AW* 91).[2]

Newman soon discovered that ignoring Froude's recomendation had been a mistake. "Newman, at the very moment of his friend Dr Hawkins's entering upon the Provostship, became conscious for the first time of his own congeniality of mind with Keble, of which neither Mr. Keble nor he had had hitherto any suspicion, and he understood at length how it was that Keble's friends felt so singular an enthusiasm for their Master" (*AW* 91). Ironically, Newman's belated discovery that Keble's "theory of the duties of a College towards its alumni" coincided substantially with his own (*AW* 91) paralleled an unexpected change in character in the new Provost.

> [Hawkins] when a member of the Common Room, had ever used the language of a Tribune of the people; he had been strongly on the side of Fellows and Tutors; . . . . Yet now, on the contrary, that he was Provost, he did not shrink from declaring that all was as it ought to be, . . . that no reform was called for.
>
> (*AW* 96-97)[3]

Such a change in character rankled Newman who felt: "Keble would not have so acted" (*AW* 97).

Much later, Newman privately admitted that the quarrel was unnecessary or at least avoidable:

> Yet it might have been averted or remedied, had that intimacy continued which had once existed between Dr. Hawkins and Mr. Newman; but by 1829 their relation towards each other had become very different from what it was in 1824, when the latter had been the unpretending and grateful disciple of the former.
>
> (*AW* 101)[4]

Apparently their differences in personality provided the raw material for a dispute. At a later date, even the usually mild-mannered John Keble felt it necessary to caution Newman about "going too fast, and with too little regard to the feelings and wants and state of information of persons in general"; Keble pointed out not only Newman's failings in communication but also "the keenness of your feelings—(for you know, my dear N. you are a very sensitive person—" (*LD* 6:348).

Newman's sensitivity seems to have collided with what he considered a stubborn streak in the Provost's personality: Hawkins "with admirable command of temper and composure of manner, refused to retire one hair's breadth from the position which he had taken up, with a stern obstinacy which made any accomodation impossible" (AW 102).

Personality differences aside, another ground for the dispute was their different intepretation of college procedures. On the one hand, Newman felt that it was within the tutors' province to schedule lectures and to advise each student. Indeed a more sagacious administrator might well have tolerated such a procedure: "It would seem to have been wiser in the Provost, had he let them [the tutors] have their swing, and make their experiment and experience the failure of the complications to which they had committed themselves . . . " (AW 104).

Not only did Hawkins miss a strategic opportunity; he seems to have seriously underestimated Newman's tenacity when principles were at stake: "But what irritated Newman most was his [Hawkins'] imputing Newman's conduct to irritation, and refusing or not being able to see that there was a grave principle in it earnestly held, and betraying a confident expectation that what was, he considered, mere temper in Newman, would soon pass away, and that he would eventually give in" (AW 103).

Yet whatever his short-sightedness, Hawkins had, as Maisie Ward has observed, "a case for being on his side aggravated by his high-minded young colleagues!" (W 181). In fact—and hardly to their credit—Newman and the other tutors did not inform the Provost about the "new system" that they had put into operation; rather, "they determined then to let the matter take its course, and to leave the Provost to object, if he wished" (AW 100).

If such was really their reasoning, they should not have been surprised when Hawkins later objected to their actions. Or

perhaps, as Meriol Trevor has suggested, the tutors really hoped
to present the Provost with a *fait accompli*:

> Newman feared Hawkins would not approve it [the tutors'
> plan] and did not discuss it with him. He thought if the
> scheme was put into operation and the result turned out
> well, the Provost might accept it—he had the opportunity of
> judging the results as it was he who conducted the terminal
> examinations.
>
> (T 1: 84)

Whatever their rationale, the fact remains that the tutors did
not inform Hawkins of the changes they had made; Hawkins
was understandably angry when he discovered what his
subordinates were doing behind his back. Moreover, as Marvin
O'Connell has pointed out, Hawkins had good grounds for
complaint; if tutors like Newman, Hurrell Froude and Robert
Isaac Wilberforce were both talented and dedicated, "Newman's
system depended upon the ability of the tutors" (O'C 115).

In addition, as Thomas Mozley (1806-93), Newman's
brother-in-law, later observed, the Provost could hardly have
helped feeling that "the tutors would thereby have the tuition
entirely in their own hands, and that he might find himself left
out of the actual course of studies and out of the current of
college thought and feeling" (M 1:230). And finally, as Newman
later acknowledged, it seemed to Hawkins that the new system
"was sacrificing the many to the few, and governing, not by
intelligible rules and their impartial application, but by a
system, if it was so to be called, of mere personal influence and
favoritism" (*AW* 92). Perhaps what Hawkins feared even more
than the problems potentially arising from the new procedures
was Newman's growing personal influence, not only at Oriel and
Oxford but beyond.

The third dimension of the debate was a conflict between two different sets of principles, one administrative and academic, the other pastoral and pedagogical. Thomas Mozley thought that there was something to be said for each side; on the one hand, "it cannot be denied that the Provost seemed to be justified by the event in not virtually resigning the education of his college into Newman's hands;" on the other hand, Newman, Froude, and Wilberforce, "the three tutors had both right and the public interest on their side" (M 1:233).

For Newman, "the quarrel between the two parties was based on principle, and rested . . . on theological differences, as to which neither party was likely to surrender its own view, but rather to be more firmly rooted in it, as time went on" (AW 98). In any case, the tutorship-dispute was hardly Newman's finest hour; as Marvin O'Connell has commented, "the quarrel demonstrated how tough and unyielding he could be on what he considered a matter of principle; 'flinty' was the word Frederic Rogers used to describe this quality" (O'C 116).

Yet if Newman would not, indeed could not, concede a matter of principle, he soon came to repent of the manner in which he had defended that principle; he recalled reflecting during his sickness in Sicily in 1833: ". . . I was lying there the very day on which three years before I had sent in my resignation of the Tutorship (or something like it) and, though I could (and do not) at all repent doing so, yet I began to understand that the *manner* was hasty and impatient" (AW 118).[5]

Such reflections eventually led Newman to admit that he "might have acted more generously towards a man to whom he owed much . . ." (AW 101).[6] Such memories came to the fore at the time of Hawkins' death in 1882, when Newman wrote his widow:

> Your dear husband has never been out my mind of late years. . . . These standing reminders of him personally

sprang out of the kindness and benefits done to me by him
close upon sixty years ago, when he was Vicar of St Mary's
and I held my first at St. Clement's.

(*LD* 30:152-53)

THE PRINCIPLES AT STAKE

With his two appointments—in 1826 as a Tutor of Oriel
College and two years later as Vicar of St. Mary's—Newman,
though still in his twenties, had acquired positions of influence
and prominence. However, rather than regarding these positions as "stepping stones" to even more prestigious placements
in the Church of England, he considered these positions "permanent appointments"; as he later reflected:

> He did not look beyond them [these two positions]. He
> desired nothing better than such a lifelong residence at
> Oxford, nothing higher than such an influential position,
> as these two gave him.
>
> (*AW* 86)

For Newman, these two positions, one academic the other
pastoral, were not incompatible. Cognizant of the "standing
difference of opinion among religious men of that day, whether
a College Tutorship was or was not an engagement compatible
with the Ordination Vow" (*AW* 87), Newman opted for a "view
of the substantially religious nature of a College Tutorship" (*AW*
88). Indeed, Newman came to this conclusion during his first
month of "being engaged in the Oriel Tuition":

> I think the Tutors see too little of the men, and that there is
> not enough of direct religious instruction. It is my wish to
> consider myself as the minister of Christ. May I most
> seriously reflect, that, *unless*, I find that opportunities occur

of doing spiritual good to those over whom I am placed, it will become a grave question whether I *ought* to continue in the Tuition.

(AW 209)[7]

Newman justified his acceptance of a tutorship by recalling "that in the Laudian statutes for Oxford a Tutor was not a mere academical Policeman, or Constable, but a moral and religious guardian of the youths committed to him" (*AW* 91). The University Statutes described the tutor as "a man regarded for his uprightness and erudition" who "would instruct the students entrusted to his guardianship in good morals, and teach them from approved authors, especially in the basic articles of religion and doctrine."[8]

As Newman interpreted them, the University Statutes meant that a tutor "was not a Lecturer to a mixed multitude of Undergraduates, with whom he had no definite relations, but as the Latin word implies, a guardian of certain given pupils or wards" (*AW* 106). Thus, for Newman, "the office of a tutor was itself sacred—that it should involve not merely supervision of the studies of his pupils but also a true pastoral office towards them" (W 112).

To exercise such a guardianship, a tutor obviously needed considerable authority; in Newman's judgment, that was not only what was intended by the statutes but what was customary at Oxford: "When I look round at Other Colleges, I found the Tutors possessed of an almost unlimited discretion, a discretionary power committed (allowed) to them by the Head of their House, when he appointed them to their situation" (*AW* 100). Consequently, Newman concluded that "the tutorship, as far as the College was concerned, was a substantive, self-dependent office; . . . it necessarily involved a discretionary action and a personal responsibility; . . . " (*AW* 106).

This view of the tutorship was the source of contention between Newman and Hawkins. Newman considered the tutorship as a pastoral office, and demanded the discretionary latitude necessary to fulfill this religious responsibility. On the other hand, "Hawkins tended to see religious education as moral training, and he was afraid that a tutor who considered himself a pastor might think it his right to impose Evangelical or Anglo-Catholic views upon his students" (O'C 114-5).

In effect, Newman's pastoral interpretation of the tutorship set the stage for a conflict between principle and practice: "the principle was the question of whether a special pastoral relationship existed between a tutor and his own pupils"; the practical consequences—"whether it was lawful for tutors to concentrate on the ablest men" and the "question of the arrangement of time-tables"—were the areas of practical policy where the battle with Hawkins was actually fought (W 179).[9]

THE PROVOST'S PYRRHIC VICTORY

In fact, Newman initiated the first round of changes while Coppleston was still Provost. On the one hand, these changes occasioned a certain amount of objection; on the other hand, a lack of support from the Provost. With the election of Hawkins as Provost, Newman had another chance to push his planned reforms. In brief, his strategy was to give attention to the more promising students.

> With such youths [those pupils who "wished to work for academical honours"] he cultivated relations, not only of intimacy, but of friendship, and almost of equality, putting off, as much as might be, the martinet manner then in fashion with College tutors, and seeking their society in outdoor exercise, on evenings, and in Vacation.
>
> (AW 90)

Apparently during the first year after Hawkins's election, the new tutorial system worked satisfactorily; in a letter to Samuel Rickards (1796-1865), a former Fellow of Oriel, Newman described the achievements under the new plan:

> We have gone through the year famously, packed off our lumber, parted with spoilt goods, washed and darned where we could, and imported several new articles of approved quality. Indeed the College is so altered that you would hardly know it again.—The tangible improvements of system have been, first the diminishing the Gentlemen Commoners from 20 to 8 or 9—Then the dismissal of the Incurables—Then the rejecting unprepared candidates for admission—the number is awful, some twice. Then the giving chance vacancies to well-recommended and picked men . . . The most important and far reaching improvement has been commenced this term:—a radical alteration (*not apparent* on the published list), of the lecture system. The bad men are thrown into large classes—and thus time saved for the better sort who are put into very small lectures, and principally with their own Tutors quite familiarly and chattingly. And, besides, a regular lecture system *for the year* has been devised. But we do not wish this to be talked about.
>
> (*LD* 2:117-8)[10]

In spite of Newman's desire that the new tutorial system not be discussed, Hawkins learned of it, and, according to Meriol Trevor, "refused to see anything in Newman's system but 'favouritism'—he was making favourites of his clever pupils at the expense of the others. Hawkins himself was inclined to favour the gentlemen commoners, who were not usually candidates for academic honours" (T 1:85).

As Provost, Hawkins, of course, had to think of the welfare of all of the College's students. Perhaps, he was also thinking

of the College's income, since the parents of gentlemen commoners were also likely benefactors. In any case, the Provost had
the administrative advantage; he settled the dispute by not
assigning Newman and two of the other tutors any more
students; Newman reported this decision in a letter to his
mother on June 18, 1830:

> It is at length settled that the Provost gives us no more
> pupils—us three (Wilberforce, Froude and me)—and we die
> off gradually with our existing pupils. This to me personally
> is a delightful arrangement—it will materially lessen my
> labours, and at length reduce them within bearable limits,
> without at once depriving me of resources which I could not
> but reckon upon, while they lasted. But for the College, I
> think it a miserable determination.
>
> (*LD* 2:244)

For Hawkins, the immediate advantage was that he was rid
of three troublesome tutors and their controversial system. The
immediate problem was that he had to make special arrange-
ments for a substitute tutor. Such arrangments did not prove to
be beneficial at least as measured by success in the baccalaureate examinations; the number of Oriel students gaining first
class honors soon dropped.[11] Hawkins' victory was pyrrhic.

Newman as Tutor

On May 7, 1826, four weeks after Newman became "engaged
in the Oriel tuition," he recorded his initial impression of the
students:

> The College is filled principally with men of family, in many
> cases of fortune. I fear there exists very considerable profli-
> gacy among them. There is much too in the system which
> I think wrong.

(*AW* 209/*LD* 1: 286, n.4).

Newman was not one to let profligacy go unchallenged; he "began by setting himself fiercely against the Gentlemen-Commoners, young men of birth, wealth or prospects, whom he considered (of course, with real exceptions) to be the scandal and the ruin of the place" (*AW* 89).

Nearly six decades later, on October 24, 1884, Newman vividly desribed the situation in a letter to the editor of the *Daily News*:

> The truth is, that when I came into office, the discipline was in a very lax state, and I, like a new broom, began sweeping very vigorously, as far as my opportunities went. This aroused the indignation of certain high and mighty youths, who, relying on the claims of family and fortune, did their best to oppose me and to spread tales about me.
>
> (*LD* 30:423)

Half a century later, one of these "high and mighty youths," apparently still prone to tale-telling, recalled his former tutor's efforts at reform. James Howard Harris (1807-1889), who bore the title Lord FitzHarris while a student at Oriel and who later became the third Earl of Malmesbury, in his *Memoirs* published the following portrait of Newman as tutor:

> He used to allow his class to torment him with the most helpless resignation; every kind of mischievous trick was, to our shame, played upon him—such as cutting his bell-rope, and at lectures making the table advance gradually till he was jammed into a corner. He remained quite impassive and painfully tolerant.
>
> (*LD* 30: 409, n.3)

After Newman publicly challenged Malmesbury's account in a letter to the *Daily News* (*LD* 30: 422-423), it was discovered that Malmesbury's recollections really concerned incidents involving, not Newman, but another tutor.[12]

Fortunately for Newman's reputation, other students retained more pleasant memories of their former tutor. Frederic Rogers (1811-1889), who became Baron Blachford in 1871, recalled:

> I went up to Oriel in October, 1828 . . . and I then attended Mr. Newman's lectures for three years. . . . He was very kind and retiring, but perfectly determined (as might be expected from his subsequent history)—a tutor with whom men did not venture to take a liberty, and who was master of a formidable and speaking silence calculated to quell any ordinary impertinence.
>
> (*LD* 30: 410, n.1)

SNAP-DRAGON VERSUS IVY

Like many teachers bent on reforming an educational system, Newman experienced a serious refusal of support from "the high authorities of the college" (*LD* 30:423). Over-esteeming his position and under-estimating the power of the Provost, Newman found himself ousted from his tutorship by an administrative end-play.

And like many teachers who demand hard work of their students, Newman found that his pedagogical efforts met with mixed response. Some students not only opposed him, but used their families' influence to remove him. Others appreciated Newman's personal concern; for example, in a personal letter, Thomas Mozley wrote: "My new tutor has been very attentive and obliging, and has given me abundance of good advice" (W 112). This mix of opposition and appreciation indicates how influential a teacher he was—how many teachers find their students still arguing about their effectiveness a good half-century after they have left their position?

Such a reputation was presumably the reason why Newman was invited to head the Catholic University in Dublin. For Newman, the rectorship of the Catholic University provided a sort of second chance to realize his pedagogical ideals. What Newman did not foresee was the fact that his effort to implement those ideals would once again be thwarted by the very people who had prevailed upon him to accept the rectorship in the first place.

Nonetheless, his Irish rectorship gave him the "especial call" that he needed to memorialize his educational ideals in *The Idea of a University* (*AW* 272). Thus, long after his rectorial battles ended, his voice is still fighting for his ideal of a university education that combines academic excellence and personal religious commitment.

The irony of the tutorship dispute is that Newman probably would not have had time for such reflections, nor for many other contributions, had he continued in the time-consuming task of tutoring undergraduates. The Provost's triumph had a long-range effect that neither party could have predicted at the time; it was only much later that Newman realized that his ousting from the tutorship had been a blessing in disguise:

> In the year after his relinquishing his College office, on his return from abroad, the Tract Movement began. Humanly speaking, that movement never would have been, had he not been deprived of his Tutorship; or had Keble, not Hawkins, been Provost.
>
> (*AW* 96)

Endnotes

1. For the use of this expression in a quite different context, see Robin Selby, *The Principle of Reserve in the Writings of John Henry Cardinal Newman* (Oxford University Press, 1975). A clear account of the tutorial dispute is given by Ian Ker (K 37-41).

2. Newman made similar statements over a half century later in his correspondence with both Lord Blachford (4 November 1884, in *LD* 30:431-433) and Pusey (29 June, 1882, in *LD* 30:106-107) to whom Newman acknowledged: "I certainly was sorry I had helped in electing Hawkins" (107).

3. As Louis Bouyer has pointedly observed, "it is . . . by no means uncommon in colleges and similar communities for men to vote a colleague into a position of authority in the belief that they will be able to count on his good offices to help them bring about certain reforms which they have at heart, and then to find him, when well in the saddle, exhibiting a narrow-minded conservatism as uncompromising as unexpected" (B 91).

4. Newman mentioned 1829, the year of Peel's re-election, as the date of the formal break between Dr. Whately and me" (*Apo* 24); Newman's opposition to Peel apparently occasioned a break with Hawkins as well.

5. In another assessment in his autobiographical memoire, Newman stated: "I thought I had been very self willed about the Tutorship affair — and now I viewed my whole course as one of presumption" (AW 125).

6. Louis Bouyer has commented: "He always maintained that his position was in principle, a perfectly sound one, but, as the years went on, he blamed himself more and more for the attitude which he had taken up. It was Hawkins, after all, who had brought him out, Hawkins who had given him post as tutor and finally, it was Hawkins who had appointed him to St. Mary's in succession to himself. When he came to look back on these things, it seemed to him that his response to all these benefits had been singularly thankless" (B 93).

7. Italics in original; reprinted in LD 1: 286-287, n. 4 (May 7, 1826). Newman later added a note indicating that this statement "illustrates my view in dispute with the Provost (Hawkins) about the Tutorship" (AW 209).

8. According to the Statutes [the tutor] was intended to be a "vir probitate et eruditione perspecta, religione sincerus", who "scholares tutelae suae commissos probis moribus instruat, et in probatis authoribus instituat, et maxime in rudimentis religionis et doctrinae articulis" (AW 106).

9. In effect, "Newman's plan . . . called for a reassessment of the tutor's position within the college and a new emphasis upon his post as a religious and personal responsibility. Instead of a tutor's merely lecturing a few times a week on certain classical texts to a group of college undergraduates—the customary practice—he should take upon himself the obligation of the direct religious training of the undergraduates assigned to him, and, at the same time, see to their secular instruction in a detailed and personal way" (O'C 114).

10. 6 February, 1829; however, the University Calendar for 1829, 'corrected to December 31, 1828', names sixteen Gentlemen Commoners at Oriel" (*LD* 2:117, n.5).

11. Newman recorded the following statistics on students gaining first class honors at Oriel (*AW* 107):

    1825-29:   2 Firsts
    1829-33: 11 Firsts [when the new system was in effect]
    1833-37:   5 Firsts [when old system was partially restored]

12. Malmesbury retreated in the face of such evidence and subsequently offered an apology of sorts to Newman (29 October 1884, *LD* 30: 427, n. 2), who accepted it "without insisting upon questions of fact" (3 November 1884, *LD* 30: 430-431).

WORKS CITED

Bouyer, Louis. *Cardinal Newman: His Life and Spirituality.* New York: P. Kenedy, 1958. (B)

Ker, Ian. *John Henry Newman: A Biography.* Oxford: Clarendon Press, 1988. (K)

Mozley, T. *Reminiscences, Chiefly of Oriel college and the Oxford Movement.* London: Longmans, Green and Co., 1882. 2 vol. (M)

Newman, John Henry. *Apologia Pro Vita Sua.* Ed. David J. DeLaura. New York: W. W. Norton, 1968.

—. *Autobiographical Writings.* Ed. with intro. Henry Tristram. New York: Sheed and Ward, 1957.

—. *The Letters and Diaries of John Henry Newman.*

Volume 1, *Ealing, Trinity, Oriel, February 1801 to December 1826.* Ed. Ian Ker and Thomas Gornall. Oxford: Clarendon Press, 1978.

Volume 2, *Tutor of Oriel, January 1827 to December 1831.* Ed. Ian Ker and Thomas Gornall. Oxford: Clarendon Press, 1979.

Volume 6, *The Via Media and Froude's Remains, January 1837 to December 1838.* Ed. Gerard Tracey. Oxford: Clarendon Press, 1984.

Volume 25, *The Vatican Council, January 1870 to December 1871.* Ed. Charles Stephen Dessain and Thomas Gornall. Oxford: Clarendon Press, 1973.

Volume 30, *A Cardinal's Apostolate, October 1881 to December 1884.* Ed.Charles Stephen Dessain and Thomas Gornall. Oxford: Clarendon Press, 1976.

O'Connell, Marvin. *The Oxford Conspirators: A History of the Oxford Movement, 1833-1845.* Macmillan; London: Collier-Macmillan, 1969. (O'C)

Trevor, Meriol. *Newman, The Pillar of the Cloud.* Garden City, New York: Doubleday, 1962. (T)

Ward, Maisie. *Young Mr. Newman.* New York: Sheed & Ward, 1948. (W)

Moral Education in the Thought of John Henry Newman

Clifford Stevens

John Henry Newman was deeply influenced by Greek Patristic thought, particularly the pedagogical genius of St. Basil of Caesarea, St. Gregory Nazianzus and St. Gregory of Nyssa. It is not often realized that the spiritual genius of these towers of early Christian thought was not divorced from life, but was aimed at the formation of the *anima Christiana*, ὁ Χριστομαθής—a human person who is Χριστοδίδακτος, Χριστοειδῶς, Χριστοφιλής, Χριστόφρων, Χριστοφόρος, taught by Christ, after the likeness of Christ, Christ-loving, Christ-minded, Christ-bearing. Patristic literature is filled with expressions of this kind, inculcating and articulating a unique kind of pedagogy: uniquely Greek, eminently Christian, profoundly human, the final goal of a Christian *paideia*[1], shot through with the brilliant insights into the human psyche that were the backbone of Greek classical thought (Cf. Jaeger, *Paedeia* and *Early Christianity* ch 7).

This body of Christian literature, amazing in its scope, astonishing in its depth, the high point of a Christian culture unparalleled in twenty centuries of Christian history, fell into Newman's hands during his years as a tutor of Oriel. In 1827, his friend, Pusey, while on a visit to the Continent, obtained for him beautiful bound volumes of the Fathers in Greek and Latin. Between 1827 and 1831, he amassed a total of thirty-six volumes, in handsome bindings, including a St. Athanasius

49

which had once belonged to Bossuet. In October of 1827, he wrote to his mother: "My Fathers are arrived all safe—huge fellows they are, but very cheap—one folio costs a shilling!" (Bouyer 112). In his *Autobiographical Memoir*, speaking of himself in the third person, he says: "As to the Fathers themselves, much more did he ever delight . . . to find himself brought into their company" (Bouyer 113[2]).

It is incorrect to speak of *moral education* in the thought of John Henry Newman, because the concept of *paideia* goes much deeper and broader than that. *Paideia* is the total development of the human person: body, mind, heart, will, senses, passions, judgments, instincts, aimed at what the Greeks called *arete*, excellence in living. It is this concept, with all its Christian implications, that the young John Henry Newman drew from the Fathers, and it is this concept that runs through his writings like a thread of gold from the first sermons that he preached from the pulpit of St. Mary's at Oxford, which made him the sensation of the university when he was scarcely thirty years old, to the mature lectures that constitute the *Idea of a University*. It is significant that one of the major achievements of his life was the founding of the Catholic University of Ireland, and that the one great desire of his heart which was never accomplished was to return as a Catholic to Oxford, to carry on his mission of *pedagogue* as he understood it.

The first conviction that rings out of Newman's many writings on the subject of education is that morality, moral character, what the Greeks called *sophrosyne*, cannot be taught. It is the result of personal association and influence; it is the conjunction of person with person, mind with mind, soul with soul. It was in his work at Oriel that he began to realize the power of personal influence and the specific role that the tutor fulfilled in the university system.

Later, when he founded the Catholic University of Ireland, he saw in his role of rector a broadening of the tutor's role, and his influence upon the first students of the university was massive. *Pedagogy*, in the classical Greek sense of fashioning the total personality of the student, was his unique gift, and his university sketches, published in the *University Gazette* in 1854 and 1855, were his exploration of the subject. These sketches became, in fact, the charter of the university he founded and contain some of his best thinking on the subject. The purpose of moral education is *moral character*, a firm disposition for the good, for moral excellence, for all that is noblest and best in human existence. It is *cultivated* excellence, not mere inclination or inherited disposition. It is rooted in intellectual insight and rational judgment and is the product of deliberate choice. And one of Newman's startling discoveries, one that fashioned his whole concept of education, was that the primary element in the cultivation of character was the personal influence of another human being.

In 1826, he was considered for the post of tutor to the future King of Hanover, but he was too young: he was only 25 and the position required someone at least 27. Instead, he was appointed tutor of Oriel, in place of the man who went to Germany. In his diary, he records his impression of the role he was expected to fulfill:

> There is much in the system which I think wrong; I think the tutors see too little of the men, and there is not enough direct religious instruction. It is my wish to consider myself as a minister of Christ. Unless I find that opportunities occur of doing spiritual good to those over whom I am placed, it will become a grave question whether I ought to continue in this tuition
>
> (*LD* I: 133)

In the carrying out of this responsibility as tutor, Newman discovered that his paramount task was moral and spiritual, and he realized that his own manner and his own relationship with his students were critical factors in their spiritual and moral formation. This is how Louis Bouyer, Newman's biographer, wrote about this discovery:

> He had learnt from his recent experience . . . that to have any spiritual influence over his pupils, over and above the mundane teaching of them, it was necessary to discard the authoritarian attitude, and still more any suggestion of the high-and-mighty manner . . . . He therefore started working with his pupils on a system which, novel and startling enough to begin with, gained him before very long . . . first their respect, and finally their affection. He began by putting himself wholly at their disposal as far as their work was concerned. As he got to know them better, he strove, by discerning and persuasive sympathy, to draw out from each whatever he was able to offer. With regard to those who looked upon their studies as a kind of obstacle that had to be got over with somehow or other, he confined himself to doing just as much as his official duties demanded, and no more, letting them see, however, clearly enough what he thought of them. On the other hand, there was no limit to what he would do for the more promising ones among them, even those who, without being specially gifted in any way, showed signs of a genuine desire to get on. With regard to these latter, 'he cultivated'—to use his own words— 'relations, not only of intimacy, but of friendship, and almost of equality, putting off, as much as might be, the martinet manner then in fashion with College tutors, and seeking *their* society in outdoor exercise, on evenings, and in Vacation'
>
> (Bouyer 86-7).

Moral character involves a certain artistry in living, the living of life to the fullest, with a passion for what is noble and good and a constant refusal to live below one's full potential, from an instinct for the beautiful, the good, and that which is expressive of the noblest and the best. *Character* proceeds from a passion for life, is expansive and free and puts the stamp of conviction and careful judgment on the whole business of living. It is a cultivated quality that faces life in its totality and is capable of unprecedented decisions and decisive action. It is the finest and final fruit of a profound moral education and preserves the sheer *goodness* of things.

This is certainly descriptive of John Henry Newman at the beginning of his teaching career, as he began to glimpse the power and influence of a good teacher. He put some of his convictions together on the subject in a sermon that he preached at St. Mary's, Oxford, in 1832, when his Sunday sermons were beginning to cause a stir at the university.

His topic was "Personal Influence, the Means of Propagating the Truth," and at the very beginning of the sermon, he asks several pointed questions. Speaking of the amazing spread of the Gospel throughout the Mediterranean world by the Apostles at the beginnings of Christianity, he asks:

> How is it that in spite of all [the] impediments to their success, still they succeeded? How did they gain that lodgment in the world, which they hold to this day, enabling them to perpetuate principles distasteful to the majority of those who profess them? What is that hidden attribute of the Truth, and how does it act, prevailing, as it does, single-handed, over the many and multiform errors, by which it is simultaneously and incessantly attacked?
> (*Reason* 61)

After a number of those marvelous passages of superb English for which he is noted, Newman answers: "Its real influence consists directly in some inherent moral power . . . . the *personal influence* . . . . of those who are commissioned to teach it" (*Reason* 64-5).

Character, then, according to Newman, cannot be taught: it is the crowning achievement of parenthood and of that education which mirrors parenthood. Its fashioning power comes chiefly from personal influence, even though it requires as well every other human art and skill available to genuine education.

Even though this moral fashioning is the work of personal influence, it is something that blossoms from the *inside*, it is an acquired quality by which the child begins to fashion his own relationship to the world around him and determines the *quality* with which he will taste reality and make it a part of himself. What it does precisely in the complicated business of living is to put the stamp of true nobility upon every element of personal life. Newman would agree with St. Thomas Aquinas in his description of the classical Greek concept of *arete* or *virtue*: "Virtue is called the limit of potentiality . . . . because it causes an inclination to the highest act a faculty can perform."[3] And Aquinas's follow-up to this: "The nature of virtue lies in the good more than in difficulty" (*Summa* II-II, Q. 123, 12 ad 2; qtd. in Pieper 65).

Moral character or *virtue*, in this sense, lays the basis for any form of human happiness. Without it every human gift is spoiled and every human gift wasted. Character is the fruit of knowledge and experience and the exercise of *judgment*, in the beginning the knowledge and experience and the judgment of the parent or teacher, but ultimately the knowledge, experience and judgment of the person himself.

This radical view runs all through Newman's writings. In one of his most pointed commentaries on the subject, a sermon entitled "Human Responsibility, as Independent of Circumstances," he expresses his view on the matter:

> "That we are accountable for what we do and what we are . . . . is a truth certified by both Nature and Grace. . . . It has always been the office of Religion . . . to preserve . . .

both the freedom and responsibility of man . . . the sovereignty of the law of conscience . . . and the irrelevancy of external circumstances in the judgment which is ultimately to be made of our conduct and character"
(*Reason* 126).

Notice that this concept of moral character is far removed from a certain kind of *stoicism*, in which the *autonomous reason* and moral judgment is poised above all the circumstances and events of life. This concept of moral character is *involved* in the human drama, immersed in the events and circumstances of an individual life and history. With a sure hand on the rudder, it navigates the rivers of life with all the skill of a master-boatsman.

Moral character, in this sense, is skill and artistry in living, looking at the totality of life, *recta ratio agibilium*, just as *art* itself is skill in making, *recta ratio factibilium*. A man of *character* is a master in the art of living, a skilled craftsman in the fashioning of a truly human life.

In his educational theory, it was Newman's achievement to have tapped the wellsprings of Western civilization and to bring into focus the humane tradition of the Greeks and the religious traditions of the Greek Fathers. In this sense, Christian means fashioning the human being in the image of Christ, not in *intention* only, as is the custom with much "Christian" propaganda, but in *reality*. At the heart of this *Christian character* is a moral education that transforms and develops the full human potential and brings every human gift and every human event into the orbit of a profound relationship with God.

"From first to last", wrote Newman, "education has been my line" (Bouyer 358). Nowhere is this shown more than in the founding of the Catholic University of Ireland, where he put his ideas into practice and out of which came the most masterly expression of his thought on education: *The Idea of a University* and his *University Sketches*.

In studying this period of Newman's life, it is evident that he differed widely from the Irish bishops who commissioned him to found the university. They visualized it as something of a seminary where Catholic young men could receive a professional education in a Catholic atmosphere, free from moral contagion and free from the unCatholic and unreligious atmosphere of the secular university.

Newman visualized something far different: a vast paideia of sciences and disciplines, to develop the total person, to cultivate virtues of intellect as well as virtues for moral living and to introduce the student to the totality of human knowledge and wisdom. This was exactly what he set out to establish, and reading his letters and writings of this time, it is clear that he enjoyed himself immensely. Here he was uniquely the teacher, the pedagogue, the molder of minds and men, the very mission he had hoped to set up for himself at Oxford, his beloved Oxford, but a mission which was also frustrated by the opposition of narrow men:

He thus introduced his intention to the Irish public:

> I have it in purpose to commit to paper, time after time, various thoughts of my own, seasonable, as I conceive, when a Catholic university is under formation, and apposite in a publication which is to be the record and organ of its proceedings. An anonymous person, indeed, like myself, can claim no authority for anything he advances; nor have I any intention of introducing or sheltering myself under the sanction of the Institution which I wish to serve. My remarks will stand amid weightier matters like the non-official portion of certain government journals in foreign parts; and trust they will have their use, though they are but individual in their origin, and meagre in their execution.
> (*US* 1)

I am sure if the Irish bishops who commissioned him to found the university read these university sketches, they were completely baffled by their scope and intent. This was scarcely the project they had in mind: a kind of Catholic protective preserve where Catholic young men would receive a professional education away from those influences that might be a danger to their faith.

Listen to Newman: "If I were asked to describe . . . . what a University was, I should draw my answer from its ancient designation of a *Studium Generale*, or *School of Universal Learning*." This description implies an

> assemblage of stangers from all parts to one spot—*from all parts*; else, how will you find professors and students for every department of knowledge? and *in one spot*; else, how can there be any school at all? Accordingly, in its simple and rudimental form, it is a school of knowledge of every kind, consisting of teachers and learners from every quarter. Many things are requisite to complete and satisfy the idea embodied in this description; but such a University seems to be in essence, a place for the communication and circulation of thought by means of personal intercourse, through a wide extent of country . . . . Mutual education, in a large sense of the word, is one of the great and incessant occupations of human society . . . . one generation forms another; and the existing generation is ever acting and reacting upon itself in the persons of its individual members.
>
> (*US* 6)

Well! What had the Irish bishops gotten themselves into? A huge *paideia*, where teachers influence students and students influence each other and where the influence of *person on person* is the paramount activity.

And then in one superb section, filled with that glittering prose of his, standing words on their head and juggling concepts and images and matchless metaphors, he first makes what seems to be an obvious observation: "Now, in this process, books, I need scarcely say . . . . are one special instrument" (*US* 6-7). And then he proceeds to bury "popular education" in a grave worthy of its contrived purposes:

> A University is a place of concourse, whither students come from every quarter for every kind of knowledge . . . . it is the place . . . . in which the intellect may safely range and speculate, sure to find its equal in some antagonistic activity, and its judge in the tribunal of truth. It is a place where inquiry is pushed forward, and discoveries verified and perfected, and rashness rendered innocuous, and error exposed, by the collision of mind with mind, and knowledge with knowledge. It is the place where the professor becomes eloquent, and a missionary and a preacher of science, displaying it in its most complete and winning form, pouring it forth with the zeal of enthusiasm, and lighting up his own love of it in the breasts of his hearers . . . . It is the place which attracts the affections of the young by its fame, wins the judgment of the middle-aged by its beauty, and rivets the memory of the old by its associations. It is a seat of wisdom, a light of the world, a minister of the faith, an Alma Mater of the rising generations.
> (*US* 15-16)

Whew! What indeed had the Irish bishops gotten themselves in for? They wanted a haven of religion in a hostile world. Newman wanted an *Alma Mater*, to nourish in the minds of his students that quality of *arete* which he had discovered in the Greek Fathers, that *arete* which brings the thirst for living and for knowledge to the ripeness of a bursting plum.

And that is why Newman remains the great teacher, the master pedagogue, the superb fashioner of minds. He left in Dublin a glowing memory, a striking church on St. Stephen's Green which he paid for with his own money and on which he lavished his exquisite good taste and his love of simplicity. He left a generation of students who adored him, a staff hand picked by himself, who worshiped him, and hundreds of ordinary Irishmen who loved him.

For Newman, education is the passing on of a culture and the creation of a culture, at the heart of which is that personal influence which first of all fashions *character* by a living association with moral excellence, and then opens the mind to the fullness of knowledge and the fullness of its own possibilities. His last word on the subject shows his own educational genius and the depth of his own remarkable character.

> It is . . . education which gives a man a clear, conscious view of his own opinions and judgments, a truth in developing them, an eloquence in expressing them, and a force in urging them. It teaches him to see things as they are, to go right to the point, to detect what is sophistical, and to discard what is irrelevant. It prepares him to fill any post with credit, and to master any subject with facility. It shows him how to accomodate himself to others, how to throw himself into their state of mind, how to bring before them his own, how to influence them, how to come to an understanding with them, how to bear with them.
>
> (*Idea* 192; qtd. in Bouyer 310)

Newman's Catholic University of Ireland failed, because of the shortsightedness of those who invited him to launch the project. But we have for all time his idea of education, which he drew from the riches of the Patristic tradition that he loved and from the years of experience at his beloved Oxford and Oriel.

ENDNOTES

1. *Paideia*, a word and a concept that has been lost to the vocabulary of education, but which, with its wealth of meaning, impressed itself upon the intellect of the budding genius of John Henry Newman.

2. This passage was deleted in Mozley.

3. "Questiones disputatae de virtutibus in communi," 9 ad 15; "Questiones disputatae de virtutibus cardinalibus" (Pieper 59).

WORKS CITED

Bouyer, Louis. *Newman: His Life and Spirituality*. New York: P.J.Kenedy and Sons, 1958.

Jaeger, Werner. *Early Christianity and Greek Paedeia*. Cambridge: Harvard UP, 1961.

—. *Paedeia: The Ideals of Greek Culture*. Oxford: Cambridge UP, 1945. 3 vols.

Mozley, Anne. *The Letters and Correspondence of John Henry Newman during his Life in the English Church*. 1891. 2 vols.

Newman, John Henry. *A Reason For the Hope Within: Sermons on the Theory of Religious Belief*. Danville: Dimension Books, 1985.

—. *The Idea of a University*. Ed. George N. Shuster. New York: Doubleday, 1959.

—. *The Letters and Diaries of John Henry Newman*. Vol. 1. Eds. Ian Ker and Thomas Gornall. Oxford: Clarendon P, 1961.

—. *University Sketches*. Westminster: Newman P, 1953.

Pieper, Josef. *The Human Wisdom of St. Thomas*. New York: Sheed and Ward, 1948.

The *Idea* and Modern Ideas: *Newman and Higher Education in the 1990s*

Francis Fennell

Perhaps the real genesis of this essay was a conversation I was having one warm August afternoon four or five years ago. Part of my duties as Dean of Humanities at my home institution was to explain to incoming transfer students how the courses taken at their prior college would be applied to Loyola's core curriculum requirements. The young man in my office was indignant. Why, he asked in polite but insistent language, would this college not give him core credit for the three hours of Intermediate Guitar which showed on his transcript? It was then that the voice began to speak to me, that little voice in the back of my mind which summoned up—God knows from where—a sentence out of Newman's *Idea of a University*: "[P]laying stringed instruments is an elegant pastime, and a resource to the idle, but it is *not* education" (128).

Well, a sophomore's mind is not easily turned, so I did not try out that sentence on *him*. But it was an immense comfort to me. And that was the beginning of a process which has continued ever since. Because as issues have come up which call for some kind of judgment, nothing has been more helpful than the observations by Newman which this little voice keeps whispering in my ear—observations which might almost serve as kind of Arnoldian touchstones for finding a steady course or shaping a proper reply.

In particular, this voice has been of inestimable value in helping me survive endless council and committee meetings. The Academic Council of the college, for example, was once debating the wording of a policy statement on faculty teaching loads. Quite predictably, the draft contained language about how teaching and research could never be in tension, would always enhance one another. "To discover and to teach are distinct functions," the voice averred; "they are also distinct gifts, and are not commonly found united in the same person" (8). On another occasion a dean's meeting was devoted to still another discussion about whether and how to revise the core curriculum. "I will tell you," said the voice sharply, "what has been the practical error of the last 20 years— . . . distracting and enfeebling the mind by an unmeaning profusion of subjects; implying that a smattering in a dozen branches of study is not shallowness, which it is, but enlargement, which it is not" (127).

This last instance of the core curriculum brings me to the subject which I wish to address in this essay. On those public occasions when I have had to represent the university during the last few years, no subject—with the possible exception of the fortunes of the basketball team, with which I am presumed to be familiar—has come up more often than Allan Bloom's *The Closing of the American Mind*. Respectfully but seriously, my interrogators want to know what we in academia think of this indictment of our purposes and our proceedings. Sometimes but less often names like Hirsch and Cheney and Giamatti also come up, and again the question is how we who are in these institutions plan to respond to what our critics ask of us. The questions are offered gravely, by people who are genuinely concerned about the state of higher education. And as I have reflected on the issues they raise, the existence of the small voice which I have been describing has suggested an approach. Going beyond touchstone phrases, what if anything does John Henry Newman have to contribute to our conversations about college and university education in America in the 1990s? Are there ways in which Newman's *Idea of a University* can become a participant in our discussions, can speak to our concerns? When I say "our discussions," I am talking about the controversies generated by specific people. Allan Bloom has already been named. For our purposes here I want to add two others: Lynne Cheney, author of *The Humanities in America*, and the late A. Barlett Giamatti, whose book of the same year was entitled *A Free and Ordered Space: The Real World of the University*. I have chosen these three voices out of many because all three are excellent controversialists, because all three have among them points of continuity as well as discontinuity, and especially because all three lay claim, directly or indirectly, to the mantle of the first Rector of the Catholic University of Dublin.

The methodology here might be called "intertextual studies," if that term is limited to what has been called "discursive and rational dialogue between literary texts" (Plottel vii), in other words, the referential relationships that can exist between texts from different places and times. The assumption is that some *meaning* arises, for example, out of a reader's realization that Newman stands in the background to Bloom, Cheney, and Giamatti, and additional meanings arise out of the realization that these references are reversible. Furthermore, such a methodology has the advantage of allowing Newman to take his place in our modern dialogue about higher education. To borrow from Arnold again, it allows Newman to become once more a "voice in the air," this time not in the Oxford of the 1840s or the Dublin of the 1850s, but in the equally contentious United States of the 1990s.

Grafted onto this methodology will be a structure which borrows from classical rhetoric in ways that Newman would have found familiar. Those with an eye for such things will probably decide that I begin with a forensic approach, but then move into thinly disguised ceremonial rhetoric, as befits a centenary, and finish with a perhaps somewhat-too-hortatory conclusion.

I

The hermeneutical task of retrieving Newman is naturally a complicated one, given the differences between his place and time and culture and ours. Especially difficult for modern readers are Newman's differing assumptions, assumptions which condition and limit our encounter with him. I want to begin by taking note of two kinds of limiting assumptions: theological and institutional.

Theological first. The Newman who can speak so confidently of theology as simply "the truths we know about God put into a system" (65), the Newman who evinces no hesitation about listing God's characteristics, is not a figure with whom we feel comfortable in an age accustomed more to a Karl Barth than to a Thomas Aquinas. Moreover when Newman draws from these assumptions practical conclusions about higher education, modern readers can sometimes only shake their heads. If the question today were one of the expediency of any particular university undertaking, for example, who of my colleagues in administration could think to end the debate by declaring, as Newman did at a similar juncture, "I have one ground of hope, just one stay, which serves me in the stead of all other argument whatever: . . . the Holy See . . . has spoken" (28)? Or my colleagues in philosophy—would they, like Newman, be content to "do" their philosophy, as the jargon has it, "under indeed the shadow of the Church," without which philosophy forms "a will of its own, . . . and attempts to form a theory, and . . . does but abet evils" (174)? Or what historian would be as comfortable as Newman was in accepting Noah's ark as an historical fact because Revelation demands it? Or who of my colleagues in theology would abandon process entirely in favor of Newman's assumption that "the Divine Voice has spoken once for all" (190) and everything else can be reached by deductive reasoning? When this theology shades over into Catholic apologetics, the difficulties are only compounded. Most of us would feel enormously uneasy with Newman's assumption of a permanent war in universities between Protestants and Catholics, and even more uneasy with the martial metaphors by which he expresses this assumption in the *Idea*—his pitting of the Catholic David against the Protestant Goliath, for example, or his view of other Christians as "the enemy's camp," where "the arming and the maneuvering, the earthworks and the mines, go on incessantly" (313). Complementing this religious insularity is a remarkable cultural insularity which allows Newman to dismiss Chinese culture, for example, as "huge, stationary, unattractive, [and] morose" (191).

We are also blocked off from Newman because of his assumptions about institutions, especially educational institutions. Many of these assumptions grow out of his familiarity with and attraction to the Oxford model, as he himself recognized. The consequences of holding to the Oxford model have been identified before, but it is worth mentioning some of them again briefly: his assumption that in speaking about higher education one focuses on a university rather than a college; his assumption that there will be few such institutions, thus giving each of them a major role to play in the intellectual life of the country; his assumption that higher education is for the culturally homogenous few rather than the culturally diverse many. Furthermore Newman had different assumptions about what goes on inside those institutions: that they will be places marked by controversy over intellectual issues, but intramural controversy rather than controversy between its members and the extramural world; that chief among those intramural controversies will be the implications of new discoveries in natural science; that pre-professional training has no direct role to play in undergraduate education. This last assumption especially is a hard one for us to let go. But we must freely confess that on this issue the utilitarians have carried the day; to pretend otherwise is an exercise in pointless nostalgia.

So these are ways in which Newman's assumptions differ from ours, and differ in ways that restrict our access to him and limit our ability to retrieve him for a contemporary reader. I propose that we simply put a bracket around this Newman, which is to say that we have taken note of these aspects of his thought but have agreed to keep our concerns separate while we examine those areas of Newman's *Idea of a University* where the assumptions do not stand in our way so much, where Newman can speak more directly to our needs and our concerns. In nineteenth century language this means we can turn from blaming our author and start to praise him. As noted before, I will treat Newman as one voice among others, the others being, specifically, Allan Bloom, Lynne Cheney, and Bart Giamatti. And I propose to consider all of them under four headings: the philosophical basis for a university education; the sociology of higher education; the psychology of the learning process; and the moral ground for the teaching-learning enterprise.

II

Under the first heading, the philosophical basis for a university education, we can begin with quotation. "It must be said," announced the university's head to its assembled students and faculty, that "there is first a broad, deep base of shared assumptions and perceptions . . . " (216). Chief among these assumptions is the belief that a university is a place for "open and free conversation, between young and young, young and old, scholar and scholar, present and past—the sound of voices straining out the truth" (45). Truth *can* be discerned, in part because these voices feel the "internal connectedness of all learning," an interconnectedness which means that "humane studies" and "religious studies are bound each to each; it is impossible to acquire a complete knowledge of the one science without the other" (139). And the fruit of an education which sees the unity of all knowledge will be a person whose mind is sophisticated, flexible, open, considerate, and principled, a person who can "affirm connection and not . . . sway to the music of fragmentation" (280).

The university head in this case was Bart Giamatti, not Newman, and the faculty and students were assembled in New Haven rather than Dublin. His words so closely parallel Newman's because both share what is today a rather unfashionable belief, namely that all knowledge forms one whole. Implicit in this belief is the assurance that, no matter how difficult the road, no matter how partial and obscured the view, truth can be approached. Not *reached*, of course, but approached, and approached only because it *exists*. Allan Bloom stands on the same principle: "The problem of the humanities . . . [is] the unity of knowledge" (371), a unity of which the core curriculum is a "threadbare [but indispensable] reminiscence" (320). Lynne Cheney too argues for what she calls "the interconnection of ideas and events," for the existence of "truths that pass beyond time and circumstance; truths that, transcending class, race, and gender, speak to us all" (14).

Such convictions are, to put it with reserve, unfashionable. Philosophers like Richard Rorty argue that the search for truth is simply an illusion and an obsession—every approach, he claims, is just one more human project, just one more set of metaphors. Literary critics like Stanley Fish rail against any notion of determinate meaning and any faith in the possibility of progress, whether historical or personal. Historians like Hayden White see their enterprise as simply the invention of a story, a story which uses and interprets historical data but reveals nothing more than the genetic or social predispositions of the storyteller.

Of course we cannot and will not resolve such immensely important and complex questions here. I simply want to establish that what Newman believed was his inarguable premise, the existence of universal truth and universal knowledge, has indeed become arguable, but also that his premise is being advanced just as vigorously as he advanced it by the three contemporaries I have named. Even if one accepts the contention that all interpretations have equal claims upon us, what is interesting about *this* interpretation is that its defiant restatement has gained a wide and responsive hearing outside the walls of the academy. The genetic and/or social predisposition to accept it must be endemic to the body politic, and other and later interpretations have not displaced it. However uncomfortable we may otherwise feel with Bloom and Cheney—and for political and other reasons I for one am often quite uncomfortable—we cannot deny that in this case their arguments, and perforce Newman's, strike at our institutions with all the force of Dr. Johnson's boot: "Thus do we confute them!"

For our three contemporaries this principle carries with it curricular implications. Cheney urges an intellectually coherent curriculum which emphasizes Western Civilization. Bloom concurs, and adds the requirement that students take philosophy and religion. Giamatti emphasizes a logocentric education in which the humanities, using a philological method, join eloquence to wisdom.

Here Newman offers a salutary caution. For him the university is a place where no branch of learning goes unhonored, but he argues *against* the *ex*clusion of certain subjects rather than *for* any required *in*clusions. While the *end* of education can be specified, viz. the cultivation of the mind, to prescribe studies is to determine *means*. Although he names grammar and mathematics as good starting points and later on gives a preliminary sketch of a possible curriculum, Newman finds the real key in learning-to-be-systematic, in making things good as one goes. Much better, he argues, to proceed slowly, in a small area, than to exchange depth for breadth. So when Bloom announces that every student must read Plato, Newman would say that such a project is a fine way to become educated—but it is not the *only* way. In the words of Tennyson's Arthur, "God fulfills Himself in many ways, / Lest one good custom should corrupt the world."

The subject of the curriculum brings us to the very heart of how a university works, and therefore to my second heading, the sociology of higher education. If in the case of first principles we found agreement among our four, and disagreement only on what implications we should draw from it, here we find two quite different understandings of how universities work, especially in terms of the question of how they relate to the world at large.

For Giamatti and for Cheney the university relates to the world outside by severance, by isolation, by seclusion. The university becomes what Giamatti calls "a free and ordered space," in other words a *playing field* if one follows out his metaphor, a playing field which has its own rules and constructs its games for the benefit of those who wish to play them, the games in turn depending on the willingness of the players to be sportsmanlike. Civility and collegiality are for Giamatti the great virtues: one engages in "free-swinging" debate—the boxing or perhaps baseball metaphor is his—but one abstains from wishing to do harm (an exhibition match, as it were). Society at large will benefit from this contest, but only indirectly insofar as its citizens may have profited from the intellectual training that such wits combat can provide. In other words, the political wars of Washington may be won on the intellectual playing fields of New Haven. For Lynne Cheney this self-prescribed isolation is both a privilege and an opportunity. She reserves special scorn for those who mesh their academic concerns and their political concerns, or those who carry this conviction a step further and see academic interests as essentially and always a form of politics.

Newman and Bloom suggest a different view, albeit in dissimilar ways. For Bloom the university serves as society's antidote. Whatever the disease of the moment, the task of those in the academy is to counteract the poison. An education makes one the disloyal opposition; standing against the prevailing current makes it possible for the river to change course. He argues for a university which is "an unpopular institution in our midst . . . that resists our powerful urges and temptations" (252). The crisis in higher education comes because we have failed our mission, have made too many accommodations, have imitated or pandered when we should have controverted.

For Newman the university does indeed have its obligations to society as a whole. An education can never be undertaken in isolation, for what students or scholars debate should connect vitally to the concerns of all. But the images in Newman are less medicinal, are much gentler, more tempered by sweet reasonableness. And that is because our task is neither to approve nor to oppose, but rather to engage in that kind of inquiry which Arnold blessed with the term "disinterestedness." Where for Bloom the type is Nietzsche, self-condemned outcast and iconoclast, for Newman the type is St. Philip Neri, who recognizes the evils of his time but who chooses "to yield to the stream, and direct the current, which he could not stop, of science, literature, art, and fashion, and so to sweeten and to sanctify . . . " (200).

And what of those who carry the largest burden of this sweetening and this sanctifying, in other words the faculty? Here the four voices speak in quite different tones.

Newman's is the calmest, most respectful assessment of the profession. He can on occasion chastise those faculty who embrace expedience at the expense of principle in order "to humour a spirit which they could not withstand, and make temporizing concessions at which they could not but inwardly smile" (127). But in general his attitude is one of respect tempered by affection. At the very least faculty members help cultivate in students those habits of mind which suit them for participating in intellectual discourse. And at their best or most fortunate moments, they can speak or bring to others those words "by means of [which] the secrets of the heart are brought to light, pain of soul is relieved, hidden grief is carried off, sympathy conveyed, counsel imparted, experience recorded, and wisdom perpetuated" (245).

But alas such a sympathetic view comes cheek-by-jowl with and grows out of the premise which I noted so lightly back at the beginning: the idea that teaching and research are separate gifts. For Newman research should be carried on in academies or institutes or what we today would call "the private sector." Universities are for teaching and learning.

I will not trouble the reader with yet another summary of the effects, pernicious or otherwise, of holding to the model of the German research university. Some faculty come from institutions in which Newman's ideal could still live. But others exist in quite different environments where the publication of research is a necessity. And if we are to talk about the role of the faculty we must, to use Newman's words, "take things as they are, if we take them at all" (255).

Giamatti accepts the principle of dual obligations with considerable cheerfulness, because for him "Research . . . is the essential source from which teaching is drawn" (149). If he evidences a concern it is not with institutional demands but rather with the faculty's attitude towards itself. There are two dangers: on the one hand a tendency toward priestliness, toward a new clericalism, with all the arrogance that often goes with it; and on the other hand a temptation toward fainthearted-ness, toward a loss of morale which leaves in its wake only "uncertainty, anger, at worst self-hatred" (201). But a faculty's best product, says Giamatti, is its innate idealism. It needs to and can throw off fatigue, confident that this idealism "fructifies and charges . . . with a strange and wonderful coherence."

Lynne Cheney is less sanguine, and for her the villain is not arrogance or faintheartedness but rather overspecialization in subject, in method, and in language. Having lost a common language, in her view faculty are condemned to speak only the tribal tongue of their specialties and therefore to value only what the tribe values. Hence the overemphasis she sees being placed on research. For her it is a question of proportion and of audience. Research has its place, no one should doubt that; but it should not be given a disproportionate emphasis, particularly vis-a-vis teaching, and as a profession faculty should give greater credit to publications which address a wider audience and lesser credit to publications which address only the small tribe. Still, her tone is one of cajolery: faculty members have gotten off on the wrong track, but a little reordering of priorities can get them back on course.

For Bloom the matter is not merely misplaced priorities: it is a much more serious case of "servility, vanity, and lack of conviction" (313). Faculty, he claims, have sold their birthright for a mess of liberal pottage. Bloom is fueled by a Swiftean rage against what he perceives as the fatuities of the day, and proceeds out of a similarly Swiftean faith in the powers of human reason rightly applied. In Bloom's view the problem is not institutional failure, and not a failure of priorities, but rather an intellectual and a moral failure of the first magnitude.

And if you detect a strange energy in those who ask you what you think of Bloom, I suspect it is because he taps a deep reservoir of anger in the public at large. If there is an equally strange energy in faculty who attack Bloom, one can sense the rage of denial. When so much tension manifests itself, important issues are sure to be lurking.

To raise the question of the powers of human reason is to shade over into my third heading, the psychology of the learning process. What, we must ask, goes on in the classroom, the laboratory, the office, the dorm room? What happens when we say learning is taking place?

Cheney's view is a simple one—one might almost want to say simplistic. For her, learning is a matter of making connections. If faculty can help students see links and patterns they might not have seen on their own, and if further they provide a generous helping of those perennial human truths, they will have met students' needs and their own. Begged is the question of where faculty derive the patterns they help students see or how they decide which truths are perennial and which are not.

Bloom's faith, as noted before, is in reason. The Socratic dialogue helps students outgrow easy answers, outgrow the culture, so that they can become autonomous. Teachers therefore are "midwives"—the metaphor is his—midwives who help students be delivered of their own autonomous selves, largely by telling them when to push. Here are some of the nouns and noun phrases that describe the result of this Socratic method: "satisfaction," "fullness of pride," "certitude drawn from within oneself," "self-sufficiency," above all "liberation." Good American goals all. The reliance on the Socratic method necessitates the primacy of philosophy mentioned earlier.

Where Bloom proceeds by noun phrases, thus emphasizing what students should be acquiring, Giamatti reveals his understanding of how education takes place more through his verbs and his adjectives. The verbs are "clarify," "test," "seek," "feel," "judge," "proceed," "reveal." The adjectives are "discerning," "flexible," "tough-minded," "open-hearted," "responsive," "civilized." Education is more process than product, more doing than having. In these ways Giamatti echoes Newman and gives public acknowledgment of his debt to him. Readers will remember Newman's verbs: "enlarge," "pursue," "respect," "consult," "aid," "interpret," "guide," "open," "refine," "digest." And they will remember his still more famous list in the passage which cites freedom, equitableness, calmness, moderation, and wisdom.

Philosophically and temperamentally Giamatti and Newman are kindred spirits. But Newman, I would argue, carries his analysis to a level of sophistication beyond what Giamatti achieves. My own view of Newman would place perhaps its greatest emphasis on his subtlety as an educational psychologist. There is scarcely a chapter of the *Idea* that does not allow me to advance my case. Consider Discourse IV, where Newman shrewdly describes the tendency of scholars to leap to generalizations "[n]ot from self-will only, nor from malevolence, but from the irritation which suspense occasions" (75). Thus they are led into misconceptions, even in their scholarship, because what the Buddhists call the "monkey mind" cannot stop chattering and thus speculating. Or consider Discourse VI, where Newman establishes that the conclusions scholars draw come not from their data so much as from the pattern—the interpretation—they impose on the data. Here Newman comes remarkably close to Fish's position. Or consider the lecture on "University Preaching," where Newman makes fascinating connections between reading and writing that I often recommend to my colleagues when the subject is writing across the curriculum. There are important passages too where Newman demonstrates the need for activity rather than passivity if learning is to take place, and where he develops an epistemology that in today's parlance we would call "left-brain" while still acknowledging the importance of those looks and sounds which melt us and move us. Most remarkable of all, consider the account which Newman provides, again in Discourse VI, for what it is like to first come across ideas which challenge our whole way of thinking. The initial shock, even anger; then the shy allure of the forbidden; then the sudden rush of free speculation, culminating in the exultant sense of deliverance and the intoxicating feeling that one has stepped out of the cave, has made common cause with the gods: all this Newman offers us, truthfully and sympathetically, as a description of what a young religious mind experiences when it first encounters the theories of unbelievers. It is a passage of singular breadth of vision and penetration of insight.

One other aspect of Newman's educational psychology warrants mention, and that is his belief that intellectual pursuits can be a "homeopathic medicine for the disease [of sensuality]" (161). While Newman is otherwise skeptical about education making us better people, he does in this instance hold out hope that Aristotle and the erotic can be deadly enemies. I will leave it to the readers' experience to decide whether this has proven to be so on his or her own campus or even in his or her own life. I want to raise it here simply because it points up that despite his protestations to the contrary, Newman really did see relationships between our intellectual lives and our moral lives. And this brings me to my fourth and final heading, the moral ground for the teaching-learning enterprise.

If truth be told, Newman gives evidence of a profound ambivalence on the question of how learning relates to the development of a person's moral life. On the one hand, we associate him with skeptical judgments like "Liberal education makes not the Christian, not the Catholic, but the gentleman" (110), which he advances in Discourse V. But then in Discourse IX he warns about the tendency of liberal knowledge toward a "rebellious stirring against miracle and mystery" (186), such that indifference can lead to laxity and eventually to heresy. Teachers bear culpability for such an intellectual failure; this is a serious matter for Newman and is hardly counterbalanced by the homeopathic effects of learning mentioned a moment ago. And Newman is ever the moralist when he reflects on what is characteristic of the life of the scholar. That famous passage on quarrying with a razor, for example, bears upon Newman's conviction that, just as sensuality might be the temptation of the young, the besetting sin as scholars is the far more serious sin of pride. Insofar as he deflates their pretenses to greater virtue because they claim to have greater knowledge, Newman performs an invaluable service. What may be virtuous intellectually is at best neutral morally.

Newman of course offers remedies. A strict adherence to the subjects of one's discipline reduces the inclination to decide "on facts by means of theories" (62), and a willingness to listen to the voice of revealed religion can act as a further check. I leave it to the reader's judgment whether we can or should accept those remedies. I must confess to having quoted to some of my colleagues in the business school Newman's strictures on teaching "sordid and unchristian principles . . . of moneymaking" (85). We laugh together, they and I, but the existence of required courses in what is oxymoronically known as business ethics serves as a faint curricular echo of that now-unfashionable belief.

Bloom and Cheney do not offer much food for reflection on this matter, the former because his claim about refusing to moralize is patently false, the latter because she seems unaware of the serious problem of definition raised by her argument for "perennial truths." It is Giamatti who brings us to the heart of the matter when he can say in one place that the university should not teach moral values and in another place that an educational process fails when it does not urge a student to "freely educate oneself for a life of some benefit to others" (29, 215). Confusing and contradictory? Of course. So is Newman. If we examine these writers carefully, and perhaps if we examine ourselves carefully too, we find at bottom a very basic ambivalence toward these questions. We cannot say that an education should make us, or even could make us, better people. But we are equally reluctant to say it cannot.

III

I come, then, to a summary of what this analysis has yielded by way of conclusions. If we focus simply on Newman, but with the other three voices often lending resonance, I have offered at least the following propositions:

- That in terms of higher education Newman's applied theology no longer has the relevance it may once have had, and in fact is more of an impediment than a help;

- That Newman's assumptions about the purpose of education and about the nature of educational institutions have been at least partially betrayed by history, which means one of his great adversaries, the utilitarians, can on some issues claim to have carried the day; but also

- That Newman's premises about universal truth and universal knowledge, while under strong challenge, still carry immense weight and suggestive power, and furthermore they have curricular implications—but surprisingly more in the area of depth than of breadth;

- That for faculty the burden and the glory is the task of "sweetening and sanctifying" the lives of their students, whether or not they pursue research in addition to their vocation as teachers; and finally

- That education is more a getting than a having—it is an exciting *process*, one fraught with moral implications which we can sense better than we can define.

To read Newman's *Idea of a University* in 1990 is, with regard to our institutional environment, a counter-cultural act, an act I believe is far more important for faculty to perform than for students. He is a force against our tendency to splinter, our tendency to overspecialize, our tendency toward neoscholasticism and neoclericalism, our tendency to lose sight of the audiences with whom we should communicate. His is also a voice for tolerance and for the academic freedom which is its *sine qua non*. Above all, Newman's is a voice of encouragement, a voice which says that, whatever may be the "infidelities of the day," these too shall pass, and in the meantime teaching and learning will go on: that mysterious process which is ultimately so complex because it is so personal—on one end of the log a student, in the famous formula for a liberal education, and on the other end Mark Hopkins, or you or I. And then the good talk begins.

WORKS CITED

Bloom, Allan. *The Closing of the American Mind: How Higher Education Has Failed Democracy and Impoverished the Souls of Today's Students*. New York: Simon and Schuster, 1987.

Cheney, Lynn. *The Humanities in America: A Report to the President, the Congress, and the American People*. Washington: National Endowment for the Humanities, 1988.

Giamatti, A. Bartlett. *A Free and Ordered Space: The Real World of the University*. New York: Norton, 1988.

Newman, John Henry. *The Idea of a University*. Ed. I. T. Ker. Oxford: Clarendon Press, 1976.

Plottel, Jeanine, and Hanna Charney, eds. *Intertextuality: New Perspectives in Criticism*. New York: New York Literary Forum, 1978.

Twentieth Century Research Specialization in the Context of John Henry Newman's Nineteenth Century Philosophy of Education

David R. Stevenson

The seminal idea of this essay is that our late 20th century (late 2nd millennium) intellectual difficulty with John Henry Newman at the centenary of his death is that he seems strange to us because he he lived on "the far side of 1905." This statement is based on analysis of historical context with reference to only one text, an undelivered address in 1855 to a Dublin clerical audience about "Science and Religion." This can be characterized as stemming from and more than a mere *apercu* but is less than a full-bloom thesis because space does not permit us to sustain it. After we establish the "beyond 1905" idea, we will pose the question whether Newman's attitude toward education as "teaching" rather than"research" bridges the gap between Newman and us today.

In the 19th century Mark Pattison argued that Newman had "no real sense of the scientific method and temper" and that the scholarship he has always in mind "is of the delicate but narrow 'English' description," which meant that it did not produce the steady train of German researchers and scholars. He alone of

Newman's contemporaries argued that the university is a dead place if its teachers were not engaged in doing research. Opposing Newman's dictum that "To discover and to teach are distinct functions," Pattison retorted that "The Professor of a modern University ought to regard himself primarily as a learner and a teacher only secondarily" (*Idea* xxv).

In the 20th century this has become orthodox dogma as a whole host of academicians headed by such men as Jacques Barzun have presumed that the liberal arts ideal is associated with the humanities while research specialization is associated with the experimental (and hard) sciences. This is true even though rigorous research called academic scholarship with its attendant specialization is practiced by humanists as well as scientists.

John Henry Cardinal Newman has remained the outstanding 19th century spokesman for what we in the 20th century call "liberal arts education," "humanities education," development of "the whole man" (properly understood to include "woman" too). The purpose of this essay is to explore Newman's attitude toward research, a 20th century concern, in the context of the 19th century intellectual *milieu*. In what must serve as a preliminary foray, I am going to focus upon just one of Newman's essays. This is one of his obscure ones that he never delivered.

In 1855 Newman wrote a lecture entitled "Christianity and Scientific Investigation" (*Scope* 235-59). He intended it to be an address for the School of Science in Dublin. The fact that this was a lecture not delivered indicates that its topic was indeed touchy if not taboo.

Newman presented his point of view in the long opening sentence:

> This is a time, gentlemen, when not only the classics, but much more the sciences, in the largest sense of the word, are

looked upon with anxiety, not altogether ungrounded, by religious men, and since I for my part wish to stand on good terms with all kinds of knowledge, and have no intention of quarreling with any . . . therefore, as I have been making overtures of reconciliation, first between polite literature and religion, and next between physics and theology, so now I would say a word by way of deprecating and protesting against the needless antagonism which sometimes exists in fact between divines and the cultivators of the sciences generally.

(235)

Perhaps nowhere else in the canon did Newman express himself in such intellectually tolerant terms. Not only was he trying to encompass all points of view, he was trying to reconcile them.

On the other hand, there is Newman's commitment to authority. After all, Newman, at great personal expense in career and agonizing introspection, had recently joined the Roman Catholic Church, for whom authority was shortly to be incarnated in the dogma of Papal Infallibility. This made the question a matter not only of "Science and Religion" in the 19th century sense, but a matter of "Reason and Faith" in the 13th century sense.

Newman's conversion to Roman Catholicism committed him to support the neo-medieval outlook, which was already considered anachronistic by many in the burgeoning community of researchers, scientists, and educators. Newman's concern is exemplified by this pronouncement: "Great minds need elbow room, not indeed in the domain of faith, but of thought. And so indeed do less minds, and all minds" (256). Reason and faith were separated. This led into an encomium to geniuses, to great minds who must not be curbed in their thinking and creating, viz.

> Yet if you insist that in their speculations, researches, or
> conclusions in their particular science it is not enough that
> they should submit to the Church generally, . . . you simply
> crush and stamp out the flame within them, and they can do
> nothing at all.
>
> (256)

However, moving toward the end, he snuffed out 19th century
"liberalism" with this assertion:

> Now if any such thinker starts from radically unsound
> principles, or aims at directly false conclusion, if he be a
> Hobbes, or a Shaftesbury, or a Hume, or Bentham, then, of
> course, there is an end of the whole matter. He is an
> opponent of revealed truth, and he means to be so; nothing
> more need be said.
>
> (257)

Newman, the humanist, subscribed to the dogma of reason;
Newman, the Christian, insisted that the dogma of reason points
toward, justifies, reaffirms, and is altogether reconcilable with
the dogma of faith.

But hold on. In the very next sentence Newman backs away
from his medieval dogmatic pronouncement. While this is
standard casuistry, medieval and modern, Newman seems to be
leaping back into the 19th century cauldron:

> But perhaps it is not so; perhaps his errors are those which
> are inseparable accidents of his system or of his mind, and
> are spontaneously evolved, not pertinaciously defended.
> Every human system, every human writer, is open to just
> criticism. Make him shut up his portfolio; good! and then
> perhaps you lose what, on the whole and in spite of inciden-
> tal mistakes, would have been one of the ablest defenses of
> revealed truth (directly or indirectly, according to his
> subject) ever given to the world.

(*Scope* 257)

There are two ways to interpret this lecture. Either Newman defended freedom of thought, almost to the Socratic extreme of "Follow the argument wherever it leads!" because he has the faith that it will lead to the Truth; or he defended freedom of thought only insofar as it did not contradict Christian doctrine, which means that he did not really defend it at all. His language, his neo-scholastic terminology, albeit aimed at a conservative Irish audience, certainly makes him appear to be the kind of Roman Catholic who would be judged adversarially by Protestants and free-thinker "scientists."

How can we evaluate Newman's position? We can perform either *explication de text* or *l'analyse du context*. In this essay we will attempt the latter. In this historical analysis of context let us set forth two basic themes:

a) Newman occupies the "metaxyal" (in between) place in the age-old tradition of Classical-Christian hermeneutics, which can be characterized as the age-old tension between the realms of secular and sacred.

b) Newman occupies the same kind of "metaxyal" position in the modern European battle between science and religion, which is a 19th century version of the 17th century war between "the ancients" and "the moderns."

In the first place, let us agree that Newman stands with a foot in Athens and a foot in Jerusalem. We shall venture to label this as the "*metaxy*" (a personal coinage from the Greek language) tradition of Classical-Christian hermeneutics. Newman stands at the opposite pole from Origen. Origen, according to Eusebius (*History* Book 6, Chapter 3), "decided that the study of literature did not harmonize with training in theology, and promptly broke off his lectures on literature declaring them to be useless and a hindrance to his sacred studies."

Let us acknowledge that both this author (*c'est moi!*, or rather more precisely, the editorial *nous*) and our subject (JHN) of this essay stand together, albeit at different levels, in the so-called "*metaxyal*" tradition. We must aver that it is indeed a venerable academic tradition started by St. Jerome, the tempted scholar turned Christian, if not by St. Paul himself, the original defender of Jerusalem at Athens. And this hermeneutical tradition is star-studded by such variegated luminaries as Aquinas of Paris, Erasmus of Rotterdam, Calvin of Geneva, Lessing of Wolfenbuttel, just a few of those religious scholars and scholarly religious who have tried to steer the *via media* between the poles of the secular and the sacred.

Next, let us agree that according to his lecture, written and prepared for Dublin in 1855, Newman stood between science and religion. Ever since the rise of rationalism in the West, there has been intellectual warfare between two kinds of "priests." There are those apostles of the mind called philosophers and scientists who believe in logic and practical thinking, pitted against those apostles of the spirit or soul who believe in intuition and feeling. At the dawn of our scientific age in the 17th century, this duel was characterized as the quarrel between "the Ancients and the Moderns." In the 18th century it evolved into the battle between "Science and Religion." In the late 19th century and into the 20th century, it has been waged as a war between the scientist and the artist. The 20th century version of this war has been characterized as follows: a) eruditely, the age-old war between the natural scientist and the human and social artist and humanist; b) mundanely, as the battle between the specialist and the generalist, and disparagingly, as the squabble between the dilettante and the scholar-squirrel; c) "pop" philosophically, as the battle between the "two cultures" in a book of that name by C.P. Snow.

Insofar as Newman is concerned we must pay special attention to the controversy between "Science and Religion. This was true even though "Science" was invoked by humanists (such as Ranke, Renan, and Taine, among others) as well as by the more accurately labeled natural scientists.

How are we to assess the impact of Newman's religious belief on his place in the the development of human thought? Is this a question of development or direction? A 20th century Newman scholar named Harold Weatherby has seen this as a matter of continuation and development rather than right or wrong direction from the outset. In his *Cardinal Newman and His Age*, Weatherby concluded that "Newman has done for modern thought what Aquinas did for Aristotle—except that Aquinas Christianized Aristotle by taking his arguments to their logical conclusion whereas Newman achieved an orthodox modernism only by securing modern thought against the consequences of its full development" (286).

What does Weatherby mean by "full development"? Without sharing his teleological presumption or adumbrating his fleshed out interpretation, let us survey the historical context and look at the research issues of the mid-19th century. Some were in Newman's purview and some were not. Like many other Victorian Age intellectuals, and all churchmen, Newman battled to preserve his faith in a milieu of reason, science, secularism, etc., all of which were espoused with an anti-clerical, anti-Catholic, and especially anti-Papal zeal. On the basis of general knowledge far beyond that of the text of his imprudent lecture in Ireland, we can adjudge that Authority, Nature, and the Bible were the major issues to be investigated by the scholarly methods of the day.

Authority in Newman's thought is shaped by the dogma question of the Church in mid-century. Far beyond the scope of this paper is the examination of the cardinal issue of Newman's intellectual life which marked his conversion to Roman Catholicism in the early 1840's and his encounter with Papal Infallibility in the early 1870's. Suffice to say, Newman stood on the basic Roman Catholic position that Nature and Grace, Reason and Revelation, come from the same Divine Author, whose works cannot contradict each other. Perhaps, we summarize the issue as follows: Newman tried to keep the Medieval dogma of faith and doctrine from smothering and strangling the Enlightenment dogma of reason.

Nature is more complicated for Newman and scholars disagree. Diametrically opposed interpretations of Newman's view of Nature still exist. C.F. Harrold's essay entitled "Newman and the Alexandrian Platonists" draws upon Newman's historical study of the Arian heresy in the 4th century to conclude that Newman emphasized the gulf between "Nature" and God.

Weatherby, on the other hand, averred that Newman studied "Nature" in the shadow of Coleridge, which meant that he espoused a romantic idealism which tended to blend together "Nature" and the divine reality. The Bible in Newman is relegated to the periphery of obsolescence and anachronism. This is because Newman studied the Bible before the literary revolution of "higher criticism" wrought by F.C. Baur, D.F. Strauss, Ernest Renan, et alia., and before the scientific revolution of "natural selection" fashioned by Wallace and Darwin. Dwight Culler reinforces Weatherby's view of Newman when, in *The Imperial Intellect*, he entitles his Bible chapter (XIII), "Secular and Religious Knowledge" (244-70). .

What do we mean when we say that John Henry Cardinal Newman is on "far side of 1905"? In the first place, we observe that although Newman is closest to us in chronological time he does seem curiously farther removed from us than his "*metaxyal*" predecessors. For example, at an elementary, if not elemental level, Newman seems not to have been provoked by the sexual temptation of the Patriarchs. He did not seem to have the thorn-in-the-flesh affliction often attributed to St. Paul, spectacularly extirpated by Origen, and most lamentably celebrated by St. Augustine. Nor did he rage against the vocational celibacy so spectacularly repudiated by Abelard and Luther, chaffingly endured by Erasmus and many post-Tridentine scholars of the church, and so voyeuristically and morbidly condemned by all non-Tridentine scholars of the Protestant-secular academy. Moreover, Newman was not angered by clerical authority as he embraced the discipline of Rome, although like most would-be reformers and scholars generally, he was often vexed by Papal authoritarianism and ecclesiastical politics. In sum, Newman, when compared to fellow intellectuals of the Victorian age, appears to us to be the quintessential Victorian scholar, i.e., neither sex-ridden nor rebellious. At a higher level, Newman was intellectually farther removed from us than many other figures who "lived on the farside of 1905." Quite obviously, he was pre-Freud in his psychology, as is evident from his decision to eschew sex and never mention it. He was pre-Marx in his politics as is illustrated by his propensity to disregard economic dimensions in his thought. And he was pre-Einstein in his metaphysics. This last point is central to his thought. While he would consider it of negligible importance to eschew the sexual turmoil that Freud associated with personality and would be equally inclined to disregard the class conflict that Marx discerned to be basic to politics, he would have to accept as fundamental the metaphysical revolution wrought by Einstein.

Newman sought the harmony integral to the Aristotelian and Newtonian universes. He sought certainty as defined by Cartesian clarity and Newtonian definiteness. This metaphysical certainty was both anchored and presaged by Classical and Christian authors' concepts of reason and virtue. Not for Newman is the Pascalian anguish in ambiguity as a spiritual condition. Not for Newman is the secular version of the Christian vision "through the glass darkly" as defined by Einstein's statistical probability in a universe of mathematical relativity.

'Tis time to draw these strands toward a conclusion. Let us venture this statement about Newman: He is a "constructionist" thinker, and his "constructionism" shaped his philosophy of education.

Newman would characterize himself as a "constructionist" thinker. He was living during and grappling with the the intellectual dimensions of a paradigmatic shift (to use Thomas Kuhn's expression). It was the paradigmatic shift from perceiving reality and measuring it as a clock running according to "natural" laws of mathematics and physics (18th century) to perceiving reality and measuring it as an organism growing according to equally "natural" laws of biology and history (19th century). Living and writing as he did almost a full hundred years before the 20th century's "deconstructive" interest in language and communication, Newman participated in the 19th century's "constructive" thinking. His thought was rooted in the new organic evolutionary assumptions which were supplanting the 18th century's equally "constructive" thinking, which was based upon the no-longer-new mechanistic universal assumptions about the nature of reality.

There are two ways to illustrate this. In the old-fashioned way, Newman may be seen as changing the thinker from master craftsman (18th century) to master artist (19th century). Immersed as he was in the transition, he would find no meaning in the linguistic mode of thought which has emerged to dominate the late 20th century. He would find incomprehensible the surge of secondary literature work about him which talks about his "language." Not for Newman is the reduction of reality to the "deconstruction" of texts, whether they be documents and certainly whether they be institutions. He was grappling with the intellectual transition between the 18th century notion that one discovered truth through building ideas as a master craftsman and the 19th century notion that one created truth through developing concepts as a master artist.

In the new-fangled way Newman may be seen as follows: Far from deracinating the subject from the object in order to study the object, as the 18th century physicists tried to do to achieve "objectivity," but rather to study the subject as the 19th century psychologists were beginning to do, Newman presumed to study the subject as subject, as the mind of the liberally educated person (*Bildung* in German), as "imperial intellect" (Culler's intellectual biography). He was grappling with the intellectual transition between the 18th century notion that one expressed the objective reality "out there" by discovering it and creating the expression for it, and the 19th century notion that one created the objective reality "out there" by creating it through encompassing objective reality in the subject "in here."

One conclusion. This is why Newman is a teacher instead of a researcher. He was interested in the subject as subject, i.e., the student as learner instead of as a receptacle of objective knowledge. Thus, his emphasis on the "whole man" is not only a reflection of the pastoral concern of religious belief. It derives from his philosophical notion that thinking is a human act from a human agent or "subject."

There are further questions to ask, of course. We should ask, following Weatherby, whether the "before 1905" character of his thought is a matter of direction, not development? Putting it one way, does "1905" represent a dead end for Newman, or does Newman's "constructivist" thought contain the elements of what we can call "post-poststructuralist, postmodernist, post-etc." thinking? Putting it another way, do we disregard the "1905 watershed" and consider whether Newman blocked the consequences of his thought by rejecting the notion of specialization and research?

If so, we ought to put pedagogy before religion in our analysis of Newman's philosophy of education. Is it indeed possible that Newman's view of education was shaped more by his pedagogical commitment than his religious belief? Does it follow, then, that Newman resisted science and research specialization because he was primarily a teacher?

We should ask, following Culler, whether "the imperial intellect," which entertained and encompassed the transition from 18th century mechanism to 19th organism, can comprehend the transition from 19th century constructionism to 20th century deconstructionism?

In summary, we argue that John Henry Newman lived on what we label "the far side of 1905" and is therefore a "constructionist" thinker who would seem quite alien to the "deconstructionist" thinking today. We argue that Cardinal Newman's "constructionist" thinking shares the credit with his religious belief for shaping his "*metaxyal*" Christian humanist philosophy of education.

WORKS CITED

Culler, Dwight. *The Imperial Intellect: A Study of Newman's Educational Ideal*. New Haven: Yale UP, 1955.

Harrold, C.F. "Newman and the Alexandrian Platonists." *Modern Philology* XXVII XXXVII (1939-40): 279-91.

Newman, John Henry Cardinal. "Christianity and Scientific Investigation." *On the Scope and Nature of University Education*. London: Dent, 1915.

—.*The Idea of a University*. Ed. May Yardley. Cambridge: Oxford UP, 1955.

Weatherby, Harold. *Cardinal Newman and His Age*. Cambridge: Oxford UP, 1973.

"Growth the only evidence of life": *Development of Doctrine and* The Idea of a University

Philip C. Rule, S.J.

"The rubric 'development of doctrine' has been in use since John Henry Newman, *An Essay on the Development of Christian Doctrine*," observes George A. Lindbeck (13n). Fellow theologian Jaroslov Pelican observes that Newman's essay is "the almost inevitable starting point for the investigation of the development of doctrine" (3). Thus Newman and the idea of development in religious doctrine are almost synonymous. This raises a most fascinating question. Why Newman? Why at this particular time in the middle of the 19th century? Surely the idea itself was not new. Under the various terms of growth, change, process, progress, evolution, and development the concept was current in the late 18th and early 19th centuries. It has in fact been around since the beginning of western civilization as John Nisbet has shown exhaustively in his two general studies of the idea. Karl Weintraub has demonstrated that around 1800 "our modern sense of history and of individuality grew from the fusing of an emergent genetic sense and a growing concern for singularity" (332). So, if the idea was in the air, why was Newman the first one to thus exploit it in theology?

A similar question arose some twenty years ago for Erik Erikson in his reflections on "Autobiographical Notes on the Identity Crisis" in a seminar dedicated to the questions of "how major transforming concepts or theories developed, and what [is] the climate propitious to such developments" (v). His essay attempts to "lay out some of the possible reasons for my having been the person who, at a given time in his life and in the history of psychoanalysis, came to observe and to name something by now so self-evident as the identity crisis and to explain, in fact, why it now seems so self-evident" (730). Apart from clinical and anthropological observation, Erikson finds the concept rooted concretely and autobiographically in his identity as an adopted son of his step-father and his subsequent "adoption" by Anna and Sigmund Freud. To the best of my knowledge, no biographer or scholar of Newman has asked that question in any detail about Newman. The question could, of course, also be asked of Darwin. As Richard Altick has pointed out, with the admitted exception of some "crucial additions," *Origin of Species* "was largely a brilliant synthesis of many scientific ideas already current. What was new was Darwin's explanation of organic mutability" (226). Walter Ong, for example, in discussing the intellectual milieu of *An Essay on the Development of Christian Doctrine* (hereafter referred to as *Essay*), rightly points out that it is imminent in his early works and anticipatory of subsequent writing, thus giving "a unified significance" to the history of his writings, but like others before and after, Ong does not ask about the autobiographical origins of so pivotal an idea; he simply assumes Newman borrowed it from the current discourse ("Newman's Essay" 3).

This neglect of the autobiographical origins of the idea of development is no more dramatically exemplified than in Ian Ker's recent and otherwise authoritative biography which devotes only 53 of its 750 pages to the first thirty-two years of Newman's life, and in those 53 pages he nowhere deals explicitly with the formation of the key insight of his personal and intellectual life. Even Henry Bremond's life, which purported to study Newman's "intellectual, emotional, and inner life" (37), says nothing about the idea of development. Wilfrid Ward's biography, which devotes 118 pages to the *Essay*, spends only 53 pages on the first forty-four years of his life. And yet he calls it "a record of the genesis of his thought" (I, 3). Maisie Ward tried to redress such obvious neglect in *Young Mister Newman* where she says, quoting Newman himself, "we rarely know much of men in their most interesting years—the years when they were forming—'from eighteen to twenty-eight or thirty'" (vii). One need not be much of a psycho-biographer to find this designation of the "formative years" rather naive, especially when dealing with someone as emotionally and intellectually precocious as Newman. Much had happened in Newman's intellectual development before he reached the ripe age of twenty. Meriol Trevor, of all biographers up to her time, comes closest to suggesting what I am addressing here. Newman, she writes, "had transferred the idea of growth from the individual to the group on the highest personal level, before it was discovered on the lowest and basic level of biology." She then suggests a line of pursuit, saying that "it is possible to trace the course of this growth because of his exceptional self-awareness, which some have considered self-preoccupation" (4). Unfortunately, having put her finger on one of the key sources, she fails to follow through in her otherwise excellent narrative biography.

It is my intention here, therefore, to trace the origins and conceptualization of Newman's fundamental, almost self-defining, insight in the first twenty-five years of his life before suggesting how both the *Essay* and later *The Idea of a University Defined and Illustrated* (hereafter referred to as *Idea*) grew out of the gradually shaping insight and are both rooted in it, exemplifying that both in the unfolding of revelation and the cultivation of the intellect, development is the central guiding insight.[4] I am suggesting in what follows that certain traits of character and temperament, certain practices, and certain experiences all converged to make Newman the right person with the right idea at the right time in the study of the history of Christian doctrine, and somewhat incidentally in terms of magnitude, in the contemporary ongoing dialogue about what university education should be. My procedure will be to pursue him through what I see to be the formative years, from birth to the age of twenty-five, by following him through volume one of the *Letters and Diaries*, like a gleaner looking for what previous biographers and scholars have, I am convinced, overlooked.

II

We might begin with a seemingly trivial entry into a boyhood pocketbook. In 1810, at the age of nine, he pencilled in his first entry, a biblical truism which upon reflection might well be seen as emblematic of his life to come: "Train up a child in the way he should go, and when he is old, he will not depart from it" (*LD* I, 5). In the *Autobiographical Writings* there is a small passage of some twenty-one lines written over a period of 72 years. The initial entry written in 1812 at the age of 11 suggests how precociously self-conscious he had become at so early an age: "John Newman wrote this just before he was going up to Greek on Tuesday, June 10, 1812, when it wanted only three days to his going home, thinking of the time (at home) when looking at this he shall recollect when he did it" (5). This projecting of the future moment occurs in later years when, for example, he writes his mother from Oxford: "I have no doubt I shall look back with regret to the time I was at Oxford and my birthday of 18" (*LD* I, 62).

In the notebooks and diaries and letters written throughout his life, there is a definite pattern of looking back to the past and forward to the future. In 1807 he left his home at Ham near Richmond for good, going off to school at Ealing. Almost 60 years later, he wrote, "it has ever been in my dreams" (*LD* I, 4). In 1886 he said it was a place "Which I dreamed about when a schoolboy as if it was Paradise" (*LD* I, 4). In 1816 after his father's financial failure, Newman wrote to his aunt Elizabeth about leaving Norwood saying, "he must have been conscious to himself that he would never see it (as his home) again" (*LD* I, 26). To his brother Frank he wrote in 1820 from Oxford: "For the calm happiness I now enjoy I cannot feel thankful as I ought. How in my future life, if I do live, shall I look back with a sad smile at these days!" (*LD* I, 82). What one senses here is a vivid consciousness of his being on the move—of moving from one place to another, of reaching back from a present point to a past one in a sort of Augustinian consciousness of the self stretched across time. It is as if he was ever in the presence of himself growing, a phenomenon poignantly borne out by an 1874 memo scribbled on a Latin oration delivered at Oriel in 1823: "I read this now for the first time these 51 years with sad tenderness, as if I loved and pitied the poor boy so ignorant of the future, who then wrote and delivered it before the Provost and Fellows, now almost all dead, but to whom I then looked up with great reverence and loving pride (*LD* I, 157). In this "sad smile and "sad tenderness" one hears echoes of the Virgilian time-bridging exhortation "*Haec olim forsan et meminisse juvabit*" (One day you will enjoy looking back even on what you now endure") (*Aeneid* 3), or of the Wordsworthian vision "That in this moment there is food and life / For future years" ("Tintern Abbey" 64-65).

A second important aspect of Newman's early years is his dedication to the arduous task of composition. In an autobiographical memoir of 1874, he says, "though in no respect a precocious boy, he attempted original composition in prose and verse from the age of eleven, and in prose showed a great sensibility and took much pain in matters of style" (*AW* 29).

While at Oxford "he wrote a critique of the plays of Aeschylus on the principles of Aristotle's Poetics, though original composition at that time had no place in school examinations" (*AW* 40). In an 1872 transcription of some early journal entries, he writes that "the unpleasant style in which it is written arises from my habit from a boy to compose" (*AS* 149). The highly developed sense of introspection and self-consciousness revealed in the early acts of memory and of imagining the future cited above can now be combined with an introspection or inwardness heightened and refined by sustained and rigorous efforts at original composition. As Walter Ong has pointed out, all writing—far short of the laborious kind we are witnessing here—has an interiorizing effect on a person. The cultural transition from orality to literacy literally restructures human consciousness. If as Ong says, "writing heightens consciousness," one can imagine the impact of such sustained and arduous exercise on an already self-conscious writer (*Orality* 82). It was, in fact, in the sustained experience of the writing process that Newman formally conceptualized the subjective insight of development—something growing from a seed into a full blown fruit. Two telling examples suggest this. In 1821 an essay he had submitted for an English Essay prize failed to win. Looking back thirty years later, he writes: "This Essay gives evidence I had not yet attended to composition—i.e., taking a idea and developing it. I believe the same fault is to be found in my Essay on ancient Slavery. Perhaps I did not begin to attempt this difficult accomplishment (which even now, November 1851, is what tries and distresses me in writing) till I had been writing Sermons for some time" (Culler 23). This becomes even more explicit in his struggles with Latin composition. In an 1855 essay included later in *Idea*, he records his own experiences through an imaginary obliging tutor, Mr. Black, who confesses "I had some idea of the style of Addison, Hume, and Johnson, in English; but I had no idea what was meant by good Latin style." Thus, he continues, "I was aiming to be an architect by learning to make bricks" (*Idea* 368). Newman's apparently lifelong struggle with genuine composition—unfolding an idea in his mind while committing it to writing—certainly sensitized him to the organic growth of ideas in any human mind which is itself growing and developing as it moves across a spectrum of time through heightened and expanding consciousness.

It is also clear that Newman at an early age began to see explicitly this developmental growth model at work both in the human thought processes and in the life pattern of an individual. Upon turning 21 he wrote his mother: "There is an illusion in the words 'being of age,' which is apt to convey the idea of some sudden and unknown change. That point, instead of being gained by the slow and silent progress of one and twenty years, seems to be divided by some strongly marked line, the past from the to-come" (*LD* I, 123).

Finally, another and more crucial event of his youth must be discussed—the conversion of 1816. Perhaps the best known and most often written about aspect of his early years, because of his own stressing of it in the *Apologia*, it nevertheless must be seen here as just one more element contributing to the subsequent fundamental insight about slow, progressive change in general and doctrinal development in particular. Profoundly influenced by the writings of Thomas Scott, an evangelical clergyman, Newman says, "for years I used almost as proverbs what I considered to be the scope and issue of his doctrine, 'Holiness rather than peace,' and 'Growth the only evidence of life'" (*Apo* 5). "Growth the only evidence of life." What single phrase could sum up more completely the entire tenor of Newman both intellectually and personally? His meticulous recording of the movements of his own life even at an early age, his deepening awareness of the developmental organic structure of human thought, and now a profound transition, a conversion, in his life as a Christian, which he saw at the time and would see throughout his life as continuous rather than discontinuous, as organic movement rather than static stages, as development rather than corruption. In a lengthy letter of 1817, his former school master Walter Mayers described to the young convert what this kind of spiritual change is. "The change," he writes, "is what I would call conversion, or rather what I understand the Scripture would denominate conversion,—A change which is very rarely *sudden* or *instantaneous* but generally *slow* and *gradual*, arising often times from causes which appear at the times fortuitous, but which the mind when enlightened will discern to have been directed by God" (*LD* I, 32). This conversion is explored in autobiographical notes written in 1820-21 and later transcribed with editing in 1874. The following entry suggests how the stuff of life makes its way into his subsequent writings: "The reality of conversion—as cutting at the root of doubt, providing a chain between God and the soul (i.e., with every link complete) I know I am right. How do I know it? I know I know. How? I know I know I know &c &c (vide *Grammar of Assent* 195-97, ed 4)." (*AW* 150). In the *Apologia* he writes, "a great change of thought took place in me" (4), but this change is elsewhere described as both quiet and continuous. The personal influence of Mayers and the writings of Scott, while conducing to the feeling of election to eternal life, also grows out of his longstanding "mistrust of the reality of material phenomena" (4). Newman describes the particular circumstances of the conversion as quite serene. Finishing the school term at Ealing early, "thereby I was left at school by myself, my friends gone away—(that is, it was a time of reflection, and where the Influences of Mr. Mayers would have room to act upon me. Also, I was terrified at the heavy hand of God which came down upon me" (*AW* 150). In June or July 1821, he writes, "I speak of (the process of) conversion with great diffidence, being obliged to adopt the language of books. For my own feelings, as far as I remember, were so different from any account I had ever read, that I dare not go by what may be the individual case" (*AW* 166). Commenting on these very lines five years later, July 1826, he adds this reflection:

> I am persuaded that very many of my most positive and dogmatic notions were taken *from books*. In the matter in question (conversion) my feelings were not violent, but a returning to, a renewing of, principles, under the power of the Holy Spirit, which I had *already* felt, and in a measure acted on, when young.
>
> (*AW* 172)

The converging pattern we have seen above—continuity of consciousness in recollecting the past and projecting the future, compositional activity, and conversion—come together in the combined concerns about his own spiritual growth and the unconscious shifting of his theological positions brought about by regular preaching. A diary entry for February 21, 1825, notes "dined in rooms and reviewed the past year" (*LD* I, 211). In a fuller entry for that date in *Autobiographical Writings*, he writes that "the necessity of composing sermons has obliged me to systematize and complete my ideas on many subjects." He expresses regret that "this change of opinion" is occurring with "little opportunity for devotion or private study," that he lacks time for prayer and "stated self-examination" (204-5). On Sunday, July 17, of that same year he writes that "I may add to my above remarks on my change of sentiments as to Regeneration, that I have been principally or in great measure led to this change by the fact that in my parochial activities I found many, who in most important points were inconsistent, but whom yet I could not say were altogether without grace" (*AW* 206). In the Autobiographical Memoir of 1874, he points to this period also as the beginning of "a great change in his religious opinions" (*AW* 73). Acknowledging "the force of logic and the influence of others," he credits personal pastoral experience for his growing conviction "that the religions which he had received from John Newton and Thomas Scott would not work in a parish; that it was unreal; that thus he had actually found as a fact, as Mr. Hawkins had told him beforehand, that Calvinism was not a key to the phenomena of human nature, as they occur in the world" (*AW* 79). This pattern of adult theological reflection would continue. In February 21, 1827, he reviews the previous year focusing on his religious growth (*AW* 210). By the time he was twenty-four, the pattern of Newman's mind was clearly set. In *Loss and Gain*, Newman's thinly veiled conversion biographical novel, he writes of his hero that "it is impossible to stop the growth of the mind. Here was Charles with his thoughts turned away from religious controversy for two years, yet with his religious views progressing, unknown to himself the whole time" (202).

From this point in time, we can date the twenty-year intellectual and spiritual Odyssey that would culminate in the *Essay*. In August, 1825, he was engaged in a long correspondence with his brother Charles who was undergoing a crisis of faith. At one point he counters Charles's qualms about the authenticity of certain texts in Scripture by pointing out that "the New Testament is not *Christianity*, but the *record* of Christianity" (*LD* I, 254), a statement that would no doubt have offended many conservative ears of the times. This position is clearly echoed again in 1845, when he writes in the *Essay* that "it may be objected that the inspired document at once determines the limits of its mission without further trouble; but ideas are in the writer and the reader of revelation, not the inspired text itself" (56), a statement startling perhaps even for many today. Granted the earlier statement was directed to the genuineness of the gospels and the latter to the transmission of ideas and their subsequent growth in the minds of readers, the principle at stake is the same—the revelation of transcendent truth is caught up in the very complex and finite historical process of human understanding.

These twenty years preceding the *Essay* fall into three periods: 1826-1833, from the Oriel tutorship to the Publication of *Arians of the Fourth Century*; 1833-1841, from the beginning of the Tractarian Movement to the publication of *Tract 90*; and from his rejection by the University and the Bishops to his publication of the *Essay on the Development of Christian Doctrine*.

In May 1826, he wrote to his sister Harriet, announcing, "I am about to undertake a great work perhaps" (*LD* I, 284), referring her to a letter to his sister Jemima for a fuller explanation, a letter in which it is described as " a work which may take me—t!e!!-n!!!—years??? perhaps twenty—but that is a long time to look forward to—perhaps too long—for a reader and thinker must not look for a long life, and I reflect with a sigh that half my life is gone, and I have done nothing.—I hope I have laid the foundation of something" (*LD* I, 285). With Coleridgean bravado he lays out this immense task: "But what after all is the subject?-it is to trace the sources from which the corruptions of the Church, principally the Romish, have been derived—It would consequently involve a reader of all the Fathers—200 volumes at least—(you saw some good stout gentlemen in Oriel Library—Austin 12 folio volumes Chrysostom 13 do.—) all on the principal Platonists, Philo, Plotinus, Julian, etc—an inquiry into Gnosticism—Rabinnical literature—and I know not what else—perhaps much, much more—am not I bold?" (*LD* I, 285). This boldness prompted him to write his friend Samuel Rickards about an encyclopedic and systematic review of the Old English divines (*LD* I, 309-10), a task to which he would in fact address himself almost ten years later, but first he had to produce what would be his initial albeit implicit application of the theory of development to doctrinal change.[5] *The Arians of the Fourth Century*, a work which had been commissioned for an historical series, when finished evoked from William Rowe Lyall, one of the editors, the comment that "Mr. Newman's views seem to me more favourable to the Roman writers, than I should like to put forward in the Theological Library" (*LD* III, 105). If his initial study of the early church and the Fathers led him to a Catholic reading of doctrinal history, his subsequent reading of the Anglican Fathers backed him into it. Attempting to use these theologians systematically in presenting the Anglican "via media" in *Prophetical Office of the Church* (1837) and *Lectures on Justification* (1838), Newman discovered that they were not historians when they dealt with history.[6] Actually, as early as 1831, writing to Samuel Rickard, to whom he had initially proposed such use of these theologians, he commented that "the standard Divines are magnificent fellows, but then they are Antiquarians or Doctrinists, not Ecclesiastical Historians—Bull, Waterland, Petavius, Baronius and the rest—of the historians I have met with I have a very low opinion—Mosheim, Gibbon, Middleton, Milner, etc—Cave and Tillement are highly respectable, but biographers" (*LD* II, 371).

Clearly Newman had found no adequate model for reading that past and its texts and was gradually articulating his own, a theory that would explain the facts, rather than twist the facts to fit a theory. It is indeed a felicitous coincidence that the year 1845 witnessed not only the publication of Newman's *Essay* but also of Poe's short story "The Purloined Letter, " for both exemplify what may be fairly called a "Romantic" epistemology, one which considers the role of imaginative insight as equal to or superior to reason and logic. Poe's master sleuth, M. Dupin, tells his companion why the Prefect of Police failed to find the stolen letter: "The measures, then, . . . were good in their kind and well executed; their defect lay in their being inapplicable to the case, and to the man. A certain set of highly ingenious resources are, with the Prefect, a sort of Procrustean bed, to which he forcibly adapts his designs," (I, 19). Later, Sherlock

Holmes, in a story clearly echoing and parodying Poe, "A Scandal in Bohemia, " provides a similar answer to Dr. Watson as to why he has not yet solved his case: "I have no data yet. It is a capital mistake to theorize before one has data. Insensibly one begins to twist facts to suit theories, instead of theories to suit facts," (3). Newman's own experientially based theory of development, ultimately based on his concept of the illative sense, would be the paradigm for this new reading and explanation of the facts of doctrinal history.[7]

Thus, as Erik Erikson's insight into "identity" and "identity crisis" emerged from his "personal, clinical, and anthropological observations" (747), so Newman's insight into "development" grew out of his personal experience of the self as a developing entity, gathering and incorporating, so as to achieve a personal continuity of consciousness over space and time.[8] As the individual, so the social phenomenon. Revelation is made to developing spiritual beings embedded in history—in space and time—and as he says with conviction in the *Essay*, "in a higher world it is otherwise, but here below to live is to change, and to be perfect is to have changed often" (63). This is only a maturer articulation of the insight achieved thirty years before: "Growth the only evidence of life."

III

In the *Essay* we find a convergence of the private and the public. Written as a personal synthesis of those arguments which brought him from the Anglican to the Roman Catholic Church, it is at once autobiography and theology. Karl Weintraub says that the proper form of autobiography is one "wherein a self-reflective person asks 'who am I?' and 'how did I come to be what I am?'" (1). What is here autobiographical in origin will become autobiography in form when in the narrative of the *Apologia* Newman traces from the inside, as it were, the forty-four years leading up to the writing of the *Essay*. Yet the autobiographical note is struck here by the highly personal tone of the original 1845 Advertisement to the *Essay*, where he apologizes for the frequent self-quotations "which are necessary in order to show how he stands at present in relation to various of his former publications" (x) and by the Dantesque echo at the end of the Introduction, where he apologizes for the fact that his evidence is far from exhaustive. The bold enterprise once envisioned by the youth of twenty-five was daunting, but "much less can such an undertaking be imagined by one who, *in the middle of his days*, is beginning life again" (31, emphasis mine).

My interest here is focused exclusively on the first two chapters of the *Essay*. The rest of the chapters in Part I are simply the application of the theory to the antecedent probability of development, and Part II is a detailed series of studies applying the notes of true development, seven notes which are in fact somewhat arbitrary and which Newman applies with decreasing degrees of thoroughness ranging from one hundred pages on the first to seven on the last. While it exceeds the limit of the present topic, it may be pointed out that even the choice and arrangement of doctrines treated serve autobiographical as well as objective theological needs. But the heart of the *Essay* is the discussion in Chapters I and II of the way the human mind works.

The opening words we read are that "it is the characteristic of our minds to be ever engaged in passing judgment on the things that come before us. No sooner do we apprehend than we judge; we allow nothing to stand by itself; we compare, contrast, abstract, generalize, connect, adjust, classify; and we view all our knowledge in the associations with which these processes have invested it" (33). It is tempting here to ask, is this the beginning of a treatise on doctrinal history, or on educational theory, or on assent to truth, or even a history of one's own religious opinions? It is clear that in all these cases the starting point for Newman is the nature of the human knower, the way the human mind works in the concrete.

His method in the first two chapters is to move from the nature of ideas growing in the individual mind to the nature of teaching and learning. Newman, first of all, who in the *Apologia* describes his youthful "mistrust of the reality of material phenomena" which made him "rest in the thought of two and two only absolute and luminously self-evident beings, myself and my Creator" (4), is not now thinking of a transcendent ahistorical self receiving divine truths in their completeness from a supremely transcendent being—God. However unquestioned the reality of the human spirit and the reality of a transcendent God, the human spirit is firmly embedded in history, in space and time, with all the limitations such a predicament implies. Thus an idea, "which represents an object or supposed object is commensurate with the sum total of its possible aspects, however they may vary in the separate consciousness of individuals" (34), "but there is no one aspect deep enough to exhaust the content of a real idea, no one term or proposition which will serve to define it" (35). "When an idea, whether real or not, is of a nature to arrest and possess the mind, it may be said to have life, that is, to live in the mind which is its recipient" (36). Once such an idea is possessed by the mind of many individuals, its growth is slow and complex. This process Newman calls "its development, being the germination and maturation of some truth or apparent truth on a large mental field" (38). He explicitly rejects a logical or deterministic model of knowing when he says, this "development of an idea is not like an investigation worked out on paper, in which each successive advance is a pure evolution from a foregoing, but it is carried on through and by means of communities of men and their leaders and guides; and it employs the minds as its instruments, and depends upon them while it uses them" (38). Then, foreshadowing both his argument for infallibility in

Chapter II and his later awareness of the risks involved for a religious community in sponsoring the cultivation of the intellect, as he would recommend in *Idea*, he says that "this it is that imparts to the history of both states and of religions its specially turbulent and polemical character. Such is the explanation of wrangling, whether of scholars or of parliaments. It is the warfare of ideas under their various aspects striving for the mastery, each of them enterprising, engrossing, imperious, more or less incompatible with the rest, and rallying followers or rousing foes, according as it acts upon the faith, the prejudice, or the interests of parties or classes" (39). Ideas develop in minds, consciously or unconsciously, peacefully or contentiously, ordinarily over long periods of time, even at the end of which the complexity of a real idea is not fully exhausted or developed. Newman, like Coleridge before him, takes pleasure in pointing out that "with all our intimate knowledge of animal life and of the structure of particular animals, we have not arrived at a true definition of any one of them, but are forced to enumerate properties and accidents by way of description" (35).[9]

The analogy with teaching and learning is drawn explicitly in the opening paragraph of Chapter II which, with typical rhetorical brilliance, summarizes the previous chapter. After describing how the historical fact of Christianity impresses a real idea on the mind and that idea then expands "into a multitude of ideas, and aspects of ideas, connected and harmonious with one another," he says this occurs because "it is a characteristic of our minds that they cannot take an object in which is submitted to them simply and integrally. We conceive by means of definition or description; whole objects do not create in the intellect whole ideas, but are, to use a mathematical phrase, thrown into series, into a number of statements, strengthening, interpreting, correcting each other, and with more or less exactness approximating, as they accumulate to a perfect image. There is no other way of learning or teaching.

We cannot teach except by aspects or views which are not identical with the thing itself which we are teaching. Two persons may each convey the same truth to a third, yet by methods and representations altogether different. The same person will treat the same argument differently in an essay or speech, according to the accident of the day of writing, or of the audience, yet will be substantially the same" (55).   Thus, Newman's "classroom" is one where uniquely individual minds struggle to communicate with other uniquely individual minds amid constantly changing times and circumstances. It is not the classroom of Dickens' Mr. McChoakumchild, where one sees students sitting "like an inclined plane of little vessels then and there arranged in order, ready to have imperial gallons of facts poured into them until they were full to the brim" (*Hard Times* 12). The method of teaching, of course, becomes the method of examining the historical process of unfolding revelation.

For anyone who might object that in the case of revelation, which is in fact a sort of teaching/learning situation, at least the textbook, speaks for itself, determines "the limits of its mission without further trouble," Newman counters, as we have seen, that "ideas are in the writer and reader of revelation, not in the inspired text itself" (56). For the problem is still the same: "the question is whether those ideas which the letter conveys from writer to reader, reach the reader at once in their completeness and accuracy on his first perception of them, or whether they open out in his intellect and grow to perfection in the course of time" (56). Newman is insistent on the analogue to human learning and understanding, for he ends his point by reiterating that "unless some special ground of exception can be assigned, it is as evident that Christianity, as a doctrine and worship will develop in the minds of recipients, as that it conforms in other respects, in its external propagation or its political framework, to the general method by which the course of things is carried forward" (57).

The force of this argument within the context of the *Essay* leads to an argument for the antecedent probability of the development of doctrine throughout the history of the Church, which leads in turn to an argument for the antecedent probability of an infallible guide of that process (which is not deterministic as physical evolution would be) which need not concern us here except to point out that just as conscience for Newman is the "governor" or regulator of individual growth (George Eliot said "The strongest principle of growth lies in human choice"), so the multiplicity of opinions inevitably engendered over time by the conscious and unconscious exercise of the intellect must somehow be brought into unison if revealed truth is to be salvific and unifying. Describing the reality that results when "reason, as it is called, is the standard of truth and right," Newman concludes that individuals will tolerate no "common measure." The solution is again described in terms of teaching and learning; for it is precisely education, as he will stress in the *Idea*, which causes the diversity. "There can," he says, "be no combination on the basis of truth without an organ of truth. As cultivation brings out the colours of flowers and domestication changes the character of animals, so does education of necessity develop differences of opinion; and while it is impossible to lay down first principles in which all will unite, it is utterly unreasonable to lay down first principles in which all will unite, it is utterly unreasonable to expect that this man should yield to that, or all to one" (90). And thus "the only general persuasive in matters of conduct is authority" (90). The rest of the *Essay* grows out of this insight into the processes of human understanding, communication, and interpretation. The revelation is divine and transcendent; the medium and recipients, however, are very finite and time bound. The process of development is very human, however divinely guided to its destined end. Development of doctrine, like teaching and

learning, is a very subtle often frustrating but ultimately
enriching process.

IV

By now it should be clear how much personal and subjective
experience lies behind Newman's objective theological concept
"development of doctrine." Let me now proceed to suggest how
personal experience lies behind most of his thinking on education as expressed in *Idea* and pursue further the analogues
between it and the *Essay*.

Dwight Culler has dealt magisterially with the subject and
has shown how the writing of the *Idea* coincided with a move
Newman's Oratorian community made from one part of Birming-
ham to another. Already planning to review his long years at
Oxford—a trait we have seen before—as an acceptable model for
University education, he now had the additional opportunity to
sift through his incredible accumulation of writings and notes.
He would not be reviewing in memory only but could cull from
material ranging from his earliest exercises as a student to his
published works. During the Oxford years Newman engaged in
a confrontation with Edward Hawkins, Provost of Oriel, over the
lecture vs. the tutorial method. The two elements Newman
stressed in education, as Culler points out, were "the element of
discipline or law and the element of influence. Influence is
Mark Hopkins on one end of a log and a student on the other,
and Newman considered this to be the heart of the educational
process" (157). This role of personal influence runs deep in
Newman's thought. In 1840, writing against the substitution of
secular and scientific knowledge for religious truth, he said
"deductions have no power of persuasion. The heart is commonly reaching, not through the reason, but through the imagination, by means of direct impressions, by the testimony of facts
and events, by history, by description. Persons influence us,
voices melt us, looks subdue us, deeds inflame us" (*DA* 293). For

Newman, although he would argue vigorously for the cultivation of the intellect as *an* end in itself, it is not *the* end of education. His parting comment to readers of the *Essay* is not a call for scholarly examination of this evidence and argument but a reminder that "time is short, eternity is long" (418).

Thus Newman advocated the tutorial method because teaching is a pastoral activity and teachers and students form a community of learners. "A University is," he says, "according to the usual designation, an Alma Mater, knowing her children one by one, not a foundry or mint, or a breadmill" (144-45). Newman was interestingly enough anticipated in this by the poet William Cowper whose poem "Tirocinium or a Review of Schools" advocated the tutorial method as better suited for dealing with "adolescents," which turns out to be the first use in the English language of that term as describing a developmental stage between childhood and adulthood (Cowper 353). What both decried was the regarding of students as impersonal receptacles to be filled or products to be manufactured. "Real teaching," Newman says, ". . . at least tends toward cultivation of the intellect; it at least recognizes that knowledge is something more than a sort of passive recognition of scraps and details; it is something and it does something which never will issue from the most strenuous efforts of a set of teachers, with no mutual sympathies and no intercommunion, of a set of examiners with no opinion which they dare profess, and with no common principles, who are teaching or questioning a set of youths who do not know them, and do not know each other, on a large number of subjects, different in kind and connected by no wide philosophy, three times a week, or three times a year, or once in three years, in chill lecture rooms or on a pompous anniversary" (147-48). In real teaching one finds a "multitude of ideas" which are "connected and harmonious" such as rise out of a community reflecting over time on the content of revelation as seen in the *Essay*. One finds truths which are not impersonally dictated but lovingly and not without difficulty communicated from person to person—not the communication of fragments and bits between total strangers.

Newman's stress on the developmental model is borne out both by his explicit ideas and his choice of words. He recommends Grammar as the first step in intellectual training, "which is to impress upon a boy's mind the idea of science, method, order, principle and system; of rule and exception, of richness and harmony." The second is Mathematics, which gives him "a conception of development and arrangement from and around a common centre" (xix). In describing the history of his own views on liberal education, he speaks of "a fuller development and more exact delineation of the principles of which the University was representative" (2). His own views "have grown into my whole system of thought, and are, as it were, part of myself. Many changes has my mind gone through: here it has known no variation of vacillation of opinion, and though this by itself is no proof of the truth of my principles, it puts a seal upon conviction, and is a justification of earnestness and zeal" (4). Again the study of style, Cicero's for example, is important because "it is the expression of lofty sentiment in lofty sentences, the 'mens magna in corpore magno.' It is the development of the inner man" (281). Finally, the literature of a people is seen as a development of a nation or a culture: "The growth of a nation is like that of an individual; its tone of voice and subjects for speech vary with every age" (310).

Just as the Church runs the risk of contamination from its contact with the world, it runs an equal risk in isolating itself. So in true education one runs risks—either losing an intellect cultivated simply for its own sake or destroying or impairing it by training it only for some useful or specific task. In the *Essay* he asks "whether all authority does not necessarily lead to resistance" (50) and admits "education of necessity develops differences of opinion" (107). So in *Idea* he says "Knowledge viewed as Knowledge, exerts a subtle influence in throwing us back on ourselves, and making us our own centre, and our minds the measure of all things. This then is the tendency of that Liberal Education, of which a University is the school, viz., to view Revealed Religion from an aspect of its own,—to fuse and recast it,—to tune it, as it were, to a different key, and to reset its harmonies. . . . A sense of propriety, order, consistency, and completeness gives birth to a rebellious stirring against miracles and mystery, against the severe and the terrible" (217-18). This is the risk one takes if one conceives of the human mind as an organism and not a machine.

What Newman advocates is a philosophic habit of mind at once precise and capacious, one that can examine detail minutely and comprehend the whole systematically, one that does not look out to the world and the universe only from a limited disciplinary point of view, however adequate that may be in exploring its particular subject, but one which sees the whole as a whole. Thus he argues in Part I on University teaching for the rightful and necessary place of theology in the university faculty and curriculum if the whole of truth is to be the subject of learning, and in Part II on University Subjects he warns against the narrowing effects of Useful knowledge "which may resolve itself into an art, and terminate in a mechanical process, and a tangible fruit" (112).

V

I should like to conclude by briefly discussing another strong influence on Newman, one already suggested in passing. As late as 1872, Newman wrote that "Wordsworth's Ode is one of the most beautiful poems in our language" (*LD* XXVI, 56). In 1860, writing about the lives of the saints, he says that the real life is "a narration which impresses the reader with the idea of moral unity, identity, growth, continuity, personality" (*HS* II, 227).

Finally, in 1845 speaking of the "conservative action of the past" in the *Essay*, he writes that the "bodily structure of a man is not merely that of a magnified boy; he differs from what he was in make and proportions; still manhood is the perfection of boyhood, adding something of its own, yet keeping what it finds" (419-20). Clearly his own devout wish was that the movements both of his own life and that of the Church doctrinal life could be "Bound each to each by natural piety." Almost all of Newman's writings are, as I have been suggesting, about the two works under consideration—in particular, recollections of a past that has both a private and public dimension and significance.

As Wordsworth records in his poetry his movement from a period of youth when he saw the "splendour in the grass" and the "glory in the flower" to mature years which bring "the philosophic mind, " so Newman in his essay on "Elementary Studies" in *Idea* begins with the undifferentiated vision of an infant and moves to that mature differentiated vision which "gradually converts a calidoscope into a picture," and concludes that "the first view was more splendid, the second the more real; the former more poetical, the latter more philosophical" (331). The Wordsworthian diction is obvious. Less obvious, perhaps, is that it opens the way to the *Grammar of Assent* with its illative sense that fuses imagination and reason. In *The Prelude* Wordsworth's life and reflections would lead him to the source of that philosophic mind—at times called the "Imagination—here the Power so called / Through sad incompetence of human speech" (VI, 592-93). At other times it is called "spiritual Love [which] acts not nor can exist

> Without Imagination, which, in truth
> Is but another name for absolute power
> And clearest insight, amplitude of mind,
> And Reason in her most exalted mood

(XIV, 188-92)

Or, again, it is called "intellectual Love," for

> Imagination having been our theme,
> so also hath that intellectual Love,
> For they are each in each, and cannot stand
> Dividually.
> (XIV, 206-209)

Read in this light, the writer of the *Essay* is not a disinterested historian but a concerned reasoner. Read in this light, the writer of *Idea* is not an educational theorist but a loving and concerned teacher, concerned to bring out the full uniqueness of each individual committed to his care. What Wordsworth compressed into the word "imagination" Newman would finally call the "illative sense." In the *Grammar of Assent*, echoing both the *Essay* and *Idea* almost verbatim, he says "everyone who reasons, is his own centre: and no expedient for attaining a common measure of minds can reserve this truth" (345). Here all Newman ideas converge: doctrines tend toward their fulfillment, their perfection or individuality; education tends to bring out the uniqueness, the individuality of the human person; and now he tells us that the illative sense is the perfection of that human individuality on the cognitive level: "What is the peculiarity of our nature, in contrast with the inferior animals around us? It is that, though man cannot change what he is born with, he is a being of progress with relations to his perfection and characteristic good. Other beings are complete from their first existence, in that line of excellence which is allotted to them; but man begins with nothing realized (to use the word), and he has to make capital for himself by the exercise of those faculties which are his natural inheritance. Thus he gradually advances to the fullness of his original destiny. Nor is this progress mechanical, nor is it of necessity; it is committed to the personal efforts of each individual of the species; each of us has the prerogative of completing his inchoate and rudimentary nature, and of developing his own perfection out of the living elements with which his mind began to be. It is his gift to be the creator of his own sufficiency; and to be emphatically self-made. This is the law of his being, which he cannot escape; and whatever is involved in that law he is bound, or rather he is carried on, to fulfil" (348-49). Thus whether it be in matters of doctrine, education, or the psychology of knowing, "Growth [is] the only evidence of life."

ENDNOTES

4. In the text of my essay, for brevity's sake, The *Idea of a University* and the *Essay on Development* are referred to as *Idea* and *Essay* respectively.

5. In "Newman at Nicea," Michael Novak points out how Newman discovered in the warring theological factions represented by Antioch and Alexandria the wrong and the right way of reflecting on revelation. It was the latter party which showed him that "it is of the nature of the human mind to see things only partially; to move gradually from vantage point to vantage point; to court first one extreme and then the opposite, back and forth, in climbing the ascent of wisdom. And the irreverence of mere logicism of the Arian mind is always a threat to us enroute" (452).

6. In my "Newman and the English Theologians" I show how Newman's sustained and systematic reading of the Reformation and Caroline divines led to disillusionment with them because of their static view of history.

7. In *Bossuet to Newman* Owen Chadwick shows how the traditional Christian belief in a fixed "deposit of faith" began to yield to the pressure of a growing sense of historicism. While thoroughly conversant with this history of theorizing about change and the indefectibility of revealed truth, Newman was influenced largely if not exclusively in these matters by Bishop Joseph Butler's *Analogy of Religion* (1736) which he first read in the summer of 1823.

8. Critics such as Clifford Siskin, would, of course, claim this developing conscious self is a product and ploy of a temporally defined and conditioned Romantic discourse, all the more delusively powerful because it is so "ahistorical" (12).

9. Kathleen Coburn says Coleridge "frequently noticed with something like triumph, the difficulties in defining the edges of the mineral, vegetable, and animal kingdoms, as if here he saw evidence of the process itself, growth, continuity with change, and change with continuity. In short, in looking at nature he saw the inside of the outside, and the outside of the inside—he felt, at his best, a small but functional part of all that lives, grows, changes, and creates" (63).

WORKS CITED

Altick, Richard D. *Victorian People and Ideas*. New York: Norton, 1973.

Bremond, Henri. *The Mystery of Newman*. London: William and Norgate, 1907.

Chadwick, *From Bossuet to Newman: The Idea of Doctrinal Development*. Cambridge, Cambridge UP, 1957.

Coburn, Kathleen. *The Self-Conscious Imagination*. London: Oxford UP, 1974.

Cowper, William. *Verses and Letters*. Ed. Brian Spiller. Cambridge, Mass: Harvard UP, 1968.

Culler, A. Dw*ight*. *The Imperial Intellect: A Study of Newman's Educational Ideal*. New Haven: Yale UP, 1955.

Dickens, Charles. *Hard Times*. New York: New American Library, 1961.

Doyle, Arthur Conan. *The Complete Adventures and Memoirs of Sherlock Holmes*. New York: Bramhall House, 1975.

Erikson, Erik. "Autobiographical Notes on the Identity Crisis." *Daedalus* 99 (1970): 730-759.

Ker, Ian. *John Henry Newman: A Biography*. Oxford: Clarendon Press, 1988.

Lindbeck, George. *The Nature of Doctrine: Religion and Theology in a Postliberal Age*. Philadelphia: Westminster P, 1984.

Newman, John Henry. *Apologia Pro Vita Sua*. London: Longmans, 1895.

—. *Autobiographical Writings*. Ed. Henry Tristram. London: Sheed and Ward, 1956.

—. *Discussions and Arguments on Various Occasions*. London: Longmans, 1891.

—. *An Essay in Aid of a Grammar of Assent*. London: Longmans, 1891.

—. *An Essay on the Development of Christian Doctrine*. London: Longmans, 1894.

—. *Historical Sketches*. 3 Vols. London: Longmans, 1896. *The Idea of a University Defined and Illustrated*. London: Longmans, 1896.

—. *The Letters and Diaries of John Henry Newman*. 31 Vols. I-X: Oxford: Clarendon Press, 1978—; XI-XXXIII: London: Thomas Nelson, 1961-1977.

Nisbet, Robert. *History of the Idea of Progress*. New York: Basic Books, 1980.

—. *Social Change and History: Aspects of the Western Theory of Development*. London: Oxford UP, 1969.

Novak, Michael. "Newman at Nicea." *Theological Studies* 21 (1960): 44-53.

Ong, Walter J. "Newman's Essay On Development in its Intellectual Milieu." *Theological Studies* 13 (1946): 3-45.

—. *Orality and Literacy: The Technologizing of the Word*. London: Methuen, 1982.

Pelikan, Jaroslav. *Development of Christian Doctrine: Some Historical Prolegomena*. New Haven, Yale UP, 1969.

Poe, Edgar Allan. *The Works of Edgar Allan Poe*. 5 Vols. New York: Collier, 1903.

Rule, Philip C. "Newman and the English Theologians." *Faith and Reason* 15 (1989): 65-90.

Siskin, Clifford. *The Historicity of Romantic Discourse*. New York: Oxford UP, 1988.

Trevor, Meriol. *The Pillar of the Cloud*. New York: Doubleday, 1962.

Virgil. *The Aeneid*. Trans. W.F. Jackson Knight. Harmondsworth: Penguin, 1956.

Ward, Maisie. *Young Mister Newman*. New York: Sheed and Ward, 1948.

Ward, Wilfred. *The Life of John Henry Cardinal Newman*. 2 Vols. London: Longmans, 1912.

Weintraub, Karl Joachim. *The Value of the Individual: Self and Circumstance in Autobiography*. Chicago: U of Chicago P, 1978.

Wordsworth, William. *The Prelude*. Ed. Ernest De Selincourt. 2nd ed. Oxford: Clarendon Press, 1959.

Newman's *Apologia Pro Vita Sua: Gender, Self, and Conscience*

Mary Ellen Jordan

The historical Newman has proven to be an elusive figure. Reviewer Richard Shannon celebrates Ian Ker's recent biography of John Henry Newman as "high achievement" for its critical exposition of Newman's prose (especially Newman's skillful employment of rhetoric, imagery, metaphor, and satire), but bemoans the fact that Ker, like the many Newman biographers before him, fails to situate Newman within his historical context. This is a serious shortcoming because the historical Newman has been the subject of much controversy. According to Shannon, "the man whom a multitude of his public and private contemporaries knew, or thought they knew, in reverence, pity, or hate, is not here"; in fact, "one frequently gets a sense of a Newman temporally disembodied."

The conflicting feelings which Newman prompted among his contemporaries appear to be due to a kind of paradoxical doubleness inherent in the man. Newman was a shy man who was respectful of, even deferential to, authority; nonetheless, he was proud and ambitious. He was a mild-mannered man who was attracted to asceticism; yet, he was a skilled and combative occasional writer spurred into action by controversy. He was a traditional man who devoted his life to the dogmatic principle in religion; nevertheless, he championed the rights of conscience and prepared the way for Vatican II. Ker himself wonders about the varying reactions this doubleness has produced: "It was odd how Newman could attract such professed adulation, and yet at the same time such downright hostility" (607).

What we have at the moment are two very different schools of interpretation: the first contending that Newman possessed an extraordinary saintliness [Ward, Trevor, and Ker]; the second arguing that Newman possessed a limited, if not devious, human nature [Faber, O'Faolain, and Robbins]. Both, however, have failed to realize the historical Newman because of limited perspectives. Wilfrid Ward is wise enough to alert us to the danger of "partial" readings of the man:

> John Henry Newman is indeed himself a remarkable instance of one of his most characteristic contentions, that the same object may be seen by different onlookers under aspects so various and partial as to make their views, from their inadequacy, appear occasionally even contradictory.
>
> (I,2)

This paper is an attempt to connect Newman's acclaimed saintliness with his very human nature, that is, to show that Newman's religious strengths and insights are intimately connected with his psychological struggles as a man. A look at these struggles demonstrates a movement from a prescribed and restricting identification with oedipal father figures, to a new and creative identification with multiple figures, especially the mother/woman figure. This breakthrough signals a more expansive self and a less narrow experience of gender, which led Newman to a natural reenvisioning of the relationship between church authority and conscience.

In considering the polarized views regarding Newman, we must begin with the issue of his celibacy. To those well disposed to Catholicism and/or to the Church's stipulation (since the time of the Middle Ages) that clergy be celibate, there has been a tendency not to analyze Newman's decision in favor of celibacy. To others, Newman's celibate commitment, even as an Anglican, suggests an outdated medieval bias and possibly a psychological problem. Especially since the appearance of Darwinian theory in the nineteenth century, educated people have doubted the credibility of someone, like Newman, whose life was dedicated to a God who seemed to exist above and apart from history and biology. Thus, the celibate's decision to "imitate the Unmoved Mover" and to "refuse to perpetuate the biological stream of life . . . might even seem perverse" (Durham 418). "Newman always thought that much of the hostility that he had to face in Oxford was due less to his theological opinions than his uncompromising preaching of such an unpopular virtue" (Trevor 41).

The polarized views regarding Newman's celibacy also reflect an ongoing debate about what for many is a related issue, the relative strengths of his "masculine" and "feminine" dispositions. The gender "question" was provoked by the observation of many that Newman possessed a fascinating, "almost a feminine charm" (Robbins 83). Many also considered him feminine due to his sensitive and artistic temperament, and what seemed a puzzling "passivity—making no attempt to fashion the course of his life, but waiting on Providence" (Father Ryder, quoted by Wilfrid Ward 15). Finally there was Newman's preference for intense male friendships, most notably with Hurrell Froude and Ambrose St. John, which suggested that he was not attracted to heterosexuality. As a consequence, "slurs" regarding his "virility" (Trevor 41) plagued him through his life.

Newman's spiritual autobiography, *Apologia Pro Vita Sua* (hereafter referred to as the *Apologia*), was prompted by such a slur. In what Marjorie Durham refers to as "perhaps the most fruitful blunder in the record of Victorian literature" (417), Charles Kingsley, a married Anglican clergyman who preached a "healthful and manly Christianity" characterized by common sense and bold action rather than by spiritual discernment and intellectual acumen (Houghton 204), attacked Newman's supposed Roman Catholic subtlety as a veiled form of lying. In so doing, Kingsley linked this subtlety with Newman's celibacy, and with femininity.

> Truth, for its own sake, had never been a virtue with the Roman clergy. Father Newman informs us that it need not, and on the whole ought not to be; that cunning is the weapon which heaven has given to the Saints wherewith to withstand the brute male force of the wicked world which marries and is given in marriage.
> (*Apo* 2)

Although Kingsley's ostensible criticism is that Newman has little respect for the truth, his metaphor for cunning suggests that Newman's subtlety is a twisted logic, a defense mechanism necessitated by an underlying, unmasculine homosexuality. Kingsley's charge positions Newman, who is ironically referred to as a Saint, as a woman who chooses a specious brand of "cunning" [a euphemism for lies] to defend herself from "brute" males intent on supposedly normal sexual gratification.

The *Apologia* proved a remarkable vindication of Newman's integrity. Despite the fact that the memoir is primarily an "intellectual" autobiography and that "on the personal level, [it] conceals as much as it reveals" (Ker 559), Newman's rhetorical strategy is admirably suited to answer Kingsley's central charge by dramatizing his "masculine" self. Clearly in the *Apologia* Newman is intent on presenting an heroic *persona*, the figure of a loyal son willing to fight to preserve the heritage handed down to him by his father. Newman's choice of "the generational metaphor" was in keeping with the traditional theological view that "the family at last represents the true Church, faithfully transmitting doctrinal truth from father to son . . . " (Durham

419). Recognizing that his audience were primarily Englishmen, many of whom were not religious, Newman easily identified a famous counterpart to the metaphor in English literature, and so also depicts his religious struggle in terms of Hamlet's fidelity to the ghost of his dead father.

The *Hamlet* analogy works like this: the Anglican Church, the (supposed) Bride of Christ, is likened to Gertrude, who, after vowing fidelity to her Divine spouse, Hamlet's father, becomes involved in an alliance with the state, represented by Claudius; and, just as Hamlet believed that he had actually seen his father's ghost, talked with him, and been commissioned by him to investigate his murder and the unseemly alliance between Gertrude and Claudius, Newman—true to his life-long belief in a spiritual realm—believes in the very real existence of God, conceptualized as the Father, who communes with His son through the writings of the early Fathers, and has commissioned him to confront his Spiritual Mother, the Anglican Church, with her past glory and present disgrace ("Look on this picture and on that").

Newman's choice of the Hamlet metaphor enables us to focus attention on a psychological dimension of Newman's conversion account. Since Ernest Jones's 1949 essay on *Hamlet*, the play has been seen as dramatizing the prototypical ambivalence toward the father which is at the heart of what Freud termed the Oedipus complex. In the *Apologia,* it is clear that Newman's conversion pivots on a critique of the father figures whom he had idealized and a reappraisal of the father figures whom he had vilified. Newman is intent, of course, on proving his virility and maintaining his identification with the father, but his struggle suggests inherent problems in oedipal psychology, and especially in its central contention that male gender, and adult maturity, are measured solely in regard to identification with the father.

The *Apologia* documents that, like Hamlet, Newman is a good son preoccupied with a loving and legitimate but absent father. When Newman begins his work in the Oxford Movement, he is adamant that, not only is he a fit spokesperson ready for the intellectual debate and full of energy, but also that his moral position is impregnable—he was not among the guilty. During a bout with fever in Sicily, he repeated with bold assurance, "I shall not die, for I have not sinned against the light, I have not sinned against the light" (40). Although Newman acknowledges that he was never able to make out what he meant by these words, he is confident that he was a good son and that Providence was guiding his steps. Looking back, he links his efforts with the daring heroism and great-heartedness which he remembers in the classic heroes Odysseus and Aeneas.

The *Apologia* also documents that, like Hamlet, Newman is a culpable son obsessed with a darker image of the father. Jones's classic interpretation points to Hamlet's indecisiveness as evidence of unconscious oedipal guilt, and argues that despite the fact that he is repelled by Claudius, a violent and sexually robust man, Hamlet cannot take action against his stepfather because, like him, he has desired slaying the father and bedding the mother (45-70). There is evidence in the text that Newman was an adolescent rebel and a contentious man vehemently opposed to the Father, especially as represented by the Anglican authorities, and even more by the Roman Pontiff allied with the Biblical fantasy figure, the whore of Babylon. Both the Hamlet analogy and the mention of the "Babylon of St. John" (132) imply Newman's sexual preoccupation. In an attempt to triumph over this father, Newman is guilty of calumny and slander.

Like Hamlet, whose indecisiveness reflects doubt, Newman struggles to make sense of his conflicting reactions to father figures. Like Hamlet, Newman hopes to solidify his identification with the legitimate father, and in so doing to prove himself as a man. Newman's mind seems almost a plethora of fathers, a significant factor in allowing him room to manoeuvre as he sorts through father/son issues. Since Newman's conversion pivots on a reappraisal of his relationship to these father figures, I will clarify the different contexts in which these father images operate.

It is important to note at the outset that Newman's biological father is notable for his absence. Although Newman justified skipping over personal material in what he termed his intellectual autobiography, it is clear from many sources that he had little in common with his father and that they were often at odds. Newman's father—a banker, a bankrupt, and a brewer, and in addition, a Freemason and member of the Beefsteak Club—was an unintellectual, extroverted, highly skeptical man, and the least religious member of his family. In the *Apologia* Newman mentions his father twice in passing (15, 16). The tone in which he speaks about his father is always cool and noncommittal. The first reference presents the father as inadvertently aiding Providence by taking his son along to hear music at the Catholic chapel of the Bavarian embassy; the second reference presents the father as an establishment figure whom the son "found pleasure" in scandalizing with his free thinking (16). Although not much can be said on the basis of so little information, it is interesting that Newman aligns his non-religious father with the Roman Catholic camp of fathers in both cases. In the first instance, the father is aligned with the providential father God who led Newman to the Catholic church, and in the second instance, he is aligned with the Pope, the other figure whom Newman "found pleasure" in scandalizing. It is as if Newman largely rejects the father of the flesh who had disparaged his son's "excessive religious zeal" (Levine 204), but "redeems" him, nonetheless, by allying him with the inadvertent workings of Divine Providence.

Given the fact that Newman and his biological father felt little empathy for one another (Faber 7), and the fact that Newman lived in communities of men with a religious orientation from the age of seven until his death, it is understandable why for Newman the concept of father operates almost exclusively in a religious context. Although Newman would have known that God is spirit, and that metaphors cannot exhaust God's possibilities, as a nineteenth century Christian he conceived of God as the Almighty Father. Since Newman specialized in Patristics, it was also natural for him to feel an emotional pull toward the Early Fathers as having a special claim to represent the Word of God as revealed by Christ. In addition, the great Anglican Divines of the sixteenth and seventeenth centuries and Newman's immediate Anglican superiors served as representatives of the Father. Finally, all Christians contend with the powerful image of the Roman Pontiff, traditionally called the Holy Father of Christendom.

The strength of Newman's attachment to the father image is intimately connected with his first experience of conversion at age fifteen, when he was struck with the "thought of two and two only absolute and luminously self-evident beings, myself and my Creator" (16). This early figure of the Father is that of an all-powerful, but providential figure, a kind of benevolent monarch. It is clear from this and from Newman's pictures of his mentors and teachers that his primary image of the father is positive, loving and supportive. Much of Newman's sense of individual worth and unique destiny is derived from his sense that he is the legitimate son of the transcendent Father and the indisputable heir to the heavenly kingdom. However, this image of the father appears divorced from history and from sexuality; consequently, Newman's identification with this father image yields a somewhat disembodied male identity.

Nevertheless, Newman is also preoccupied with a punitive and more sexually threatening father image. This figure may be related to Newman's aversion to his all too fallible father, and to his life-long sense of sin, which he had imbibed with his early Evangelicalism. Newman recognized within himself a split between the image of the good and bad father and speaks of it as "an intellectual inconsistency which disabled [him] for a long course of years." He notes that early in his life he became aware of his strong, but often conflicting emotional reactions to certain readings which focused on the father figure. When he was first introduced to the Patristic Age by reading Joseph Milner's Church History, he found himself "nothing short of enamoured of the long extracts from St. Augustine, St. Ambrose, and the other Fathers which [he] found there." At about the same time, however, he read Newton on the Prophecies and found himself furious and full of spite as he "became most firmly convinced that the Pope was the Antichrist predicted by Daniel, St. Paul, and St. John" (18).

As a symbol of the Antichrist, the Pope was well suited to serve the English Newman as a figure of the bad sexual father, whom he felt free to revile and over whom he felt he must triumph. The view of the Pope as licentious and power-mad had been widespread in England since the time of the Reformation. Spenser had been among the first there to accuse the Pope of being in league with the infamous "whore of Babylon"—but he was not the last. "The more I study Scripture," Newman wrote, "the more I am impressed with the resemblance between the Romish principle in the Church and the Babylon of St. John" (132). Having thus imbibed the Protestant aversion to the Papacy, Newman could, in good conscience, vent his anger against the father as represented by the Holy Father. An older Newman, writing the *Apologia* and looking back on the boy he was at age fifteen, is both embarrassed and saddened to report that he had actually erased in his *Gradus ad Parnassum,* such titles, under the word "Papa," as "Christi Vicarious," "sacer interpres," and "sceptra gerens," and substituted epithets so vile that [he could] not bring [him]self to write them down here.

(101)

The mention of "vile epithets," and Newman's belief that his vehement hatred of the Pope had acted like a "stain upon [his] imagination" (18) which it took him years to eradicate, suggests revulsion with and anger towards the father's sexuality. Newman's embarrassment regarding this youthful "vile" language implies that, like Hamlet, he himself is implicated with the crimes which he abhors. Interestingly, during these same teen years, Newman also flirted with democratic Liberalism. He says that he developed a flippant attitude and "a certain disdain for Antiquity," which led him to prefer "intellectual excellence to moral" (24). Like a typical adolescent, Newman stood on what he calls "negative ground" (101) and flirted with rebellion against patriarchal authority.

Soon after mentioning the "stain upon his imagination" caused by his obsession with the Pope as the anti-Christ, Newman mentions "with great reluctance, another deep imagination" (19), his decision to remain celibate. He makes no connection between the two "imaginations," yet it seems fair to assume some relation between his obsession with the image of a sexually active Pope allied with the whore of Babylon, and his celibate reaction. Newman's distaste for marriage, which is well documented in Ker's biography (44, 116, 121, 135), and his long-standing criticism of Mariolatry in the Catholic Church, possibly a signal of misogyny, appear to be psychological predeterminates of his decision not to marry.

Newman's adolescent rebellion and early Liberalism were shattered when he was "rudely awakened from [his] dream . . .

by two great blows—illness and bereavement." He is not specific either about the illness or the bereavement and the reader is forced to depend on the editor's footnote to learn that late in 1827 Newman experienced one of a series of breakdowns, "partly physical and partly nervous" (24, n.7), and that a few months later his youngest sister, Mary, died. As they are associated in the text with his youthful pride and democratic fling, Newman's depression appears a kind of self punishment for his fierce attacks on paternal figures; he may well have feared that in pitting himself against what he saw as an insuperable paternal enemy he would pay an exacting price: death on the conscious level, castration on the unconscious level. Thus Newman's breakdown is like the melancholy paralysis with which Hamlet struggled. When, like Hamlet, Newman emerged from his "shell" (26), his early devotion to the Fathers returned "in proportion" (33) to his veering away from Liberalism; that is, he dropped his obsessive rage with the bad father, which is in some ways a projection of his own discomfort with sexuality, and realigned himself with the good father and the celibate life. Thus he gird himself for battle as would a knight preparing to fight for his liege lord: "I have a work to do in England" (40).

The work Newman set himself was the establishment of a *Via Media*, a middle position between Protestantism and Roman Catholicism. As part of this, Newman began a serious study of the principal councils of the Church, especially the early councils. His study of the Monophysite and Arian controversies prompted two appearances of a "ghost" (99, 114) who, like Hamlet's father's ghost, challenged Newman to distinguish and remain faithful to the legitimate father. Newman in effect judges the Anglican father figures as pretenders to the throne. He compares his great experiment to infuse Catholic truth into the Anglican church to "proving cannon" (112), and implies that the experiment's failure suggests the sterility of the Anglican church and the impotence of the Anglican fathers.

When Newman was close to conversion, his combative stance returned. He was unwilling to speak against the Holy Father whom previously he had abhorred, and instead turned on those father figures whom previously he had respected. Believing that he had played the "devil's advocate" in presenting the Anglican Church as the *Via Media*, and that he had been hoodwinked by the Anglican Divines of the sixteenth and seventeenth centuries, he lashed out in anger at his former heroes: "Anathema to a whole tribe of Cranmers, Ridleys, Latimers, and Jewels! perish the names of Bramhall, Ussher, Taylor, Stillingfleet, and Barrow from the face of the earth . . ." (97). So fierce were Newman's attacks on father figures whom he had long venerated that Hurrell Froude's dying words were an appeal to him to control his contentious language:

> I must enter another protest against your cursing and swearing. What good can it do? and I call it uncharitable to an excess. How mistaken we may ourselves be, on many points that are only gradually opening on us! (103)

Ostensibly this reappraisal of Newman's identification with the father implies a simple reversal of allegiances. That is, it first appears that Newman's conversion entails a rejection of the Anglican father figures who had been his first mentors and whom he allied with a provident, transcendent, and asexual Father God, and a new identification with the Roman father figures who once had seemed so foreign and who, in Newman's eyes, were sexual (despite their celibacy) because of their alliance with woman. However, Newman's choice of metaphors to clarify what, for him, is an important difference between the Roman and Anglican religions, shifts attention away from the father and toward the mother figure, signalling a new kind of identification process, and a more creative, and less determined personal identity. He writes:

There was a contrariety of claims between the Roman and Anglican religions, and the history of my conversion is simply the process of working it out to a solution. In 1838 I illustrated it by the contrast presented to us between the Madonna and Child, and a Calvary. The peculiarity of the Anglican theology was this,—that it "supposed the truth to be entirely objective and detached, not" (as in the theology of Rome) "lying hid in the bosom of the Church as if one with her, clinging to and (as it were) lost in her embrace, but as being sole and unapproachable, as on the Cross or at the Resurrection, with the Church close by, but in the background."

(95)

The image for Anglican theology, according to Newman, God "as on the Cross or at the Resurrection," operates much like the image of Freud's oedipal father. Truth is imagined as male, and linked with the starkest fact of Christianity (Calvary) and its most herculean (Resurrection). In both, the God image is raised up, suggesting divinity, authority, and hierarchy. Truth is considered "entirely objective and detached," linking the father with reason and science. Not surprisingly, the image is termed "sole and unapproachable"; "sole" indicates the total individuation which the father symbolizes and the son aspires to, but as it suggests a kind of self-containment, it denies the need for relationship and, thus, implies "unapproachable," the idea that the father is cold and distant. The father image dominates the scene, pushing the Church (usually symbolized as female) into the background.

Interestingly, in both the Calvary and Resurrection images the son apparently stands on the ground with eyes riveted on the father. These images remind us of Newman's early idea that there were "two and two only absolute and luminously self-evident beings, myself and my Creator" (16). Newman's identification with a transcendent father God produced a strangely disembodied "I" divorced from all that is concrete or historical. Newman himself documents the problem:

> I used to wish the Arabian Tales were true: my imagination ran on unknown influences, on magical powers, and talismans. . . . I thought life might be a dream, or I an angel, and this world a deception, my fellow-angels by a playful device concealing themselves from me, and deceiving me with the semblance of a material world.
>
> (14)

The Calvary and Resurrection images document the dominance of the father figure over Newman, the son, whose identity appears a weak reflection or mirror image of the father. Recent self theorists have pondered the inherent contradiction between the cultural prescription that the son identify with the father and that he achieve self identity. Ricoeur, noting that identification is the "great enigma" (219) of psychoanalytic theory, asks, "How can I, by starting from another—say, from the father—become myself?" (186). Feminist theorists view the son's identification with the father as a narcissistic bond intended to preserve the privilege associated with the phallus. Jane Gallop goes further when she contends that the son's identification with the father, which is based on the assumption that the phallus is the organ in relation to which both sexes are defined (women being seen as humans lacking the phallus), involves all men in a sublimated homosexuality, since only one sex is symbolically represented, and precludes them from true heterosexual relations, since these would necessitate an encounter with otherness and difference (63). The views of Paulo Freiere, a Brazilian theorist of pedagogy, suggest that identification with the father stymies the development of the self, since those who have internalized another's consciousness are truly the "oppressed":

> The oppressed suffer from the duality which has estab-
> lished itself in their innermost being. They discover that
> without freedom they cannot exist authentically. Yet,
> although they desire authentic existence, they fear it. They
> are at one and the same time themselves and the oppressor
> whose consciousness they have internalized.
> (32)

Newman's conversion to Catholicism is linked with an entirely different metaphor, the Madonna and Child, and it signals a new kind of identification and a new self. Previously Newman had opposed Roman Catholicism's emphasis on Mary, in both its theology and devotion, believing it "magnified" (155) her importance and detracted from the rightful worship of the Father. However, after his conversion, Newman chooses the Mary symbol, with its essential tie to the doctrine of the Incarnation, to explain the distinguishing feature of the theology of Rome. In the Catholic Church, according to Newman, truth is no longer conceived in the abstract, as something "objective and detached"; truth is now understood as immanent, and envisioned as an infant "lying hid in the bosom of the church as if one with her, clinging to and (as it were) lost in her embrace . . ." It is significant that truth is no longer linked with a father figure who dominates the picture and strikes awe in the heart; in Newman's mind the infant truth is like Christ and thus still probably male (in keeping with the patriarchal idea that male experience is the paradigm for human experience), but en-meshed in, in love with, and almost one with reality (literally the church) which is imagined as female. Unlike the father, who in the Calvary image appears alone and raised up, suggesting transcendence and authority, the Mary image implies a more democratic and compassionate identity centered in relationship. This idea is conveyed by stressing the horizontal (the mother holding her infant) instead of the vertical (the raised Christ), and by switching the focus, by which I mean that in images of the Madonna and Child, the mother's gaze is typically on her son (implying concern for his welfare) and there is often a sense of mutual awareness, whereas in images of Calvary the spectator gazes at the crucified, who is absorbed by his own experience and seemingly unaware of the spectator.

Although the infant truth represents the Christ figure, the God/Man, it also represents all Christians, the faithful men (and women), of whom Newman is one. This is in keeping with Newman's emphasis on himself as a legitimate son and his understanding that in the Gospel "we are treated as sons, not as servants" (29). In fact, the Christ figure is also conceived of as the brother of God's people, who share in his dignity to the extent that they are aware of God within themselves. This clarifies that the truth is in Newman and that it is spread among the rest of the faithful, an idea which is in line with his defense of conscience and the important role to be played by the laity (men and women).

Newman, the Catholic convert, identifies with this metaphor for a number of reasons. First of all, he identifies with this infant, this New/man, since his own religious development had led him to separate himself from past allegiances and embark on a new course: "The cord is binding and compelling, till it snaps" (131).

In addition, the Madonna/child metaphor allies Newman with heterosexuality in a way that the Calvary and Resurrection metaphors do not. The relationship between man and woman is legitimated, partially because it yields new life and hope for the future. As the infant is locked in an "embrace" of the Church, a woman figure, the metaphor bolsters further a traditional sense of masculinity, giving credence to the title, Father Newman, which Kingsley could not abide. Paradoxically, however, the father, long associated with truth, is likened to the babe who is still developing and who is dependent on the material (here linked with the female) context. The father's authority to speak the truth is thus tempered by the human context in which he is situated; in other words, the father has no mythic relation to truth, since his understanding is human and still evolving in relation with woman.

Furthermore, the metaphor suggests that the infant truth is identified with Mother Church, and thus that Newman, who is this infant, and who is part of the Church, identifies with woman. Although the Madonna is understood as wedded to the father, she appears alone, without her spouse at her side. This is important because it allows her measure to be taken separately, and because it rectifies the subordination of woman under patriarchy. The Madonna's symbolic virginity implies that her gender has its own integrity, and that it is not merely a complement to a more privileged masculinity. According to Mary Daly, "the woman who is defined as a virgin is not defined exclusively by her relationships with men"; virginity becomes a prophetic "vision of the free and independent woman" (See 91, 82-85).

To put it another way, the metaphor suggests that women's self experience provides an/other self paradigm, one in which the self is developed and enhanced within relationships. This idea is in contradistinction to the widely accepted view that the self is developed by separation and individuation, and that boys especially develop their gender identity by means of separation from the mother and identification with the father. As Jean Baker Miller has pointed out, women's psychological development has to a large extent followed a different pattern: "women's sense of self becomes very much organized around being able to make and then to maintain affiliation and relationships" (83). In Janet Surrey's view, Baker Miller's recognition that "women in Western society have been 'carriers' of certain aspects of the human experience" means that "a full understanding of human development can be derived only from a thorough elucidation of both female and male experience" (1). Hence, Newman's identification with woman allows him to empathize with, even develop within himself, more than one perspective; this, in turn, enables him to critique, along with to support, the paternal perspective. This double identification appears responsible for Newman's spirited defense of both infallibility (an idea related to orthodoxy and patriarchal authority) and individual conscience (an idea associated with heterodoxy and the liberation of oppressed minorities, one of which is women).

The final chapter in Newman's spiritual autobiography, which recounts his prophetic understanding of the relationship between authority and conscience, should also be read as evidence that Newman's self identity, and even his gender, are determined in relation to both father and mother images. Remnants of his former exclusive identification with the father remain, and Newman appears a typical Victorian as he justifies the image of the Roman Church as a strong *paterfamilias*: "then, as now, [the Roman Church] might be called peremptory and stern, resolute, overbearing, and relentless" (See 109-11). There is still plenty of evidence of oedipal struggles with authority figures and of the necessity for dissent in his view that the Church remains vital precisely because it is "an arena for both combatants [religious authority and private judgment] in that awful, never-dying duel" (194, 193). And surely his strong defense of infallibility is a sign of his filial love for, and identification with, the father as represented in the person of the pope.

However, Newman's position on infallibility owes an even greater debt to his identification with woman, as symbolized by the Madonna/child metaphor. Newman envisions infallibility within the context of "the vast Catholic body itself" (193) and thus grounds the discussion within history and emphasizes the physical and multiple reality of the people of God. His argument suggests that "the only infallibility the Pope possessed was the infallibility of the Church" (Ker 673), which has always been symbolized by the maternal figure:

> In defining doctrines, Popes and Councils enjoyed an'active
> infallibility', but more was involved in the infallibility of the
> Church than that, since a "passive infallibility" belonged to
> the whole Catholic people [theologians and laity], who had
> to determine the force and meaning of these doctrinal
> definitions.
>
> (Ker 682)

Newman's defense of infallibility, in fact, evolves into a celebra-
tion of the sovereignty of the individual conscience, which both
prompts and interprets each exercise of infallibility. Newman's
famous after-dinner toast clarifies the importance he attributed
to the self and conscience:

> Certainly, if I am obliged to bring religion into after-dinner
> toasts, (which does not seem quite the thing) I shall
> drink—to the Pope, if you please—still, to Conscience first,
> and to the Pope afterwards.
>
> ("Letter to the Duke of Norfolk," quoted in Ker 690)

Thus, despite that fact that Newman himself seems to
"disappear [in Chapter V], except in so far as he believes the
doctrines he explains" (Durham 430), Newman's new self is in
operation via the metaphor which he aligns with his conversion
to Roman Catholicism, the Madonna and Child. Conversion
means to switch direction.   Thus, the Madonna metaphor
suggests that identification with the father is inadequate to
express the new self signalled by Newman's decision. This new
self is not "heroic" in the classical sense.   It appears less
substantial and more fluid. It is neither encapsulated nor fixed.
It is not merely the product of the cultural prescription that the
father's values be internalized. This new self lives in relation to
a multiple of phenomena. It is both male and female, child and
adult. It is related both to tradition and to the future. Although
the father is implied by the metaphor, he has been replaced by

the Mary figure, powerful in her own right (virgin) but existing in and supportive of relationship (mother). The self which comes alive in this context is not threatened by connections with others, but enhanced by relationships. This new self, because it is new, like a child in this way, is necessarily more geared to the future than it is to the past. It is developing, and thus creative. In keeping with his personal struggle with identification issues, Newman's conversion and his choice of the Madonna and Child metaphor signal a new definition of the manhood he wrote his *Apologia* to celebrate: one no longer limited by the patriarchal tradition though growing out of that tradition; one cognizant of oedipal struggle but already envisioning a new relation between Authority and the Individual; and one that today we can say is in keeping with feminism in its appreciation that gender definitions must be open to multiplicity and conscience.

WORKS CITED

Daly, Mary. *Beyond God the Father: Toward a Philosophy of Women's Liberation.* Boston: Beacon, 1973.

Durham, Margery. "The Spiritual Family in Newman's *Apologia.*" *Thought* 56 (1981): 417-432.

Faber, Geoffrey. *Oxford Apostles: A Character Study of the Oxford Movement.* London: Faber, 1933.

Freud, Sigmund. *The Standard Edition of the Complete Psychological Works of Sigmund Freud.* 24 vols. Ed. James Strachey. London: Hogarth, 1974.

Freiere, Paulo. *Pedagogy of the Oppressed.* New York: Continuum, 1990.

Gallop, Jane. *The Daughter's Seduction: Feminism and Psychoanalysis.* Ithaca, New York: Cornell UP, 1982.

Houghton, Walter E. *The Victorian Frame of Mind: 1830-1870.* New Haven: Yale UP, 1976.

Jones, Ernest. *Hamlet and Oedipus.* New York: Norton, 1949.

Ker, Ian. *John Henry Newman: A Biography.* Oxford: Clarendon, 1988.

Levine, George. *The Boundaries of Fiction: Carlyle, Macaulay, Newman.* Princeton: Princeton UP, 1968.

Miller, Jean Baker. *Toward a New Psychology of Women.* Boston: Beacon, 1976.

Newman, John Henry Cardinal. *Apologia Pro Vita Sua.* Ed. David J. DeLaura. New York: Norton, 1968.

O'Faolain, Sean. *Newman's Way.* London: Longmans, 1952.

Ricoeur, Paul. *Freud and Philosophy.* Trans. Denis Savage. New Haven: Yale UP, 1977.

Robbins, William. *The Newman Brothers.* Cambridge: Harvard UP, 1966.

Shannon, Richard. "A Mind of Genius and Power." Rev. of *John Henry Newman: A Biography*, by Ian Ker. *Times Literary Supplement* 10 March 1989: 242.

Surrey, Janet. "Self-in-Relation: A Theory of Women's Development." Wellesley, Mass.: Stone Center, 1985.

Trevor, Meriol. *Newman: The Pillar of the Cloud.* Garden City, New York: Doubleday, 1962.

Ward, Wilfrid. *The Life of John Henry Cardinal Newman.* 2 vols. London: Longmans, 1913.

Newman, Science and Personalized Learning: *Retaining the Spiritual in Experience*

Julia A. Smith

In reading John Henry Newman's *The Idea of a University*, both students and teachers naturally examine first the positive ideal of liberal education that Newman has created. But *The Idea* also represents Newman's response to a number of prevalent opinions that he saw as undermining both secular studies and theology. Newman once lamented the fact that he seemed to be most frequently cast in the role of "controversialist." True to form, in *The Idea*, he systematically addresses several controversies associated with the rapid development of the physical sciences and related philosophical schools. Martin Svaglic suggests in his introduction to *The Idea* that Newman, like Aristotle, usually envisions the mean as the ideal. As he recognized the growing hostility between science and faith, Newman sought to avoid the two extremes of Evangelical suspicion of intellectual achievements on one side and the proud skepticism of many intellectuals on the other.

As was often the case with Newman, personal experience may have deepened his concern for this problem. Throughout the first volume of his letters in the Dessain series, at least beginning with his first year at Oxford, Newman describes his personal concern that he may not succeed academically or that intellectual success may lead to unchristian pride. He accepts his inglorious performance on exams at Trinity College as a providential check on his developing pride. In addition, the Trinity system seemed to overwhelm the young student with a plethora of undigested knowledge. By contrast, Oriel College, in allowing Newman to attempt exams after his poor showing at Trinity, came to represent for him the true alma mater.

In these early years Newman also records his interest in the emerging natural sciences such as geology. He describes geology lectures that lacked structure because of the very newness of the science. But he was sufficiently fascinated to travel some distance to see an exhibit of minerals. In a letter near the end of this volume, Newman makes his first reference to a work he planned to write on the early Church Fathers. As Svaglic points out, the Fathers came to represent for Newman the perfect balance between intellectual pursuits and religious devotion. In addition, their writings were often enlivened by a personal, imaginative style like that Newman chose for his own best work.

Throughout *The Idea of a University* Newman responds with argumentative skill and imagination to five problems involving science: 1) The irrational reaction of some clergymen to the imagined dangers of science, 2) The real threat of science to theology, 3) The attack of utilitarian and empirical thinkers on traditional liberal education, 4) The establishment of the new universities and other institutions attempting to bring higher education to a broader segment of the population, and 5) The "natural religion" of the modern rationalist. The elaborate defense of theology in the opening lectures of *The Idea* is sometimes omitted in modern anthologies, yet ironically it is here that Newman defends science against those overly cautious theologians who fear every new scientific advance. In the Preface he asks rhetorically concerning papal authorization of the Irish university, "Is the Vicar of Christ bound by office . . . to be the preacher of the theory of gravitation or a martyr for electro-magnetism?" (xxxviii). His reply, rather than attacking science, sets up Newman's basic argument for a moderate position as one endorsed by the Pope: "He rejoices in the widest and most philosophical systems of intellectual education, from an intimate conviction that Truth is his real ally, as it is his profession; and that knowledge and Reason are sure ministers to Faith" (xxxviii).

As he argues for the inclusion of theology in his ideal university, Newman draws parallels between various natural sciences and theology, culminating in a reductio ad absurdum in which anthropology is eliminated from the curriculum because of controversy. By stressing this analogy and other arguments for the inclusion of theology, Newman wins the support of his religious audience for the general conclusion that no legitimate science should be barred from a university. Those clergymen who might be wary of the natural sciences would applaud Newman's defense of theology, perhaps overlooking his implication that no science should be excluded.

In two of the occasional lectures now published as part of *The Idea*, Newman further addresses the unwarranted fears of the clergy that scientific discoveries will destroy religion. He describes in "Christianity and Physical Science" a total separation of the worlds of theology and physical science. As long as each remains in its proper sphere, real collision is unlikely. Only rarely does Holy Scripture refer to the material universe. When it does describe a phenomenon such as the creation of the universe in six days, the Church makes no official pronouncement on the topic. Popular interpretations may be contradicted by scientific discoveries, but, says Newman, "We may wait in peace and tranquility till there is some real collision between Scripture authoritatively interpreted, and results of science clearly ascertained" (330).

Similarly, in the lecture "Christianity and Scientific Investigation," Newman urges both scientists and religious writers to acknowledge that apparent collisions between forms of Truth are distressing to the Imagination but not to Reason. Seeming contradictions fall into three categories: scientific pronouncements not really proved, discoveries not really contradicting Revelation, and those contradicting only popular opinions that have become confused with official doctrine. In the past, for example, the Copernican system at first appeared to contradict Church teaching, but in fact, the Church had made no official pronouncement on the matter. Newman argued that free discussion in the sciences is not only harmless to religion but is absolutely necessary for scientific progress. "The investigator should be free, independent, unshackled in his movements" (354). When religious writers become uneasy about science, they give inapporiate, supposedly scientific interpretations of Scripture. Perhaps Newman had in mind the clergyman who argued that if fossils were found in ancient rocks, God must have put the fossils there to confuse arrogant scientists.

Contrasting with the imagined dangers of scientific progress, Newman recognizes that science can pose a real threat to religion if it is allowed to move beyond its assigned territory. In *The Idea* Newman's frequently repeated image of the university as a circle divided into parts serves to remind his audience that each science must observe its proper limits. If theology should be eliminated in a university, other sciences would tend to occupy the space created, moving into areas of thought the natural scientist is not qualified to deal with. Newman elaborates on this danger in the lecture "A Form of Infidelity of the Day." If scientists regard theology as mere opinion rather than as a science, they may consider religion to be an enemy of knowledge. Instead of conducting open warfare, the enemies of religion may simply ignore theology, while luring students to the newer sciences through the appeal these studies have to the imagination. Throughout this lecture Newman employs the imagery of battle to dramatize the conflict.

Again, in the lecture "Christianity and Medical Science," he portrays the Church as the visible antagonist of a secularized world. For the physician, the danger lies in vlewing the human being as merely a physical animal. In his care for the body he may ignore his patient's moral needs. Because the physical world confronts us directly, reigion is at a disadvantage. Compared to the overwhelming evidence of the material universe, faith has an evanescent quality. But the Church remains the outspoken advocate for the spiritual world.

Although the truth of Physical science cannot really conflict with the truth of religion, Newman admits in Discourse IX that "there always has been a sort of jealousy and hostility between Religion and physical philosophers" (167). He agrees with Francis Bacon that the very nature of science leads the scientist to focus exclusively on the natural world. In addition, the method of science differs from that of theology. While science is inductive, theology is necessarily deductive since religious truth is revealed by God. The great successes achieved by the inductive method almost inevitably lead to skepticism about the validity of religious teachings. However, Newman attacks Protestantism for employing the inductive approach in allowing each person to draw conclusions from his own reading of the Scriptures.

If the rapid development of science had threatened religion, it had also led to attacks on the traditional content of university studies. Newman's defence of the older Oxford model of higher education lies at the heart of Discourses V through VII in *The Idea*. Through eloquent definitions of a liberal education, Newman defends the concept of such an education as an end in itself rather than as a means to some more utilitarian end or as a method of character formation. Those who misunderstand the aim of education may argue that it has failed through the ages to develop men of high moral character.

If Francis Bacon himself became a corrupt Lord Chancellor accused of accepting bribes, at least experimental science never claimed to produce men of moral stature. Says Newman: "It aimed low, but it has fulfilled its aim." This sidelong attack on Bacon may be part of Newman's response to a laudatory essay on Bacon by Macaulay. In fact, Newman adds a rather sarcastic footnote: " . . . on the whole I agree with Lord Macaulay in his Essay on Bacon's Philosophy. I do not know whether he would agree with me" (89). In his review of a new edition of Bacon's works, Macaulay had ridiculed Aristotle's philosophy as impractical in contrast to Bacon's scientific method. Newman retaliates not only in this passage but throughout *The Idea* by holding up Aristotle as the model of excellent reasoning.

Of course, in reply to those who say that some liberally educated men are immoral, Newman argues that secular education cannot really make students virtuous. The error is one he had discussed at length in 1841 in "The Tamworth Reading Room." At the opening of the library, Sir Robert Peel had expressed confidence in the power of science to edify. Newman argued that because Peel was a religious person, he imagined that science would lead others to religion. In fact, Newman concluded, "Intrinsically excellent and noble as are scientific pursuits, and worthy of a place in liberal education . . . still they are not . . . the instruments of an ethical training."

In *The Idea* Newman expands this argument to show that not only physical science but liberal education as a whole does not necessarily create a moral person. The real aim of such education is intellectual rather than moral. Through the striking images of granite quarried with razors and a large ship moored with silk threads, Newman argues that mere reason cannot control giant passion or pride. If liberal education does not serve moral ends, neither should it be viewed as simple career training. In Discourse VII, by employing the language of the economist, Newman implicitly characterizes Utilitarian thinkers as cold and materialistic. "They argue as if everything, as well as every person, had its price." They ask "what is the real worth in the market of the article called 'a Liberal Education'" (ll5-116). Utilitarians expect education either to provide immediate benefits to industry or to result in scientific discoveries.

In fact, Newman is not merely anticipating objections to his ideal university. As he indicates, the controversy he outlines actually occurred earlier in the century, when *The Edinburqh Review* attacked the traditional curriculum of Oxford. In contrast to the language cf economics used to represent these attacks, Newman personalizes the Oxford side by revealing his own ties to Oriel College before introducing the name of Dr. Copleston, Oriel defender of the Oxford tradition. Of those selected as Oriel fellows, Newman says, "Such persons did not promise to be the disciples of a low Utilitarianism" (118). By applying the title of Alma Mater to Oxford, Newman further stresses the personal nature of education in a college like Oriel. Through the arguments of another Oriel defender, Mr. Davison, Newman traces Utilitarian attitudes back to the philosopher John Locke, who had suggested that education is useful only if it prepares a student for his future profession. More recent opponents of classical education maintained that it "cultivated the *imagination* a great deal too much, and other *habits of mind* a great deal too little" (122-123). In *The Idea* Newman's own fine balance of reason and imaginative appeal provides the best refutation of these arguments. As a product of Oxford, Newman clearly represents the ideal he delineates.

Of the "various mistakes" Newman describes as besetting "the subject of University Education," another is the well meaning effort of leaders like Robert Peel to provide genuine education to large numbers of people through new colleges and libraries. Newman argues that "membership with scientific institutions, and the sight of the experiments on a platform" cannot be called education. Although the "superficial acquaintance" with various sciences may even be a "necessary accomplishment" in modern times, such activity should not be confused with the discipline of systematic education.

Newman's criticism is directed in part toward newer institutions of higher education, such as those where his brother Francis had taught. Because they dispense with residence requirements and expand the curriculum to include numerous modern sciences, Newman concludes that most students would do better with no formal education beyond secondary school. His description of the graduates of such colleges may sound familiar to us today: "when their period of education is passed, they throw up all they have learned in disgust, having gained nothing really by their anxious labours, except perhaps the habit of application" (108). Newman links these modern trends to developments in science and technology by using terms such as "the division of labor," "the steam engine," and "the treadmill" in contrast with the personified characterization of the older university as an Alma Mater.

Newman attacks a final error of the times in Discourse VII: the "natural religion" of the rationalist. Ironically, as Culler points out, though Newman clearly labels this "gentleman's religion" as a "heresy" and a "moral malady," his culminating definition of a gentleman became widely anthologized out of context, as if it represents an ideal to be achieved. In fact, by concluding this section with the examples of St. Basil and Julian the Apostate, Newman stresses the idea that liberal education without the aid of supernatural religion does not suffice to produce moral goodness. In Discourse IX he states more directly the perils of education without religion. It creates the belief that "human intellect, self-educated and self-supported, is more true and perfect in its ideas and judgments than that of Prophets and Apostles" (165). As Robbins has shown, Newman's correspondence with his brother Francis had personalized the experience of the intellectual who moves from faith to virtual skepticism by following his own unaided judgment.

As the Church reacts to all of these problems, Newman insists that its role is "not to prohibit truth of any kind." Instead of directly outlining the strategy the Church should employ in its universities, Newman tells the story of his Oratorian patron, St. Philip Neri, who "preferred to yield to the stream, and direct the current, which he could not stop, of science, literature, art, and fashion, and to sweeten and to sanctify what God had made very good and man had spoilt" (179). As he delineates the compelling personality of Philip, Newman implies that the best defense of the faith lies in the personal influence of devout and charismatic believers. In the case of a university that influence might come from faculty members who balance a genuine love of learning with a deep and solid religious faith. The author of *The Idea of a University*, for a brief period Rector of a university of his own, demonstrates by his own example and by his arguments the effectiveness of a moderate, rational yet imaginative approach to the problems emerging from the rapid development of modern science.

Works Cited

Newman, John Henry, Cardinal. *The Idea of a University*. Ed. Martin J. Svaglic. Notre Dame, Ind.: University of Notre Dame Press, 1982.

—. *The Letters and Diaries*. Gen. Ed. Charles Stephen Dessain. Vol. 1. Ed. Ian Ker and Thomas Gornall. Oxford: Oxford University Press, 1978.

—. "The Tamworth Reading Room." *Essays and Sketches*. Vol. 2. New York: Longmans, Green and Co., 1948.

Robbins, William. *The Newman Brothers: An Essay in Comparative Intellectual Bioqraphy*. Cambridge, Mass.: Harvard University Press, 1966.

"Steadily Contemplating the Object of Faith": *Newman, the* Apologia *and Romantic Aesthetics*

Jude V. Nixon

Critics who have observed Newman's indebtedness and, in some cases, aversion to Romantic thought have pointed either to his few remarks on the Romantics in the *Apologia Pro Vita Sua* or to his implied preference for the imagination and feeling and the subjection of reason to the Illative Sense in *An Essay in Aid of a Grammar of Assent.* For example, Merritt Lawliss and Alvan Ryan have argued that although Newman was nurtured on the Romantics, he gradually outgrew their influence. Lawliss asserts, focusing primarily on the imagination, that when Newman sets aside poetry to engage moral and religious issues, he becomes less of a Romantic and more of a Neoclassicist. When he turns to the more important "theological and philosophical discourse." he relies "mostly on reason" (77, 80). Alvan Ryan contends that the Newman of the early Aristotle essay is not the same Romantic in *The Idea of a University.* "It is clear," he claims, "that Newman was on the side of the Romantic writers in his search for a warmer, deeper view of man," a view missing among contemporary writers; "yet Newman did not rest long within the camp of Romanticism" (136).

The difficulty in pinning Newman down, in attempting to situate him within a literary tradition, stems from the fact that he possessed a comprehensive view of things. Thus, although his tradition remains essentially Romantic, one could just as convincingly negotiate for his Neoclassicism as for his Romanticism. Still, as Lewis Gates argues, not only were "Newman's youth and most impressionable years" nurtured on the Romantics, but he "took colour and tone from his epoch to a degree that has often been overlooked"; and his writings, which are "a genuine expression of the Romantic spirit," can be understood only when examined in relationship to that period (112). Thomas Vargish concurs, insisting that the intellectual affinities between Wordsworth and Newman "deserve our extended attention because they illustrate most clearly the degree to which Newman assimilated for Christian orthodoxy a vision of the mind's powers characteristic of Romanticism" (100). And, says John Beer, Newman cannot be understood unless we take "some account of the Romanticism which dominated the artistic and intellectual world of his youth" (193).

The following three passages indicate the degree to which Newman's sensibilities were shaped by Romanticism. In a 10 May 1828 letter to his sister Jemina following the death of their sister, Mary, Newman described a ride taken to Cuddesdon. a little village skirting Oxford:

> The country too is beautiful—the fresh leaves, the scents, the varied landscape. Yet I never felt so intensely the transitory nature of this world as when most delighted with these country scenes . . . . I wish it were possible for words to put down those indefinite vague and withal subtle feelings which quite pierce the soul and make it sick. Dear Mary seems embodied in every tree and hid behind every hill. What a veil and curtain this world of sense is! beautiful but still a veil."
>
> (*LD* 2: 69)

Three years later he described another trip. this one to Devonshire. Charmed by the landscape, he wished that he "should dissolve into essence of roses, or be attenuated into an echo . . . . What strikes me most is the strange richness of every thing. The rocks blush into every variety of colour" (*LD* 2: 343). And a passage from his sermon "The Second Spring," which forecasts England's return to Roman Catholicism, reads: "We mourn over the blossoms of May, because they are to wither; but we know, withal, that May is one day to have its revenge upon November, by the revolution of that solemn circle which never stops" (346).

The focus of this paper, however, is not to determine the role of the senses and the importance of nature in Newman as is the case in the above examples. Rather, it ferries out from Newman's protean corpus the significant points of intersection with Romantic aesthetics. It argues that Newman's aesthetic is consonant with nineteenth-century Romanticism. His literary influence and model is Romantic; and while he admitted a fondness of the Classics and admired the eighteenth-century writers from whose epistemological stance the Romantics departed, still his views on literature, religion, and reason remain essentially Romantic. And although this aesthetic was slightly modified when Newman converted to Roman Catholicism, it remains relatively unchanged in his writings and persisted even in the *Grammar*.

One of the first places to locate Newman's attraction to Romantic aesthetics is in his theory and practice of prose. The best prose, he believes, is conversational, spontaneous, and the genuine reflection of an individual's self, emotions, and thoughts. "Persons influence us," he writes, "voices melt us, looks subdue us" ("The Tamworth Reading Room" 204). To demonstrate this emphasis on dialogue, Newman chose as his Cardinal motto the phrase *cor ad cor loquitur* (heart speaks to heart). First to have detected his conversational style, what he calls "talk in prose" (*GA* 186), was his disciple and protege, the Jesuit and Victorian poet Gerard Manley Hopkins. In a 20 October 1887 letter, Hopkins, analyzing Newman's style from a more Coleridgean than Wordsworthian credo, notes that it reflects a thinking aloud, a thinking with "pen to paper." Hopkins concedes that while there are advantages to such a style, overall it manifests a flawed technique, an absence of "proper eloquence," and a stylistic disruption, what he calls the fracturing of a "continuity, the *contentio*, the strain of address, which writing should usually have." Despite this censure, of note is Hopkins's view that Newman's tradition is "the most highly educated conversation" (*Further Letters* 380). Indebted to this perceptive analysis, Walter Houghton, in *The Art of Newman's "Apologia,"* finds in Newman's style a desire simply to sketch "the inner pattern and movement of his thinking." Newman's "conversational idiom, in diction and rhythm," is meant, says Houghton, to "translate the clash of ideas back into their original human context" (48). Gates too calls Newman's prose a "friendly discourse" and "the familiar talk of a man of the world with his fellows" (65-66). Newman's heart to heart style endeavors, then, to resituate literature within the arena of speech.

The concept of a speech-based poetics is quintessentially Romantic. Wordsworth attempted, the success of which remains arguable, to choose situations from common life and to present them in a language "really used by men." His purpose, he adds, was "to adopt the very language of men," "to keep the Reader in the company of flesh and blood"; for true poetry is dialogic, "a man speaking to men" (Noyes 358-61). The Romantics and Newman understood that the subtle and enigmatic ways the mind moves require a new poetic medium, a conversational one. Thus Newman self-consciously admits having a "lounging, free-and-easy way of carrying things on" (*Apo* 58), and advised J. B. Mozley when writing to "be somewhat conservational and take a jump into your subject" (*LD* 6: 281). Newman's conversational style is at work in such homely expressions as "I came out of my shell; I remained out of it till 1841," speaking here of his emergence as a public figure (*Apo* 26); and before proceeding to flesh out the controversy between Rome and the Anglican Church, he warns the reader: "This will involve some dry discussion" (89). Regarding the formulation of his apology, Newman asks: "What then shall be the special imputation, against which I shall throw myself in these pages" (7), a phrase he again uses to describe his peculiar reason for writing Tract 15: that its subject was provided by a friend who "did not wish to be mixed up with the publication," and so "He gave it me, that I might throw it into shape" (*Apo* 48).

Inextricably tied to a conversational style is the notion that the personableness of a work mirrors the artist. The Romantics believed that the poet's own emotions and feelings are integral to his poetry. Wordsworth saw them as "the image of man and nature" (Noyes 362). Coleridge likewise drew no distinction between the poet and the poetic artifact. "What is poetry," he asked, "is so nearly the same question with, what is a poet? that the answer to the one is involved in the solution of the other" (Noyes 427). Newman's own biopoetic instances this. In a biographical sketch of Newman, James Anthony Froude tells us that the greatness of the man is matched by his poetry: "he was himself all that the poetry was" (182). Newman himself makes this connection: "Literature is to man in some sort what autobiography is to the individual; it is his delight and Remains" (*Idea* 193-94). He calls literature the "personal" use of language. Because a writer's "thought and feeling are personal . . . . so his language is personal," for it "expresses not only his great thoughts, but his great self." He further adds: "His page is the lucid mirror of his mind and life" (*Idea* 231; 235; 244). This tripartite metaphor of the page as the mirror of life is Newman's conception of autobiography, a device I will later explore in the

Apologia. And in fact the conversational and personal together comprise autobiography, as when Newman in remarking on the Ancient Saints states that they left behind them the kind of literature "which more than any other represents the abundance of the heart, which more than any other approaches to conversation; I mean correspondence" ("St. Chrysostom" 221). But more germane to this context is Newman's reputed affable personality, his "personal intercourse" that infused his prose, conveying in it the "warmth, and elasticity, and colour of life" (Gates 67).

The personableness in Newman's prose is advanced by the friendliness of his conversational idiom, which intends to establish an intimate relationship between himself and his reader. The *Apologia,* what Newman calls "my own testimony" (207), is, Gates points out, "intensely personal in its tone and matter, persuasive because of its concreteness, its dramatic vividness" (81). In his treatment of the attitude of Victorian autobiographers to their audience, Howard Helsinger asserts that their suspicion of deceit caused them to conceive of autobiography "not as intimate speech but as public discourse" (40). Newman, however, seems equivocal here. He does admit public concern in the *Apologia*—"pleading my cause before the world" (1)—but placed in an apologetic posture, he wishes to bridge any aesthetic fissure between himself and his audience. Thus he quite often appeals directly to his English readers, as in this case to their sense of fairness: "Whatever judgment my readers may eventually form of me from these pages, I am confident they will believe me" (7). Newman desires to engender sympathy for himself and his cause. To do so demands vicariously involving his reader with the details of his life. This joint private and public narrato-logical stance distinguishes Newman from many of his Victorian contemporaries, who beginning often with a private cause soon sublimate it to a larger public mandate. Thus while the *Apologia* does not at the outset presume a relationship with an audience, the progression of its narrative intends to forge that relationship.

Constituting the personableness of a style and work, the Romantics believed, is the sincerity pursued by the writer. Repeatedly, Wordsworth and Coleridge talked about poetry striving to achieve fidelity to fact and experience, colored by the imagination, but then to awaken "the mind's attention," directing it "to the loveliness and wonders of the world" (Noyes 423). Wordsworth himself informs us in his *Preface to the Lyrical Ballads* that "I have at all times endeavoured *to look steadily at my subject*; consequently, there is I hope in these Poems little falsehood of description" (Noyes 359; italics mine).   Believing then that no one could write well without observing closely, he tells us that the best poetry comes from an individual who has "thought long and deeply" (Noyes 358).   Or, quoting Ruskin, a writer much indebted to the Romantics, "To see clearly is poetry, prophecy, and religion—all in one" (Part 4, ch. 16, 333).

A telling feature of Wordsworth's poetry is the emphasis on the concrete, the concern with rendering particulars with sensual accuracy, but without murdering to dissect. Counterbalancing this overly clinical approach to poetry is the exercise of the imagination. Take, for instance, the particularization of the landscape in "Tintern Abbey": "these steep and lofty cliffs," "These plots of cottage-ground, these orchard-tufts," "These hedge-rows," "these pastoral farms," and "These beauteous forms." Such obsession with the concrete, W. R. Castle finds, is the Romantic "reaction against the abstract philosophy of the Eighteenth Century" (140). Recalling in *The Prelude* his second trip to France and the Reign of Terror under Robespierre, Wordsworth addresses the anonymous Coleridge: "I speak bare truth, / As if to thee alone in private talk" (1805, 10: 371-72); and. speculating on Coleridge reading the poem, writes: "With heart how full / Will he peruse these line, this page—perhaps / A blank to other men" (1805, 2: 353-55). These admissions and others like them in *The Prelude* prompt Howard Helsinger to call the poem a defense "*ex vita*," a "private, privileged discourse" in which Wordsworth's readers are "merely eavesdropping" (43).

Newman's keenness for details, what Hopkins described as his "charm of unaffected and personal sincerity" (*Further Letters* 380), owes much to the Romantics. This is evident in his 1849 sermon, "The Glories of Mary for the Sake of Her Son." The sermon not only broaches the theme of Wordsworth's sonnet "The World is Too Much with Us"—that man's materialistic pursuits distract his devotion to God and nature—but also uses the language of sincerity and particularity:

> And, as ignorant men may dispute the beauty and perfection of the visible creation, so men, who for six days in the week are absorbed in worldly toil, who live for wealth, or name, or self-indulgence, or profane knowledge, and do but give their leisure moments to the thought of religion, never raising their souls to God, never asking for His enlightening grace, never chastening their hearts and bodies, never *steadily contemplating the object of faith.*
>
> (364; italics mine)

At work here and in Newman's overall style, one that "steadily contemplates truths" ("Implicit and Explicit Reason" 277), and, in the case of the *Apologia*, concerns "the one object of relating things as they happened to me in the course of my conversion" (97), is an urging forward "towards the individual and the actual," writes Gates. Newman's mind "does not lag in the region of abstractions and formulas, but presses past the general term, or abstraction, or law, to the image or the example, and into the tangible, glowing, sensible world of fact" (105). Newman himself envisioned this an important criterion for a writer: "does he image forth, to all does he give utterance, in a corresponding language, which is as multiform as this inward mental action itself and analogous to it, the faithful expression of his intense personality" (*Idea* 232).

Newman's concern with the correct perception of a subject and with sincerity is nowhere more evident than in the *Apologia*. He held that prose is more suitable than poetry in presenting truth. "Fidelity," he avows, "is the primary merit of biography and history; the essence of poetry is fiction" ("Aristotle's Poetics" 9). Thus his prompting for writing prose is "the sight of a truth, and the desire to show it to others" (Ward 1: 638). Called upon to vindicate himself against charges of disingenu-ousness, to exorcise the "phantom" from the real person, to be perceived as "a living man, and not as a scarecrow . . . dressed up in my clothes," Newman purposed in the *Apologia* to "set nothing down in it as certain, of which I have not a clear memory, or some written memorial." Holding as his model Thomas Scott's *The Force of Truth*, Newman was convinced that while "False ideas may be refuted indeed by argument," only by "true ideas alone are they expelled" (*Apo* 12-13), for one is influenced most by what is "direct and precise" ("Tamworth" 205). Newman there-fore relies on letters of his and those from Catholic friends, both of the clergy and laity, as "witnes-ses enough" to verify, or correct, or complete" his claims.

Disregarding logic for autobiography, and presenting his life as his only defense by the fusion of the personal and polemical, Newman sought in the *Apologia* to be "simply personal and historical . . . , doing no more than explaining myself, and my opinions and actions. I wish as far as I am able, simply to state facts" (13). Thus in "History of My Religious Opinions from 1833 to 1839," the chapter treating the conception of the Oxford Movement, Newman opens with the disclaimer, meant to forestall any accusation of Romanticizing his life: "In spite of the foregoing pages"—containing recollections of Newman's youthful fantasies, the shaping influences on him, his belief in a sacra-mental principle, and his memorable trip to the Mediterranean—"I have," he claims, "no romantic story to tell; but I have written them, because it is my duty to tell things as they took place. I have not exaggerated the feelings with which I returned to England, and I have no desire to dress up the events which followed, so as to make them in keeping with the narrative which has gone before" (42). Newman's reticence about calling the *Apologia* romantic is meant more to emphasize the factual rather than the fictive character of the work. But he seems unwilling to acknowledge the fact that telling a life involves fictionalizing—if not in substance, at least in technique. By examining closely Newman's use of epic allusions, Robert Colby notes that Newman succeeds in "'romanticizing' the historical account . . . by ingenious analogizing" (48).

Concerned with "matters of belief and opinions" (*Apo* 31), the *Apologia* identifies notable figures, important places, significant dates, and memorable events. It documents, for example, the formative influences of Thomas Scott, who led Newman to renounce his Calvinistic view or predestination, of Richard Whately, whose rational influence on Newman delayed his conversion to Catholicism, of Blanco White and Edward Hawkins, who led him to accept inspiration of Scripture and the doctrine of Tradition, respectively. From William James he learned the doctrine of Apostolic Succession, and from Bishop Joseph Butler's *The Analogy of Religion* derived the germ for his theory on probability, later to become the central argument of the *Grammar*. Hurrell Froude, his closest friend, whom he described Romantically as "a man of high genius, brimful and overflowing with ideas and views," drew Newman to the Medieval Church and taught him devotion to the Blessed Virgin and the doctrine of Real Presence. And from the Patristic Fathers he learned the vital sacramental principle, further nourished, though with distinct differences, by his reading of the Romantics. In 1828, Newman tells us, he became Vicar of St. Mary's, and resigned on 18 September 1843 in deference to his

Bishop. He dates the commencement of the Oxford Movement Sunday, 14 July 1833, after Keble's Assize Sermon, and of his involvement with it felt that left to his supervision it would have been only a "floating opinion," never "a power." On the morning of 23 February 1846, Newman left his disparadised Littlemore and Oxford, recalling nostalgically the snapdragons that formerly grew on the walls adjacent to his freshman dorm.

The image of the snapdragon becomes connected with the sense of permanence Newman felt at Oxford, a fixity he acknowledged nineteen years earlier when he penned his "Snapdragon" poem. In it, both the poet and snapdragon assume a single identity, causing the flower's encasement in the wall to be perceived as the poet's own encagement within the walls of his college. This loss of poetic consciousness—the voice in the poem remaining consistently that of the snapdragon—successfully executes what Keats calls "Negative Capability." The poem opens with an image of rootedness, resulting, ironically, from an unnatural state of confinement:

> I am rooted in the wall
> Of buttress'd tower or ancient hall;
> Prison'd in an art-wrought bed.
> Cased in mortar, cramp'd with lead.

Echoing in countless ways Tennyson's "The Lady of Shalott" and "The Palace of Art," the passage here in Newman shows him relishing the permanence Oxford provides, but admitting also an accompanying artificiality. However, he stoically accepts the psychological paradox of mental pain:

> So for me alone remains
> Lowly thought and cheerful pains.

But Newman maintains that this sacrifice becomes a sweet-smelling savor to God, one that brings ultimate rewards:

> Ah! no more a scentless flower,
> By approving Heaven's high power,
> Suddenly my leaves exhale
> Fragrance of the Syrian gale.
> Ah! 'tis answering breath of Heaven!
> May it be! then well might I
> In College cloister live and die.

To "leave my own home" (*Apo* 81), Newman says on leaving Oxford, "the place where I began the battle of life," and "my first Oxford home from the age of 15" (*LD* 28: 284, 295), becomes more poignant because it was like being exiled from Eden, put out of one's rightful home, an institution so dear to the Victorian family and its sense of security. Now his only view of Oxford is from a distance and as an outsider, catching a mere glimpse of its celebrated spires from a train.

The snapdragon image returns in Newman's 1878 revisit to Trinity, thirty-two years later, to be honored as its only honorary Fellow. Indeed, this was to him paradise regained. In his autobiography *My Long Life,* the writer Douglas Sladen, the occupant of Newman's rooms during that revisit, recalls being invited to spend an evening with Newman to compare the Oxford of Newman's time to that of his. The snapdragons were brought up in their conversation: "He [Newman] wanted to know if the snapdragons, to which he had written a poem, still grew on the wall between Trinity and Balliol" (46). James Bryce, who attended the Trinity dinner and the one who proposed the after-dinner toast to Newman, also recalls the "mixture of sadness and pleasure" with which Newman remembered his early days at Oxford and especially the "plant of snapdragon which grew upon the wall opposite the window of the room in which he lived" (Ward 2: 430). Such reliance on "definite particulars" on people, places, and feelings gives credence to Newman's description of the *Apologia*, calling it a "documentary," one that sought to recapture "the very words" to express the "keen feeling which pierced me" (121, 138).

Newman's concern with the particular accompanies an interest in the emotions and in spontaneity. His belief that poetry appeals to passion and the imagination and has a moral center, what he calls a "right moral state of heart," is expressed in his 1829 essay, "Poetry, with Reference to Aristotle's Poetics." This early essay provides a clear account of Newman embracing the Romantic notion that poetry derives not from imitation but from inspiration. This theory, termed "Platonic" by Blanco White and disliked by the Aristotelian empiricist and Broad Church sympathizer Richard Whately (*Apo* 22), remains "fundamentally opposed," says Alba Warren, "to the theory of the *Poetics*" (36). In the essay, Newman talks of Aristotle's rules of drama inhibiting "the mind of the poet from the spontaneous exhibition of pathos or imagination" (4-5); for Aristotle views drama "more as an exhibition of ingenious workmanship, than as a free and unfettered effusion of genius" (7). In a partial repudiation of Aristotle, Newman maintains that poetic eloquence is "the sole outlet of intense inward feeling" (24). Thus a poetic mind struggles to express itself faithfully because "it is overpowered by a rush of emotions . . . . Nothing is more difficult than to analyse the feelings of our own mind" (25). This essay, Alvan Ryan finds, shows Newman "at one with Wordsworth, Coleridge, and Shelley in his search for a more emotional and more imaginative conception of poetry" (133).

Newman's expanded version of the Aristotle essay in *The Idea of a University* (1859) observes him still working with a Romantic aesthetic. Commenting on writers like Homer, Shakespeare, and Walter Scott, Newman notions that "it is the fire within the author's breast which overflows in the torrent of his burning, irresistible eloquence; it is the poetry of the inner soul, which relieves itself in the Ode or Elegy"; and the beauty of the poet's "moral countenance" reveals itself in language; and not only the language, "but even the rhythm, the meter, the verse will be the contemporaneous offspring of the emotion or imagination which possesses him." The poet "writes passionately," Newman asserts, "because he feels keenly; forcibly, because he conceives vividly; he sees too clearly to be vague . . . ; he can analyze his subject, and therefore it is rich . . . ; he has a firm hold of it, and therefore he is luminous. When his imagination wells up, it overflows in ornament; when his heart is touched, it thrills along his verse"(*Idea* 234, 244). An earlier essay, "The Mission of St. Benedict" (1858), expresses a similar idea: "Poetry does not address the reason, but the imagination and affections; it leads to admiration, enthusiasm, devotion, love" (387).

But accepting the notion that the best poetry is the spontaneous outpouring of powerful feeling does not consign Newman to the view that poetry is totally unchecked, or that it is the exercise of the free rein of the emotions. While he warms to the spiritual aspects of Romanticism, he distrusts the excesses of the senses, advocating, instead, the spiritual ascesis of the senses, as is the case in the poem "Prime":

> O Christ. securely fence
> Our gates, beleaguer'd by the foe.—
> The gate of every sense.
> . . . lest the flesh in its excess
> Should lord it o'er the soul,
> Let taming abstinence repress
> The rebel, and control.

Another poem, "Terce," articulates the same spiritual employment of the senses: "Let flesh, and heart, and lips, and mind, / Sound forth our witness to mankind." *Lyra Apostolica*, a collection of poems opting for a Romantic as well as an apostolic lyric, contends for the same control. While the words "Lyra" and "Apostolica" reveal, as G. B. Tennyson notes, "the Tractarian theologizing of Romantic poetics" and its "poeticizing of the Church," noticeably absent in the work is the waywardness and unpredictability characteristic of Romantic inspirational poetry. This is so because for Newman "inspiration is not an errant breeze, or even whisperings of the muse, but rather the breath of the divine" (123-24). Still Newman seems unwilling to disavow altogether the idea that poetry came as if inspired by nature. The poems in *Lyra*, we might recall, were inspired by the unnatural beauty of the Mediterranean landscape, and in the poem "My Lady Nature and Her Daughters," Newman toys with the idea that poetry gestated from "Nature's earth, and sea, and sky" where "Fervid thoughts inspire." It is probably for this reason that Hopkins saw the Lake School expiring in Newman (*Correspondence* 99).

The desire for control also becomes apparent in how Newman envisions poetic composition. His Aristotle essay states that creating poetry requires "that command of language which is the mere effect of practice"; and so the truly great poet must exercise "careful labour" (25). And in *The Idea of a University,* he marvels that even Shakespeare "should pause, write, erase, re-write, amend, complete, before he satisfies himself that his language has done justice to the conceptions which his mind's eye contemplated" (238). Both Wordsworth and Coleridge painstakingly revised their work, implying that the spontaneous nature of poetic creativity applies not to the final artifact but to the initial act of gestation, what Hopkins calls "the one rapture of an inspiration," or Newman a "gestation and child-birth." Wordsworth left, for example, two complete versions of *The Prelude*, the second coming forty-five years (1850) after the first. And in fact, more frequently anthologized than the earlier "spontaneous" version is the later one. In the case of Coleridge, his substantive emendations of "Dejection: An Ode" also leave two versions, the Cornell and Dove Cottage Manuscripts, questioning once more the notion of spontaneous creativity.

Although Newman advocated Romantic spontaneity in the poetic process, he too was obsessed with revising. Some one hundred pages were excised from the original *Apologia,* radically transforming the work from a spirited defense in favor of embellishing its historical and autobiographical feature, so that this procrustean version is, were one to insist on a narrow view of original creativity, more an apocryphal text than an inspired one. Speaking of the creative process, Newman said to Wilfrid Ward: "I do not think that I ever thought out a question, or wrote my thoughts, without great pain, pain reaching to the body as well as to the mind" (Ward 1: 637). Elsewhere he calls the writing process

> inexhaustible. I write—I write again—I write a third time, in the course of six months—then I take the third—I literally fill the paper with corrections so that another person could not read it—I then write it out fair for the printer—I put it by—I take it up—I begin to correct again—it will not do—alterations multiply—pages are rewritten—little lines sneak in and crawl about—the whole page is disfigured—I write again. I cannot count how many times this process goes on.
> (*LD* 6: 193)

What attracted Newman to the Romantic notion of spontaneity is the emotional and evangelical fervor it provides to religion and worship. "When the vital connection between religion and imagination is either overlooked or denied," John Coulson asserts, not only does theology suffer, but "the very life of religion ebbs and becomes infertile" (3). For all of his interest in logic and rational arguments, Newman also acknowledged the importance of the emotions—Wordsworth's "language of the heart"—in almost every area: in worship, belief, and reason. Spontaneity also makes available a refreshing alternative to a mechanized Victorian society. "There are two ways, then, of reading Nature," Newman concludes, "as a machine and as a work. If we come to it with the assumption that it is a creation, we shall study it with awe; if assuming it to be a system, with mere curiosity" ("Tamworth" 210).

But although Newman saw poetry as the expression or image of the emotion, the "spontaneous overpouring of thought" (*GA* 214), it was Keble who more fully articulated this idea. He claims that the greater the degree of influence feelings exert on our affections, and the more permanently they are, the closer they become related to and associated with poetry (480). Keble associates these characteristics of poetry with religion, seeing them as guides to nature and God. In this symbiotic relationship between poetry and religion, poetry "lends religion her wealth of symbols and similes—Religion restores these again to Poetry, clothed with so splendid a radiance that they appear to be no longer merely symbols, but to partake . . . of the nature of sacraments"; and the very exercise of poetry, Keble asserts, "will be found to possess . . . the power of guiding and composing the mind to worship and prayer" (480-83).

Wordsworth anticipated both Newman and Keble in seeing poetry and religion meet what Thomas Vargish calls "a common psychic need, the need to represent and perceive spiritual realities in material forms" (105). The passage from Wordsworth that Vargish has in mind talks of poetry being most "just when it administers the comforts and breathes the spirit of religion." It reads:

> The commerce between Man and his Maker cannot be carried on but by a process where much is represented in little, and the Infinite Being accommodates himself to a finite capacity. In all this may be perceived the affinity

> between religion and poetry; between religion—making up
> the deficiencies of reason by faith; and poetry—passionate
> for the instruction of reason; between religion—whose
> elements is infinitude, and whose ultimate trust is the
> supreme of things, submitting herself to circumscription, and
> reconciled to substitutions; and poetry—ethereal and tran-
> scendent, yet incapable to sustain her existence without
> sensuous incarnation.
>
> (*Poetical Works* 2: 411, 412)

The sacramental relationship religion and poetry share in
forging a link between man and God as between the material
and the immaterial espoused here by Wordsworth found ready
acceptance by Keble and Newman, both of whom found in the
Romantics a fitting religious paradigm for poetry: that "ideas
which in theology have become inert, may become alive and
drastically innovative when transferred . . . into the alien soil of
aesthetics" (Abrams 147). Maintaining that "Revealed Religion
should be especially poetical" ("Aristotle's Poetics" 23), Newman
felt that Keble's *Lyrica Innocentium* (1846) did for Anglicanism
what "none but a poet could do: he made it poetical"; and
because poetry, especially the Romantic type, embraces the
imagistic, emotive, and mysterious, it becomes a subterfuge,
especially for Tractarians who "have not the Catholic Church to
flee to and repose upon, for the Church herself is the most
sacred and august of poets."

But poetry is not only a sanctuary; it is also therapy.
Wordsworth notioned that "In the middle and declining age, a
scattered number of serious persons resort to poetry, as to
religion, as a consolation for the afflictions of life" (*Poetical
Works* 2: 409). Newman recognized this quality in Keble's
poetry, seeing in it "a method of relieving the overburdened
mind; it is a channel through which emotion finds expression,
and that a *safe. regulated expression*" ("John Keble" 442; italics
mine). He also embraced this theory of poetry, suggesting in his

essay on Aristotle that poetry provides a "solace for the mind broken by the disappointments and sufferings of actual life," that it is "the utterance of the inward emotions of a right moral feeling," and that it adopts "metaphorical language" as the only means available to communicate "intense feelings" (10).

Newman was not the only Victorian to recognize this feature in Wordsworth. Mill too found in his poetry a "medicine for my state of mind," for the paralysis caused by catering too scrupulously to abstractions.

Also appealing to Newman is the Romantic idea of the poet as sage. Shelley it was who saw poets as "legislators or prophets" (Noyes 1112), a view Wordsworth expressed in *The Prelude*: "poetic numbers came / Spontaneously, and clothed in priestly robe / My spirit, thus singled out, as it might seem. / For holy services" (1805, 1: 60-63). And later in Book 4: "I made no vows, but vows / Were then made for me; bond unknown to me / Was given, that I should be, else sinning greatly, / A dedicated Spirit" (1850, 4: 334-37). Newman too shared this belief. "The Greek poets and sages were in a certain sense prophets," he claims; for, and here he quotes from Keble's *The Christian Year*, "'thoughts beyond their thought to those high bards were given'" (*Apologia* 34). In *The Idea of a University*, he calls authors "the spokesmen and prophets of the human family"; an author is "the man of his age, the type of a generation, or the interpreter of a crisis" (245, 257). Newman saw himself similarly chosen. While in Rome working on the *Lyra*, he felt singled out for some divine task, one that would involve a single life. He sensed too that "deliverance is wrought, not by the many but by the few, not by bodies but by persons." Southey's poem, "Thalaba," also impressed on Newman's mind that sense of "mission," and he became convinced that he had "a work to do in England," a "presentment" that "grew stronger" on his way to Sicily. Emerging from his Baphometic condition, he was struck by the conviction that "I have work to do in England" (*Apo* 40).

Newman also recalled seeing "the shadow of a hand upon the wall" (*Apo* 99). And in fact the *Apologia's raison d'etre* is "a sacred cause" (4).

This divine sense of mission is quite often followed by a wandering, literal, symbolic, or both. Thus when Newman caught sight of that vision at the end of his Mediterranean voyage, he wrote "Lead, kindly light," indicating the end of a literal journey and the commencement of a spiritual one. The journey thus becomes an important motif in the *Apologia,* giving the work an epic shape by way of the immense task Newman confronts, through the narrative's progression, and in its reliance on classical allusions. If we view this work as charting the stages in a conversion experience, as it is, we must see it then as a pilgrimage—how the soul first discovers its lost state and then seeks salvation, confronting in the process spiritual and psychological roadblocks that threaten to impede its progress. Accordingly, the *Apologia* could well be read as a Dantesque divine journey, with Newman as pilgrim and his conscience, reason, and duty as guide. A telling feature of the work is the degree of doubt evident in Newman's countless admissions of uncertainty. Thus while the narrative moves toward assent, from loss to gain, its greatness emerges not from the quality of faith but from the degree of doubt. This paradoxical nature of faith is best expressed in Ruskin's "Our earnest poets and deepest thinkers are doubtful" (Part 4, ch. 16, 323) and in Tennyson's "There lives more faith in honest doubt" (96, 3).

The journey motif, then, binds the narrative of the *Apologia.* Newman felt himself, as a result of Whately's intellectualism, "drifting in the direction of the Liberalism of the day" (24). He describes thus the occasion for his essay on the Council of Nicea: "It was to launch myself on an ocean with currents innumerable; and I was drifted back first to the ante-Nicean history, and then to the Church of Alexandria" (33). Of his involvement with the tracts, he writes: "I felt as on board a vessel, which first gets under weigh, and then the deck is cleared out, and luggage and live stock stowed away into their proper receptacles" (47). Left to him the Movement, he admits, would have remained "but a floating opinion" (58). He calls the pain involved in retracing the past a "ripping up of old griefs" and a "venturing again upon the 'infandum dolorem' [inexplicable grief] of years" (81). The words are significantly Aeneas's as he prepares to narrate to Dido the events surrounding the fall of Troy, a catastrophe that is the prelude to Aeneas's commission to a spiritual journey, to found Rome. Recalling, then, his own spiritual pilgrimage, Newman tells us that for years he had the notion that "my mind had not found its ultimate rest, and that in some sense or other I was on journey" (100). His actual conversion to Roman Catholicism is couched in this same metaphor. "All the logic in the world," he claims, "would not have made me move faster towards Rome than I did; as well might you say that I have arrived at the end of my journey, because I see the village church before me" testifying to the miles "over which my soul had to pass before it got to Rome," my "ultimate destination" (136). By 7 November 1844 Newman notes: "I am still where I was; I am not moving" (178). One year later when he finally did move to Roman Catholicism, shattering the *via media* and forsaking his "halfway house," that ultimately unacceptable middle ground, it was like "coming into port after a rough sea" (184).

While Newman acknowledged an indebtedness to the Romantics, Byron was the one exception. Harold's pilgrimage, emerging also from Byron's Mediterranean tour, was still not to be Newman's. He disliked Byron's liberal philosophy and ideas on art and nature. "Now, as then," he writes regarding Byron's involvement with the periodical *The Liberal*, "I have no sympathy with the philosophy of Byron" (*Apo* 200). He also maintains, unlike Byron, but more in keeping with the other Romantics, that art can present at best a poor imitation of nature. Thus in reaction to Byron's aesthetics, Newman states that "nature is commonly more poetical than art . . . , because it is less comprehensible and less patient of definition" ("The Mission of St. Benedict" 387).

Newman reserved his fondest remarks for Scott and Southey, appreciating in them, says John Beer, "not simply their sense of romantic adventure," but more importantly the "combination of romance and righteousness" in their works (197). In Scott he found a writer who revived the middle ages, and whose popularity with his readers derived from stimulating their "mental thirst, feeding their hopes, setting before them visions, which, when once seen, are not easily forgotten, and silently indoctrinating them with nobler ideas" (*Apo* 84). But Newman's is not a blanket approval of Scott. He disapproves of the frivolousness in Scott's poems and romances, but insists that when contrasted with the most admired poems and novels of the eighteenth century, Scott's poems and romances "stand almost as oracles of Truth confronting the ministers of error and sin" ("Prospects of the Anglican Church" 338). Regarding Southey, Newman thought his "Thalaba" "the most . . . *morally* sublime" of English poems (*Letters* 13: 449) because it treats the eternal rewards of earthly sacrifice (Newman's "future glory"). The poem also presents, says Ward, a picture of what Newman "trusted the Movement and his share in the Movement would have been" (2: 355). In Southey's "fantastic fiction" Newman recognizes "high principles and feelings" that provide the right moral appeal and direction to readers (*Apo* 84).

Newman also admired Coleridge, though he did not endorse his skeptical stance on biblical inspiration. He saw Coleridge's originality and "higher philosophy" contributing significantly to the popularity of Roman Catholicism. He succeeded, says Newman, in influencing the best minds of his age to "the cause of Catholic truth" (*Apo* 84). Newman read Coleridge "*for the first time,*" he tells us, beginning around Christmas 1834, and was surprised how very similar Coleridge's ideas were to his (*LD* 5: 53). It was then too that he discovered Coleridge responsible for the growth and the restoration of Church principles (*LD* 5: 27). In what is perhaps the most comprehensive study of Coleridge and Newman, D. G. James, in *Romantic Comedy,* asserts that both writers view the symbol as the expression of the religious imagination, itself poetic. Not a mere signifier of truth, the symbol is consubstantial with it, achieving what Geoffrey Hartman would call an "unmediated vision." Both the signifier and the signified, the symbol and the thing it represents, then, are one. In Coleridge's and Newman's theory of symbolism, the symbol partakes of reality and history; thus it forfeits its merely metaphorical character, its sole act of representation (205-8). In his *Lay Sermon,* Coleridge notes that a "system of symbols" stem from the work of the imagination, which in turn reconciles, mediates, and organizes "the permanence and self-circling energies of the Reason" with the fluctuating images of the senses (29). He calls the imagination "the completing power, which unites clearness with depth, the plenitude of the sense with the comprehensibility of the understanding" (*Lay Sermon* 69); and it is the imagination, together with the senses and the reason, that revitalizes the symbol and with it religion. In attempting to reconcile reason and faith and to provide the latter with a rational base by dispelling whatever superstition was connected to it, Coleridge desired to show, says Harrold, that reason is not a mere "mechanical illusion" but a "dynamic faculty, which calls into play the emotions and the will as much as the analytical understanding" (xxxix).

Newman is particularly concerned with this idea of the symbol, and especially how it animates religious truth, which he perceives as currently bankrupt. In "Prospects of the Anglican Church," he asks: "How, then, in our age are those wants and feelings of our common nature satisfied, which were formerly supplied by symbols, now that symbolical language and symbolical rites have almost perished?" His response is that "the taste for poetry of a religious kind" has replaced "the deep contemplative spirit of the early Church." It may be said, he concludes, that "poetry then is our mysticism; and as far as any two characters of mind tend to penetrate below the surface of things, and to draw men away from the material to the invisible world, so far they may certainly be said to answer the same end; and that too a religious one" (357-58).

Newman also shared an aesthetic and epistemological relationship with Wordsworth. Father Ignatius Ryder fondly recalled that during a boyhood illness of his Newman read to him Wordsworth's "Intimations Ode." He sensed in his voice "a passion and a pathos . . . that made me feel that it was altogether the most beautiful thing I had ever heard." But Ryder misreads the relationship, speculating that Newman never "took cordially to Wordsworth" because of the poet's "didactic tone," near "sacerdotal pretensions," and "excessive deliberateness" (Ward 2: 354). Newman's fondness of the "Intimations Ode" is based on the philosophy of the painful loss of childhood soon replaced by a sobering adolescence, what Wordsworth calls the encroaching "shades of the prison house," and what to Newman was "the transitory nature of this world" (*LD* 2: 69). Newman sketched a more complete portrait of the Wordsworthian child in his sermon "The Mind of Little Children." The child, he says, "is but a type of what is at length to be fulfilled in him. The chief beauty of his mind is on its mere surface"; and "as time goes on . . . instantly it disappears . . . . Therefore, we must not lament that our youthful days are gone, or sigh over the remembrances of pure pleasures and contemplations which we cannot recall; rather, what we were when children, is a blessed *intimation,* given for our comfort . . . . And thus it is that a child is a pledge of immortality; for he bears upon him in figure those high and eternal excellences in which joy of heaven consists" (267-68).

In ways similar to Wordsworth, Newman's writings emphasize recollections, feeling, adventure, and childhood experiences.
Memory, he claims in the *Grammar*, "consists in a present
imagination of things that are past; memory retains the
impressions and likeness of what they were when before us . . .
. They are things still, as being the reflections of things in a
mental mirror" (22-23). Forms of the word "recollection"
punctuate almost every page of the *Apologia*. The first chapter,
Newman's remembrance of things past and the growth of his
mind, reads much like Wordsworth's *Prelude* and the "Intimations Ode." "After I was grown up," he writes, "I put on paper
my recollections of the thoughts and feelings on religious
subjects, which I had at the time I was a child and a boy,—such
as had remained on my mind with sufficient prominence to
make me then consider them worth recording." He "used to
wish," he informs us, "the Arabian Tales were true: my imagination ran on unknown influences, on magical powers, and
talismans . . . . I thought life might be a dream, or I an Angel,
and all this world a deception, my fellow-angels by a playful
device concealing themselves from me, and deceiving me with
the semblance of a material world." This attraction to the
romance was not as trivial as it might appear, for Newman
admits it had "a bearing on my later convictions" (*Apo* 14).

Elsewhere Newman observes especially among youth "a
natural love of what is noble and heroic. We like to hear
marvelous tales, which throw us out of things as they are, and
introduce us to things that are not. We so love the idea of the
invisible, that we build fabrics in the air for ourselves." In an
even more lucid Wordsworthian diction, and what could serve as
a paraphrase of the loss of the "visionary gleam" in Wordsworth,
Newman talks of youth imagining "some perfection, such as
earth has not," feelings that exist "before the world alters them,
before the world comes upon them . . . , before it breathes on
them, and blights and parches, and strips off their green foliage,

and leaves them, as dry and wintry trees without sap and sweetness." However, "in early youth," writes Newman, "we stand with our leaves and blossoms on which promise fruit; we stand by the side of the still waters, with our hearts beating high, with longings after our unknown good" ("The Weapons of Saints" 1372).

Newman also admits his childhood superstition of always crossing himself before going out in the dark, and of drawing when he was ten the figure of a cross between "Verse" and "Book," a habit, he suspects, he might have picked up "from some romance" (*Apo* 15). This early predisposition to the supernatural reminds one of Shelley's child in "Hymn to Intellectual Beauty" who "sought for ghosts, and sped / Through many a listening chamber of cave and ruin, / And starlight wood, with fearful steps pursuing / Hopes of high talk with the departed dead." Newman recalls at age fifteen "childish imaginations . . . isolating me from the objects which surrounded me, in confirming me in my mistrust of the reality of material phenomena [an idea tied to his sacramentalism] and making me rest in the thought of two and two only absolute and luminously self-evident beings, myself and my Creator"; he also remembers "fancying" the lost as simply not predestined to salvation, an opinion he held until age twenty-one "when it gradually faded away" (*Apo* 16), and of being "rudely awakened from my dream" at the discovery that he was preferring "intellectual excellence to moral" (*Apo* 24). His trip to the Mediterranean served only to intensify the recoil into the self (*Apo* 39), a retreat exacerbated by a "feeling of separation from the visible world" that accompanied his vow of celibacy (*Apo* 19). Unmistakable in this first chapter is the Romantic emphasis on, among other things, isolation and withdrawal.

Much that is here in Newman echoes Wordsworth. "I used to brood over the stories of Enoch and Elijah," Wordsworth tells us, "and almost to persuade myself that, whatever might become of others, I should be translated, in something of the same way, to heaven." He registers a strikingly similar loss of consciousness of things outside himself: "I was often unable to think of external things as having external existence, and I communed with all that I saw as something not apart from, but inherent in, my own immaterial nature. Many times while going to school have I grasped at a wall or tree to recall myself from this abyss of idealism to the reality" (*Poetical Works* 4: 463). The childhood account in *The Prelude* records the same experience: "So wide appears / The vacancy between me and those days / Which yet have such self-presence in my mind," writes Wordsworth, "That musing on them, often do I seem / Two consciousnesses, conscious of myself / And of some other Being" (1850, 2: 28-33). He notes in *The Prelude*: " Oft in those moments [during his early morning walks] such a holy calm / Did overspread my soul that I forgot / That I had bodily eyes, and what I saw / Appeared like something in myself, a dream, / A prospect in my mind" (1805, 2: 367-7 1).

Similar to Wordsworth and Coleridge, both of whom made the mind the subject of intense, self-conscious scrutiny, Newman placed emphasis on the mind and on how unpredictably it functions. "The mind," he notes, "ranges to and fro, and spreads out, and advances forward with a quickness . . . and a subtlety and versatility which baffle investigation. It passes on from point to point, gaining one by some indication . . . ; then availing itself of an association . . . ; next seizing on testimony; then committing itself to some popular impression, or some inward instinct, or some obscure memory . . . . No analysis," he discovers, "is subtle and delicate enough to represent adequately the state of mind under which we believe, or the subjects of belief, as they are presented to our thoughts." The best that can be hoped for is "painting what the mind sees and feels" ("Implicit Reason" 257). Because the mind operates in such enigmatic ways, attempting to "parcel out / [One's] intellect by geometric rules" *(The Prelude,* 1850, 2: 203-4), to take hold of that "living intelligence," "that great revolution of mind," in the *Apologia,* attempting, that is, to write autobiography, what Wordsworth calls "turning the mind in upon itself" *(The Prelude,* 1850, 3: 116), proves a challenging enterprise:

> For who can know himself, and the multitude of subtle influences which act upon him? And who can recollect, at the distance of twenty-five years, all that he once knew about his thoughts and his deeds, and that, during a portion of his life, when, even at the time, his observation, whether of himself or of the perplexity and dismay which weighed upon him . . . ? And who can suddenly gird himself to a new and anxious undertaking, which he might be able indeed to perform well, were full and calm leisure allowed him to look through every thing he had written . . . ? yet again, granting that calm contemplation of the past, in itself so desirable.
>
> (81)

How the mind operates then is fundamental to the *Apologia,* Newman's attempts to shore up through memory the fragments of his life. Like Wordsworth, trusting that his "mellower years will bring a riper mind / And clearer insight" *(The Prelude* 1850, 1: 236-37), and thus struggling with how to "trace the history, where seek / The origin of what I then have felt" (1805, 2: 365-66), how to "paint / What then I was" ("Tintern Abbey"), so Newman attempts in the *Apologia* to provide the "true key to my whole life," the "history of my mind," how opinions "developed from within," "grew," "modified," "combined," and "changed" (12). This organic work is, Newman tells us, "about myself, and about my most private thoughts and feelings" (1). He concedes difficulty in recalling his own spots of time: "How am I to say all that has to be said in a reasonable compass?" he asks (*Apologia* 12). In this "*solus cum solos*" (face to face) encounter, what in

Wordsworth was "a saving intercourse / With my true self" (*The Prelude,* 1850, 11: 34142), Newman faces the challenge of autobiography, the quandary over how to promulgate what Langbaum calls a romantic "crisis of personality" (12).

Face to face—the mirror motif in Wordsworth and Newman—is the framing of autobiography. It is a confrontation between disparate selves, either the playing off of an earlier self with a later self through the media of time and memory, or by the fictionalization of an antiself, an alter ego. Newman appears to prefer the former, Wordsworth both, the latter manifested when the self is reflected in something external to itself. That mirror of the changed self, in "Tintern Abbey" for instance, is both the landscape and the voice of Dorothy, where the poet catches "The language of my former heart" and reads in her eyes his former self. However, face to face in Newman results either by way of catching a reflection of himself in the pages of the *Apologia,* or from looking at God's face through the pages of Scripture. But whatever the encounter—and in the *Apologia* both seem always to occur simultaneously—it yields a real or imaginative apprehension of the self and the realization of autobiography.

The mirror motif in Wordsworth and Newman endeavors to effect a single identity. This identity concerns a historical perspective, the conscious identifying of an unbroken chain of events linking a life. The metaphor is strikingly analogous to Newman's description of the unity needed in the Oxford Movement: it requires, he writes, "a common history, common memories, an intercourse of mind with mind in the past, and a progress and increase in that intercourse in the present" (*Apo* 44). Newman's desire is to reconcile the past with the present, to convince his readers that his conversion was not impulsive but calculated and natural, hence his penchant for metaphors of growth and maturation. If Hopkins is right that "Self is the intrinsic oneness of a thing" (*Sermons* 146), then Newman's task is to preserve that univocity of being, to persuade his religious detractors that though changed he is much the same person. This is what M. H. Abrams calls the "Romantic genre of the *Bildungsgeschichte*, whereby "the painful process of Christian conversion" is transformed into "self-formation, crisis, and self recognition" (96). Regarding this Romantic lyrical mode as "crisis autobiography," Abrams sees the genre as "fragments of reshaped autobiography" that seek to establish a "colloquy that specifies the present, evokes the past, and anticipates the future, and thereby defines and evaluates what it means to have suffered and to grow older" (123).

The act of self-interpretation is a major preoccupation of the nineteenth-century Romantic writers. Wordsworth's *The Prelude*, Coleridge's *Biographia Literaria*, Byron's *Childe Harold's Pilgrimage*, De Quincey's *Confessions of English Opium-Eater*, and Leigh Hunt's *Autobiography* all endorse this autobiographical impulse. However the *Apologia* as autobiography is nongeneric, for its foremost concerns are Newman's spiritual birth, crisis, and rebirth. Uneven and disproportionate, the work engages mainly Newman's preparation for his defense, with a relatively limited section taken up with the actual refutation. This structural, and possibly thematic, imbalance has prompted Martin Svaglic to question the work's total autobiographical feature, for it tells nothing, says Svaglic, "of the family life, the student activities, the intellectual and artistic interests of its complex subject." Svaglic remains just as skeptical about the work as spiritual autobiography, but is more sympathetic with the work as a polemic, "designed to persuade a body of readers" (138). But these distinctions should not be emphasized. For the *Apologia* should be read, says Francis Connolly, "not only as objective history and controversial prose, but as an artistic autobiography and as the story of a soul" (111). And whatever absence of fullness the work reveals, it is compensated by a "gain in concentration"; and by excluding or marginalizing events unrelated to the religious, Newman, says Houghton, was able to strike a "powerful artistic unity" (93).

Newman did, however, envision the *Apologia* as autobiographical, and spiritually so, a sentiment George Eliot shared. Unable to set aside the book until completing it, she found it "the revelation of a life —how different in form from one's own, yet with how close a fellowship in its needs and burthens—I mean spiritual needs and burthens" (159). Newman calls the work "my own testimony" (207), the "birth of my own mind" (82), a "history of myself" (215), a "History of my Religious Opinions," and attempts to account for "how I came to write a whole book about myself, and about my most private thoughts and feelings" (1). "I must," he asserts, "give the true key to my whole life; I must show what I am," drawing out as far as possible "the history of my mind," and charting how opinions "developed from within, how they grew, were modified, were combined, were in collision with each other, and were changed" (12). Newman felt himself vulnerable to the charge of egoism, and so attempts to deflect it by the many detours away from himself, which have, he asserts, "so direct a bearing on myself, that they are no digression from my narrative" (61). Still he insists on taking this risk if he is to follow his "own lights," to speak out his "own heart" what has taken place "within me from my early years," and to share "my most private thoughts" as though it were "the intercourse between myself and my Maker" (13) with "no cloud interposed between the creature and the Object of his faith and love" (154). As autobiography, then, the *Apologia* offers coherence and meaning to life seldom found in the experience of actual life.

Newman was always fascinated with the distinct pitch of a life. "The exhibition of a person," he believes, "his thoughts, his words, his acts, his trials, his features, his beginnings, his growth, his end, have a charm to every one" (Ward 1: 207). This charm, and one might add the power, of autobiography that

Newman speaks of recalls Othello's account of winning Desdemona's ear, imagination, heart, and hand through the romantic rehearsing of his life. Similarly, Newman believed that a life, especially that of a Saint, has a "divine influence and persuasion, a power of exercising and eliciting the latent elements of divine grace in individual readers" (Ward 1: 207). This conviction not only influenced his own hagiographical writings, which he admits are romantic, but also has a direct bearing on how he perceived his own self-promulgation in the *Apologia*. "I CONFESS to a delight in reading the lives, and dwelling on the characters and actions," he writes in his biography of St. Chrysostom. "People are variously constituted; what influences one does not influence another. There are persons of warm imaginations, who can easily picture to themselves what they never saw . . . . They can go home and draw what they have seen, from the vivid memory of what, while it lasted, was so transporting." However, in so splitting apart Wordsworth's idea of the poetic process, Newman positioned himself differently: "I am not one of such; I am touched by my five senses, by what my eyes behold and my ears hear. I am touched by what I read about, not by what I myself create" (217). Still maintaining that a work is a person's blueprint, Newman notes: "A Saint's writings are to me his real 'Life,'" and by "Life" he means "a narrative which impresses the reader with the idea of moral unity, identity, growth, continuity, personality" (227). He contends with hagiographers who employ a narrative of virtue rather than one of chronology, arguing that such treatment confuses "youth, manhood, and age." Thus "I would not be able to determine whether there was heroism in the young, whether there was not infirmity and temptation in the old. I shall not be able to explain actions which need explanation, for the age of the actors is the *true key* for entering into them" ("St. Chrysostom" 230-31; italics mine).

The *Apologia* charts Newman's mental changes by way of answering Kingsley's charge not about "words," "actions," or "arguments," says Newman, but about that "living intelligence," about "my Mind" (11). But how the mind actually works is the topic not of the *Apologia* but of the *Grammar*, which argues that belief is grounded in the joint rational and sensual apprehension of probability. Michael Ryan rightly calls the *Apologia* "the practice for which the *Grammar* would be the theoretical exposition" (129). In the *Apologia,* which antedates the *Grammar* by six years, Newman broached the argument on certitude and probability. He declares, speaking in regard to his *Oxford University Sermons*, that "absolute certitude" on matters of natural theology and revelation "was the result of an *assemblage* of concurring and converging possibilities." He calls certitude a "habit of the mind," a "quality of propositions," and believes that even "probabilities which did not reach to logical certainty, might suffice for a mental certitude." Newman maintains that such mental certitude "might equal in measure and strength the certitude which was created by the strictest scientific demonstration." But such certitude, he insists, demands "plain duty" (*Apo* 29). So confident is Newman about his theory that he grounds his belief in God, in Christianity, and in Catholicism in probability; and that these beliefs, though dissimilar, yet demand "one and the same in nature of proof, as being probabilities—probabilities of a special kind, a cumulative, a transcendent probability but still probability." And it is God who willed that as we arrive at certitude in mathematics "by rigid demonstrations," so in religious inquiry we arrive at certitude on the grounds of "accumulated probabilities" (*Apo* 157).

The worship of the cult of reason by the eighteenth-century rationalists and now in the nineteenth century made an accepted religion convinced Newman that "Rationalism is the great evil of the day," (*Apo* 112), whose symptom is an "all-corroding, all-dissolving skepticism of the intellect" (*Apo* 187).

Naturally, then, Newman turned to the imagination and senses from which to derive certitude. Earlier in the Tamworth essay, he observed that "The heart is commonly reached, not through the reason, but through the imagination, by means of direct impressions, by the testimony of facts and events." He proceeded with the claim that "man is *not* a reasoning animal; he is a seeing, feeling, contemplating, acting animal" (204, 205). Taken out of context, these positions would seem to suggest that Newman devalued reason in the process toward faith and certitude. But such is not the case, for his remarks are to be understood, as Hopkins discerned, more as rhetorical devices than as an actual statement of his epistemology; they are meant, says Hopkins, "to awake the hearer's attention" (*Further Letters* 388) to the folly in pursuing natural theology.

Instead, Newman advocates not the insignificance of reason but its cooperation with the senses and the imagination in arriving at certitude. In the *Grammar* this becomes his theory of cognition, what he calls assent, the mental assertion and totally unconditional acceptance of a proposition; or, to use his exact words, "the mental assertion of an intelligible proposition, as an act of intellect direct, absolute, complete in itself, unconditional, arbitrary, yet not incompatible with the appeal to argument, and at least in many cases exercised unconsciously" (*GA* 123-24). Newman believes that to insist always on proof is to invite paralysis; to act one must "assume, and that assumption is faith." But as not to dispense of reason altogether, he refashions it, considering it not a mechanical activity but a principle tied to nature, a "living spontaneous energy within us, not an art" ("Implicit Reason" 257). Newman refuses to speculate on ~Why we are so constituted that Faith, not Knowledge or Argument, is our principle of action" ("Tamworth" 206). Still the *Grammar* undertakes to sketch how the mind operates in apprehending propositions on the way to unconditional assent.

Newman calls the two modes of apprehension—the process from images to notions—the notional and the real. The real is more effective than the notional because it "excites and stimulates the affections and passions" (14), it relies on memory, and it appeals to the imagination. The imagination then becomes tied to the principle of action, for assent to a "real proposition" is, Newman argues, "assent to imagination," which in turn supplies objects to our "emotional and moral nature" (*GA* 140). Real Assent, then, the same as "Belief," results when the imagination stimulates "those powers of the mind from which action proceeds." Assent itself does not spur action, but the "power of the concrete upon the affections and passions" (63). Newman asserts that there is no clear predictor of how the mind receives data, used either for pleasure or for certitude. In fact, what influences most our certitude are the pleasurable ways in which information is impressed on the mind. For the "acquisition of new images, and those images striking, great, various, unexpected, beautiful" is "highly pleasurable" and "quite independently of the question whether there is any truth in them" (135).

Lest he be accused of displaying a Romantic penchant for the image, an inclination that threatens the signified when the symbol replaces the real, and the figure rather than the figural is embraced, Newman again explains his sacramentalism: "'I don't worship the image *at all*, my eyes pass on to that I do not see thro' that I do see—' or 'I *identify* with the reality, I see the reality in it, I worship the reality in it, I worship what is unseen in what is seen or *through* what is seen—that is I worship the seen as the visible form of what is unseen'" (*LD* 14: 240-41). This rejection of the reality of material phenomena, deducing its value only in symbolic terms, returns us to the *Apologia*. In this passage, Newman admits that useful to him in Butler's *The Analogy of Religion* was that "the very idea of an analogy between the separate works of God leads to the conclusion that the system which is of less importance is economically or sacramentally connected with the more momentous system" (21). Embracing, then, a sacramental vision of the world—"that material phenomena are both the types and the instruments of real things unseen" (*Apo* 28); that "the exterior world, physical and historical, was but the manifestation to our senses of realities greater than itself"; and that the Holy Church is "but a symbol of those heavenly facts which fill eternity," and her mysteries "expressions in human language of truths to which the human mind is unequal" (34)—Newman becomes disheartened when he looks "out of myself" to find, like Wordsworth, some analogue of the sublime, something in the world of nature far more deeply interfused. To his consternation he encounters a universe unable to appreciate "that great truth of which my being is so full": "If I looked into a mirror, and did not see my face, I should have the sort of feeling which actually comes upon me, when I look into this living busy world, and see no reflection of its Creator" (Apo 186).

Although Newman's knowledge of the existence of God is coextensive with his discovery of himself ("myself and my Creator"), he is still troubled by the Argument from Design, a doctrine advanced by the Romantics. This epistemology not only leads to pantheism but remains too rational for Newman, denying him an "imaginative apprehension" of God: "Can I attain to any more vivid assent to the Being of God, than that which is given merely to notions of the intellect? Can I enter with a personal knowledge into the circle of truths which make up that feat thought? . . . Can I believe as if I saw?" (*GA* 71). Newman believes he can; but this crisis of faith in the existence of God cannot be attenuated by rational explanations drawn from the design argument—"these," Newman says, "do not warm me or enlighten me; they do not take away the winter of my desolation, or make the buds unfold and the leaves grow within me, and my moral being rejoice." Rather, and in a Coleridgean turning within on not finding in "outward forms" the "passion and the life, whose fountains are within" ("Dejection: An Ode"), Newman ascertains that "Were it not for this voice, speaking so clearly in my conscience and my heart, I should be an atheist, or a pantheist, or a polytheist when I looked into the world." For "The world seems simply to give the lie to that great truth, of which my whole being is so full." And to rebuff such overwhelming evidence is to disavow one's very existence (*Apo* 186). But like a persistent Romantic, Newman refuses to relinquish his search for God's manifestation of himself in nature. What he finds in this nightmarish world of nineteenth-century England, however, is "a vision to dizzy and appal," a "heart-piercing, reason-bewildering" affliction on the mind, which from his human standpoint seems insoluble. He concludes that "either there is no Creator, or this living society of men is in a true sense discarded from His presence . . . . And so I argue about the world—if there be a God, *since* there is a God, the human race is implicated in some terrible aboriginal calamity. It is out of joint with the purposes of its Creator" (187). This accusation is stunningly close to Wordsworth's incrimination of man in "The World is too Much with Us."

Clearly, then, Newman's relationship with the nineteenth century Romantics is both a stated and implied fondness of their aesthetics. The argument, it seems to me, is not that he was a Romantic, but that he, like so many of his contemporary Victorians—Carlyle, Ruskin, Arnold, and Hopkins, in particular—who for reasons pertaining to the imagination, the growing skepticism that was the product of empiricism and reason, and the increasing mechanization of society that threatens not only the dehumanization of man but the survivability or art and religion, turned deliberately to his literary predecessors. However, Newman's was not an absolute acceptance of Romantic epistemology, though, it seems, an almost total compliance with their aesthetics. His protean corpus reveals an attempt to retailor Romanticism to fit his own notions of how prose, the mind, reason, and belief should all perform if they are to remain vital. And because of this he should be included among the last Romantics.

WORKS CITED

Abrams, M. H. *The Mirror and the Lamp*. London: Oxford UP, 1953.

Beer, John. "Newman and the Romantic Sensibility." *The English Mind*. Ed. Hugh Sykes Davies. London: Cambridge UP, 1964. 193-218.

Bloom, Harold. "The Internalization of Quest-Romance." *Romanticism and Consciousness*. New York: W. W. Norton, 1970. 3-24.

Castle, W. R. "Newman and Coleridge." *The Sewanee Review*. 17 (1909): 139-52.

Church, R. W. *The Oxford Movement*. California: Stanford UP, 1960.

Colby, Robert A. "The Poetical Structure of Newman's *Apologia Pro Vita Sua*." The Journal of Religion 33.1 (1953): 47-57.

The Collected Works of Samuel Taylor Coleridge: Lay Sermons. Vol. 6. Ed. R. J. White. London: Routledge & Kegan Paul, 1972.

Connolly, Francis X. "The *Apologia:* History, Rhetoric, and Literature." *Newman's "Apologia": A Classic Reconsidered*. Ed. Vincent Ferrer Blehl, and Francis X. Connolly. New York: Harcourt, 1964. 105-24.

Froude, James Anthony. *Short Studies on Great Subjects*. New York: Charles Scribner's Sons, 1892.

Gates, Lewis E. "Newman as a Prose Writer." *Three Studies in Literature*. New York: Macmillan, 1899. 64-123.

The *George Eliot Letters*. Vol. 4. Ed. Gordon S. Haight. New Haven: Yale UP, 1955.

Harrold, Charles F., and William D. Templeman. *English Prose of the Victorian Period*. New York: Oxford UP, 1938.

Helsinger, Howard. "Credence and Credibility: The Concern for Honesty in Victorian Autobiography." *Approaches to* Victorian Autobiography. Ed. George P. Landow. Athens: Ohio UP, 1979. 39-63.

Hopkins, Gerard Manley. The *Correspondence of Gerard Manley Hopkins and Richard Watson Dixon.* Ed. Claude Colleer Abbott. 2nd ed. London: Oxford UP. 1970.

—. *Further Letters.* Ed. Claude Colleer Abbott. 2nd ed. London: Oxford UP, 1970.

—. *The Sermons and Devotional Writings.* Ed. Christopher Devlin. London: Oxford UP. 1959.

Houghton, Walter E. *The Art of Newman's "Apologia."* New Haven: Yale UP, 1945.

James. D. G. *The Romantic Comedy: An Essay on English Romanticism.* London: Oxford UP, 1963.

Keble, John. *Lectures on Poetry.* Vol. 2. Trans. Edward Kershaw Francis. Oxford: The Clarendon P, 1912.

Langbaum, Robert. *The Poetry of Experience: The Dramatic Monologue in Modern Literary Tradition.* Chicago: The U of Chicago P, 1985.

Lawliss, Merritt E. "Newman on the Imagination." *Modern Language Notes* 68.2 (1953): 73-80.

Newman, John Henry. *Apologia Pro Vita Sua.* Ed. David J. DeLaura. New York: W. W. Norton, 1968.

—. *Discourses Addressed to Mixed Congregations.* London: Longman, Brown, Green, Longmans, 1849.

—. *An Essay in Aid of a Grammar of Assent.* Ed. I. T. Ker. Oxford: Clarendon P, 1985.

—. *The Idea of a University.* Ed. I. T. Ker. Oxford: Clarendon P, 1976.

—. "Implicit and Explicit Reason." *University Sermons.* Eds. D. M. MacKinnon, and J. D. Holmes. Westminster, Maryland: Christian Classic, 1970. 251-7

—. "John Keble." *Essays Critical and Historical.* Vol. 2. New York: Longmans, 1919.

—. *The Letters and Diaries of John Henry Newman.* Vol. 2. Eds. Ian Ker and Thomas Gornall. Oxford: Clarendon P, 1979.

—. *The Letters and Diaries of John Henry Newman.* Vol. 5. Ed. Thomas Gornall. Oxford: Clarendon P, 1981.

—. *The Letters and Diaries of John Henry Newman.* Vol. 6. Ed. Gerard Tracey. Oxford: Clarendon P, 1984.

—. *The Letters and Diaries of John Henry Newman.* Vol. 14. Ed. Charles Stephen Dessain. New York: Thomas Nelson, 1963.

—. "The Mind of Little Children." *Parochial and Plain Sermons.* San Francisco: Ignatius P, 1987. 264-68.

—. "Poetry, with Reference to Aristotle's *Poetics.*" *Essays Critical and Historical.* Vol. 1. New York: Longmans, 1919. 1-26.

—. "Prospects of the Anglican Church." *Essays and Sketches.* Vol. 1. New York: Longmans, 1948. 333-37.

—. "St. Chrysostom." *Historical Sketches.* Vol 2. London: Longmans, 1840. 217.-302.

—. "The Second Spring." *Sermons and Discourses.* Vol. 2. New York: Longmans, 1949. 345-60.

—."The Tamworth Reading Room." *Essays and Sketches.* Vol. 2. Ed. Charles Frederick Harrold. New York: Longmans, 1948. 173-214.

—. *Verses on Various Occasions.* London: Longman, 1890.

—. "The Weapons of Saints." *Parochial and Plain Sermons.* San Francisco: Ignatius P, 1987. 1370-78.

Noyes, Russell, ed. *English Romantic Poetry and Prose.* New York: Oxford UP, 1956.

Robinson, Jonathan. "The *Apologia* and the *Grammar of Assent.*" *Newman's "Apologia": A Classic Reconsidered.* Eds. Vincent Ferrer Blehl, and Francis X. Connolly. New York: Harcourt, 1964. 145-64.

Ruskin, John. *Modern Painters*. Vol. 3. *The Works of Ruskin*. Ed. E. T. Cook. and Alexander Wedderburn. London: George Allen, 1904.

Ryan, Alvan S. "Newman's Conception of Literature." *Critical Studies in Arnold. Emerson. and Newman*. Eds. John Hicks et al. Iowa City: U of Iowa P, 1942. 123-72.

Ryan, Michael. "A Grammatology of Assent: Cardinal Newman's *Apologia Pro Vita Sua*." *Approaches to Victorian Autobiography*. Ed. George P. Landow. Athens: Ohio UP, 1979. 128-5.

Sladen, Douglas. *My Long Life: Anecdotes and Adventures*. London: Hutchinson, 1939.

Svaglic, Martin J. "The Structure of Newman's *Apologia*." *PMLA* 66 (1951): 138-48.

Tennyson, G. B. *Victorian Devotional Poetry: The Tractarian Mode*. Cambridge: Harvard UP, 1981.

Vargish, Thomas. *Newman: The Contemplation of Mind*. Oxford: Clarendon P, 1970.

Ward, Wilfrid. *The Life of John Henry Newman*. 2 vols. New York: Longmans, 1921.

Warren, Alba. *English Poetic Theory 1825-1865*. New Jersey: Princeton UP, 1950.

Wordsworth, William. *The Poetical Works*. Ed. E. DeSelincourt. 5 vol. Oxford: Clarendon P, 1940-49.

—. *The Prelude 1799. 1805. 1850*. Eds. Jonathan Wordsworth, et al. New York: W. W. Norton, 1979.

Education's "New" Source of Methodology: *The Rhetoric of Apologetic-Autobiography*

John Britt

> Literature is to man in some sort what *autobiography* is to the individual; it is his Life and Remains.
> *(Idea* 73)

> It is not surprising that in 1864 Newman discarded logic for the rhetoric of autobiography and decided not to expound Catholic doctrine but to be simply personal and historical . . . simply to state facts.
> *(Art* 10)

When we use apology we concern ourselves with the signs of the times in the events going on around us in light of our own meaning and when we add to this the use of rhetoric we have persuasion and finally when we add autobiography we have that which reveals the secret of that meaning in the very being of the person. We unite the hermeneutic, the justificatory and the personal. Yet as much as we would like to get to the mystery of the person, there is no assured way to discover even our own motivation much less expect another to share theirs. Instead we must depend upon the harmony and consistency of our actions and our state of mind on the one hand and the methods in relation to our principles on the other. Yet when these purposes

201

are united we have a form of persuasion which cares for the social ties which extend our personal stories beyond ourselves and the personal influence which makes our words move others to emulation and fulfillment. In taking this tack, education avoids the attempt to prove through logic and moves to the use of persuasion to convince in order that society might go into action. With this "new" methodology, the deadend of behaviorism with its dependency upon a scientific approach to education is replaced by this complex path of rhetoric of apologetic autobiography.

In order to obtain an entry into this set of propositions we will take Newman's famous lecture "Literature" from *The Idea of a University* as a test case for an apologetic-autobiographical rhetoric. This lecture gave the faculty and students of the Arts an opportunity to gain self respect at a time when *science* was joining with *professions* to capture the esteem of society. Newman put an enormous effort into this lecture in proportion to his evaluation of the coming challenge.

Just as in our time Marshall McLuhan and Walter Ong have prepared society for a new form of orality, secondary orality, so in this lecture Newman analyzed the relation of language, as the spoken word, to literature, the written word. In his analysis he came upon the necessary link between thought and language and thus between these and the person and only finally with the social ties related to this form of influence.

Section after section of the lecture broke out the basis of the principles and methods of thought which highlighted the link between thought and language until the consequences of the relation became clear in the conclusion. There Newman developed a summary by means of a series of seven conditionals. These conditionals led to a powerful double negative through which he stressed both the value and the dignity of literature. If the seven qualities of literature were as he found them, we would be right not to make light of its study. On the contrary, literature would be seen as of supreme worth.

However, this worth is not only a case of personal influence, which Newman took as paramount, but the result of our social ties. We, as a people, are shaped by our language. Our language has a tyrannous hold upon us. In "English Catholic Literature," Newman further developed this point. Despite the demand of the bishops that he justify the enormous investment of Ireland's spiritual and material capital in setting up a Catholic University in Dublin, he could not accept a charge to do the impossible. English literature was Protestant. No wishing could deny this fact of English literary history.

As St. Basil the Great's famous lecture on pagan literature used the metaphor of the bee, honey, and poison, to convince students and parents that no growth in Greek language and thought was possible without the use of classical Greek litera-ture, despite the fact it was composed by pagans, so Newman used the autobiographical fact of English literature to justify both the use of classical English literature and the acceptance of the limits of what could be hoped for from the pursuit of an English Catholic literature.

This phenomenon of the *influence* of language recently elaborated upon by McLuhan and Ong justifies Newman's Conclusion to "Literature," in which he combined "social ties" and "personal influence" in such unquestioned fashion.

His genius as well as his intuitive-introverted approach, which Samuel Wilberforce in Newman's day and the theologian Jak Walgrave in our day, noted negatively and positively respectively, revealed the connection of the personal and the social which we most frequently overlook, both in our separation of psychology and sociology and in our simplified approach to problems. While we personally influence others, and this with great effort, we ourselves depend upon the tradition of our culture and express the result of this influence in a variety of ways quite oblivious of the inculturation which has shaped our influence. Newman ended his list of influences coming from literature in his conclusion with the claim that no greater gift could be naturally given to us than language.

PERSONAL INFLUENCE THROUGH THOUGHT AND LANGUAGE

Throughout his life he examined the influence of language and thought upon himself and others. In *An Essay in Aid of a Grammar of Assent,* he three times emphasized the limits of language due to a lack of its versatility. Such study disclosed what he had earlier admitted—only by writing do we know what we know; nonetheless, our development depends upon our thought and our thought depends upon our language. But beyond the latter is the action of our illative sense in which, paradoxically, we determine what exists and is knowable before we make it explicit. In this interdependency Newman used his personal experience in the difference between rhetoric and the limits of logic from his apologetic-autobiographical analysis of influence to convince us of the defense against the usual critic's opposition to an over expectation of logic by entering complexly into the relation between inference and assent before concluding first to the need for an assent to assent and then to the limits of logic. Despite his cooperation in the writing of a textbook on logic, Newman used his phenomenal rhetorical powers with even greater effect. Thus he always kept logic in its place and accepted the English bias against it as the following quotations make clear.

> Logical inference, then, being such, and its office such as I have described, the question follows, how far it answers the purpose for which it is used. It proposes to provide both a test and a common measure of reasoning; . . . failing on

account of the fallacy of the original assumption, that whatever can be thought can be adequately expressed in words.

(212)

Science . . . In its very perfection lies its incompetency to settle particulars and details. As to Logic, its chain of conclusions hangs loose at both ends; both the point at which it should start and the point at which it should arrive, are beyond its reach; it comes short both of first principles, and of concrete issues.

(227)

Here then again, as in the other instances, it seems clear, that methodical processes of inference, useful as they are, as far as they go, are only instruments of the mind, and need, in order to their due exercise, that real ratiocination and present imagination which gives them a sense beyond their letter, and which, while acting through them, reaches to conclusions beyond and above them. Such a living *organon* is a personal gift, and not a mere method or calculus.

Great as are the services of language in enabling us to extend the compass of our inference, to test their validity, and to communicate them to others, still the *mind itself is more versatile and vigorous than any of its works*, of which language is one, and it is only under its penetrating and subtle action that the margin disappears, which I have described as intervening between verbal argumentation and conclusions in the concrete. It determines what science cannot determine, the weight of converging probabilities and the reasons sufficient for proofs. It is the rational mind itself, and no art, however simple in its form and sure in operation, which we are able to determine and thereupon to be certain, that a living body left to itself will never stop, and that no man can live without eating.

(281-282)

This autobiographical approach was one with his apologetic use of language. Early and later in his life, he collected persuasive defenses of activities in which he participated. Letters as well as diaries provided what appeared to be objective data for his life. Yet the fact that he was often under a shadow meant that much of the reason for the evidence was defensive. As he knew, his attackers would not allow him merely to use on a *prima facie* basis what he recalled. Those who place him under a cloud recalled to their advantage, therefore he had to spend much time preparing his journals for a refutation of those who misunderstood him regardless of his care in making himself clear.

APOLOGETIC-AUTOBIOGRAPHICAL RHETORIC

Nothing, then, was more important to Newman than influence and the tools for securing that influence. As an *educator*, the *rhetorician* of the Oxford Movement, and as an *apologist*, Newman used the rhetoric of autobiography as a means of fulfilling his mission in life. A quotation from the *Apologia* moves us from the starting point we have taken in the understanding of his proposition: "Universities are the natural centers of intellectual movements" (*Apo* 44). As such centers, these required both personal influence as well as social ties. Whereas literature has a predominant role to play, both science and theology share in the influence of such centers. Thus we find it important to take a quotation from *The Idea of a University* which indicates why this is necessary if we are to grasp the significance Newman found in the University for his mission. "It is a great point then to enlarge the range of subjects which a University professes, even for the sake of the students; and, though they cannot pursue every subject which is open to them, they will be the gainers by living among and under those who represent the whole circle . . . Thus is created a pure and clear atmosphere of thought, which the student also breathes, though in his own case he only pursues a few sciences out of the multitude" (*Apo* 76). Newman accepted the limits of the individual in relation to the variety of worlds of knowledge and expected that the faculty would do the same. The fact they did not is evident in the need Alfred North Whitehead, an admirer of Newman, had to write an analogous work to the *Idea* in order to reform the English educational system where students were expected to come to know a little about everything in place of Newman's "a little, but well."

Newman had hoped to convince those at the Catholic University he was forming, as well as future generations, of the relationship between knowledge and a philosophical habit of mind and influence, yet few have shown by their practice that they have understood his point.

I write this in the steps of Whitehead because in 1979 I carried out a study of the Core Curriculum at Harvard University, and I attempted a similar study of the Western Civilization program at Stanford University. The person in charge of the former program confessed Harvard was merely taking a small step in the way of Newman and the latter's program was so insignificant I had to abort the study. Since then I have watched other institutions follow Harvard's lead in taking a very small step, while the problem is that those who are in charge have an image of a *general* program rather than of the type of program Newman envisioned from his life experience at Oxford and his reflection upon the encompassing influence of a philosophical habit of mind in initiating the Catholic University in Dublin.

If we consider the significance of the "even" in the above quotation, we may well catch the point. "Even for the sake of the students" comes immediately after Newman had begun the second half of his nine discourses on a university education. At that point he had described the principle which held his work together —the *wholeness* of knowledge—assumed throughout the first four discourses in relation to the subject matter and to be used in the next five discourses in relation to the students.

Since, as we will notice in our later treatment of *Historical Sketches* (*Apo* 51), Newman understood that a university is for the professor, he began his work with the subject matter, yet he recognized that the same principle which was of such significance for the professor was also of value for the student. The reason for this is found in the influence of knowledge itself and its existence within the mind of the knower.

His growing appreciation of the influence of knowledge in the professor and through the philosophical habit of mind helps prepare us for Newman's change from a concern for the *tutor* to a concern for the *institution*. He was concerned with the institution, not as a thing outside of the persons making up the institution but as existing in these very *influential* people.

AUTOBIOGRAPHY, APOLOGY, RHETORIC

Thus we are led back autobiographically to the *Apologia*, where he rhetorically presented his changed opinions after he had given his unchanged principles; we find this change in "History of my Religious Opinions from 1833 to 1839," where he professed: "What I held in 1816, I held in 1833, and I hold in 1864. Please God, I shall hold it to the end . . . . Here again, I have not changed in opinion; I am as certain now on this point as I was in 1833, and have never ceased to be certain" (*Apo* 53). "But now, as to the third point on which I stood in 1833, and which I have utterly renounced and trampled upon since,—my then view of the Church of Rome;—I will speak about it as exactly as I can" (*Apo* 53). Newman realized the difference between principle, states of mind and methods of thought in studying his own experience of conversation. A University could do much for the latter two, but only the person was responsible for the principle upon which to base one's life. Thus he was concerned to study the principles upon which his associates acted.

INFLUENCE: FROM PLACE TO ANTECEDENT REASONINGS

While earlier Newman had argued from the significance of *place* and the possibility of unity, he went on to the more ulterior basis of unity—antecedent reasonings. Before getting to this basis, we should recall several writings bearing upon this point: *Historical Sketches,* where we find Newman provided the justification for going up to a University as to a city, hence as an argument for place; *Grammar,* where we have his most protracted treatment of antecedent reasonings; the *Idea,* where we have both points covered; later through "Elementary Studies" in the University Subjects and earlier through "Knowledge Its Own End" in the University Teaching. In the former we have the treatment of "Anabasis," where the questioning revealed the need for knowing that we go *up* to centers and the latter where we, as was partially shown already, must take into account the overriding importance of *antecedent reasonings.*

"A far more essential unity (than that of place as a condition) was that of antecedents,—a common history, common memories, an intercourse of mind with mind in the past, and a progress and increase in that intercourse in the present" (*Apo* 44).

Newman used his friend Palmer as his crucial example of the limits of place in regard to unity. Palmer was, in fact, at Oxford; he had knowledge on his side, he had a religious view, but he had come to Oxford from "*a distance, he had never really grown into an Oxford man.*" Not only that, but he lacked that "which Froude and I considered essential to any true success in the stand which had to be made against Liberalism" (*Apo* 44-45)—personal influence.

Foe of Education: Liberalism

Already on the second page of the *Idea* Newman had stressed *religious exclusivity* and *utility*; these two questions were the basis of the work. A work which was in combat with Liberalism— this same Liberalism which was at the heart of the unity of the *Idea*. Then through the whole second discourse, he laid out the history of the problem which forced him to go to Ireland to put up a *new influence* to combat Liberalism which he had had to *lose* by leaving Oxford with his departure from the Anglican church.

We find here another instance of the rhetorical apologetic-autobiographical interest evident in all of Newman's writings and ultimately clinched in the speech given at his reception of the Cardinalate.

Rhetoric of Apologetic Autobiography in Apologia

An instance of the rhetoric of autobiography which clarifies the remainder of his life and writings occurs where Newman, having returned with a mission, appeared in England as a changed person. With his health and strength renewed after the strain of writing *The Arians of the 4th Century*, he seemed, to his acquaintances at Oxford, somewhat himself and somewhat outside of himself. As he described himself he seemed to have gained a haughtiness which resulted from an excessive self confidence. The result of this was that his "behavior had a mixture in it both of fierceness and of sport; and on this account, I dare say, it gave offence to many; nor am I here defending it" (*Apo* 48). In this we find his chief need for a rhetoric of apologetic-autobiography. He had to defend himself by distinguishing a temptation to handle others ironically from any actual handling of the truth insincerely. Did he cross over? Whether he did so or not, the point for us is he used his very great rhetorical skill to defend himself by seeming *not* to do so.

His fierceness was the issue with Charles Kingsley; the latter wanted to handle the dispute as a case of a *gentlemanly* affair and hence a matter of compromise. He found Newman was fierce like a monkey tearing at his face. How could Newman be this way? By putting the influence of truth above the cause of the gentleman.

In the long and famous description of the gentleman, Newman had to use a rhetoric which made it ambivalent. At the heart of the *Idea* we cannot be certain of the degree of Newman's estimation of the gentleman. Only four years before he had had to defend fierceness without seeming to do so; now in the *Idea* he had to seem to respect the gentleman only to show that it was not an unambivalent criterion for a University.

This habit of subtlety forced him to question his harmony of motivation and behavior. Therefore we are not surprised with his confession: "This kind of behavior was a sort of habit with me. If I have ever trifled with my subject, it was a more serious fault. I never used arguments which I saw clearly to be unsound" (*Apo* 48). Just before this he had made his opponents seem to be fools. This seemed to justify him in leading people on by his use of irony and to play with those who asked him what he considered an impertinence.

Autobiographically, Newman tried to justify his irony as well as his subtlety because of his great concern with the need for influence not only through the written word but through his behavior.

Having finally arrived in our argument at this sensitive point in Newman's defense (evidenced by Martin Svaglic in his essay on the *Apologia* among others)—whether Newman betrayed the truth in his concern to defend truth—we are ready to go on to Newman's position on the Classics.

Influence of the Classics

Other than these influences was that of the Classics. We find in "English Catholic Literature" his concern with this type of influence. "The influence of a great classic upon the nation which he represents is twofold: on the one hand he advances his native language towards its perfection; but on the other hand discourages in some measure an advance beyond his own" (*Idea* 243). And to clinch this point, Newman averred that even Newton seemed to have kept the scientific mind from advancing from the power of his prestige. "If a literature be . . . the voice of a particular nation, it requires a territory and a period, as large as that nation's extent and history, to mature in. It is broader and deeper than the capacity of any body of men, however gifted, or any system of teaching, however true . . . It is the result of the mutual action of a hundred simultaneous influences and operations, and the issue of a hundred strange accidents in independent places and times" (*Idea* 232). Language is, indeed, tyrannous.

Important as this approach to language and literature is, we must balance it with the conclusion of "Literature" in the *Idea* already mentioned, where Newman united "social ties" and "personal influence" in considering what literature is and the point of "English Catholic Literature," where we find why Newman was as concerned as he was to develop a Catholic University: those who write very well due to the history of development in literature had become "anonymous" (*Idea* 246). This anonymity he specified at the end of his preface with a claim of conflict between the influence of the press and of the University. Whereas the former was chiefly anonymous, the university was geared towards a personal wisdom embodied in a tradition.

For one noted for the Oxford Movement, it is not surprising then that he favored tradition and moved his prior allegiance from the tutorial to the university. Tradition and his move clarify the significance of his introduction to the third volume of *Historical Sketches*. This passage seems sufficiently significant to lay out in a great deal of white space to recall our starting point in which we prepared the comparison between place and antecedent reasonings to make the order of influence evident.

> The general principles of any study
> you may learn by books at home;
> but the detail, the colour, the tone, the air,
> the life which makes it live in us,
> you must catch all these
> from those in whom it lives already.
> Whenever men are really serious about getting a good article,
> when they aim at something refined,
>   something really luminous,
>   something really large,
>   something choice, they go to another market;
>   they avail themselves,
> in some shape or other,
> of a visual method, the ancient method,
> of oral instruction,
> of present communication between man and man,
> of teachers instead of learning,
> of the personal influence of a master, and
>   the humble initiation of a disciple, and in consequence,
> of great centres of pilgrimage and throng,
> which such a method of education necessarily involves.
> This, I think, will be found to hold good
> in all those departments or aspects of society,
> which possess an interest sufficient to bind men together,
> or, to constitute what is called a 'world.'
>   It holds in the political world,
>   and in the high world,
>   and in the religious world;

and it holds also in the literary and
scientific world.
(*HS*)

In this specimen, we have Newman depending upon what Robert Brumbaugh's *Plato's Mathematical Imagination* made obvious—Plato always taught with visual aids. This "personal influence of a master" Newman here illustrated by the very choice of his own master—not Cicero in this instance, but Plato.

Thus Newman justified *organically* and *synthetically* the university as a place of influence where the faculty share the worlds they continue to develop for the good of their students and the non-academic world.

Conclusion

Newman's apologetic-autobiographical rhetoric enabled him to justify his claim that his whole life was that of a rhetorician in accord with his understanding of his principles and his use of methods derived from these in accord with his changing states of mind. Regardless of the tyranny of language and culture, Newman found a use of his subtlety to influence his own and future generations because he, as he claimed Shakespeare did, was able to overcome the limits of language and speak to a universal audience with a persuasion which grows with passing time and vain controversies which occasioned his writing. We as educators must be willing to assent to our assents and enter into our intellectual autobiographies in order that our students might overcome the temptation of anonymity in a society which long ago went the way of Bentham and "Americanization" at the expense of Coleridge and romanticism. In this way we can develop their personal influence within limitless social ties.

WORKS CITED

Houghton, Walter E. *The Art of Newman's Apologia.* New Haven: Yale UP, 1945.

Newman, John Henry. *Apologia Pro Vita Sua.* Ed. David J. DeLaura. New York: Norton, 1968.

—. *The Idea of a University.* Ed. Martin J. Svaglic. Notre Dame, IN: University of Notre Dame Press, 1960.

John Henry Newman:
The Rhetoric of the Real

David M. Whalen

"Thine eyes shall see the King in His beauty: they shall behold the land that is very far off." This is Isaiah, chapter thirty-three, verse seventeen, and it is the text which opens one of John Henry Newman's Advent sermons, "Unreal Words," from the *Parochial and Plain* collection. In its class this sermon is not an extraordinary one. It is buried within seventeen-hundred pages of kindred sermons, has not attracted particular attention to itself, and though I will focus upon this sermon, it does not really stand apart from its fellows in skill or excellence. This is the point. An unextraordinary sermon is especially useful in explicating what, for a particular author, constitutes major and seminal features of mind. Its very ordinariness is the source of its utility for study. But, of course, when the author is Newman, "ordinary" is by no means dull, mediocre, or uninstructive. Newman's skill as a homilist is well known (more by reputation than actual readership, today), and his ordinary prose is extraordinarily rich in thought and style—a veritable "garden of delights" for the habitual reader as well as the literary scholar. The sermon does possess a unique interest in words, language, and man's peculiar relation to them, but it does so within the context of Newman's frequent and consistent homiletic themes. One finds in it Newman's disdain for pretension and Victorian superficiality, his keen vision of psychological realities, his awareness of the significant political questions of the day and

217

his passion for integrity, or what he would call "sincerity." But
in a more broad and general sense, this sermon is typical of
Newman in that it deals explicitly with the issue of truth and
man in relation to the whole of reality. He opens with a
compressed observation:

> Before Christ came was the time of shadows, but when he
> came he brought truth as well as grace; and as He who is
> the Truth has come to us, so does He in return require that
> we should be true and sincere in our dealings with Him. To
> be true and sincere is really to see with our minds those
> great wonders which He has wrought in order that we might
> see them.
>
> (969)

Then, heralding the specific subject of this sermon, he says, "Our
professions, our creeds, our prayers, our dealings, our conversations, our arguments, our teaching must henceforth be sincere,
or, to use an expressive word, must be real" (970).

No reader of Newman can be unaware of the place "sincerity"
has in Newman's estimation, but here he suggests that sincerity
is—or can be—far more than the conventionally understood
honesty or earnestness; it is related to the intellect as well. We
are sincere, he says, when we see, realize, what God has made
for us to see. When we do see thus properly, our words are
sincere and partake of that reality created for our perception
and understanding. Our intellectual (as well as moral and
spiritual) advance is rooted in seeing things as they are, and this
conception is at the very heart of Newman's thought. He
dedicated his life to leading people to see things as they are, to
foster, in the words of A. Dwight Culler, "the full development
of man's own nature" (231), to reintegrate man with a reality
from which he had been partially severed. Newman's use of the
word "real" invokes its Latin original, "res,"—the thing, the
terminus, the object and end. What he calls "the real" is the

whole of reality, the Creator and the created, the world visible and invisible, seen and unseen.

Man, of course, is part of this reality and as such possesses a nature harmonious to both the Creator and the rest of the created order. Newman well knew that the oft-cited capacities of intellect, passions, and will, as well as the possession of body and soul, are not isolated aspects of human nature bound externally together like so many random volumes placed arbitrarily upon a shelf. His famous remark that "the whole man reasons" (and not merely some remote and procedural corner of the mind) illustrates his conception that man's various capacities are essentially integrated. This is all very well and good, but there is a flip side to this metaphysical coin. Both doctrinally and from long experience, Newman was all too aware that man was a fallen creature and that this fall had definite and immediate consequences in the daily conduct of life. Though originally integrated, the features or qualities of man suffered disorder as a result of the fall. Man was at war with himself. Intellect was clouded, passions were domineering, and will was in turns weakened and exaggerated. "Original justice," says St. Thomas Aquinas, "was forfeited through the sin of our first parent . . . so that all the powers of the soul are left, as it were, destitute of their proper order . . . which destitution is called a wounding of nature" (447). This fallen and disordered state drove a wedge of unreality, as it were, between man and the world. If truth is the "*adequatio rei et intellectus*," the proper relation of mind to thing, then not only death but also deception, untruth, insincerity and a kind of perceptual, intellectual unreality entered the world with sin. For Newman this was remedied, of course, primarily through sacramental cooperation with the divine intervention on our behalf. Thus man might be sanctified, saved by grace from the eternal consequences of original and actual sin. But this is not all. Even the redeemed carry about them the detritus of the fall—clouded mind, insubordinate passions and tendencies toward repeated falls. The work of man, then, was also a work of vigilance. As Newman notes in this sermon, "It takes a long time really to feel and understand things as they are; we learn to do so only gradually" (977). Man must strive, not only not to sin, but to ameliorate the continuing effects of the fall, even in the way we know things and express them. He must beware not only things immediately and morally deleterious but also the subtle dislocations and disintegrations of mind attendant upon his state; he must beware complacency, empty thoughts and empty words.

Newman reveals in this sermon that our very language and words partake of our fallen state and are prone to "unreality." Due in part to intellectual sloth, words and language are prone to being used lightly and without meaning in every level of discourse. This affliction of language runs very deep and has multifarious consequences. Linguist and novelist Walker Percy describes the affliction as a "hardening and closure" of a word which ultimately results in the "devaluation" of the word and even its referent (104-105). What today we would call cliches, catch-phrases (and even catch-ideas), jargon, and—in the religious sphere—pious platitudes, all result in a kind of mental paralysis. By our slipping thus over the surface of language and, I might add, the surface of thought, language ceases to facilitate and express man's relation to the surrounding reality and instead interposes itself and acts as an insulating influence between the person and that reality. The mind is numbed through the illusion created by vaguely acceptable, currently fashionable but vacuous phraseology. Just as man may be susceptible to sin yet not doomed to it, language may easily incline toward the ephemeral yet have the capacity of being "real." In fact, language can be more than real; if properly employed and directed toward good ends, it can even assist man in his constant work of becoming fully integrated with reality.

This has intriguing consequences for the nature and use of language and words. Though the word does not occur in the sermon, a "rhetoric" of reintegration, as it were, is inferred. In fact, rhetoric in its broadest and most esteemed sense is an enormous component of Newman's entire habit of mind. In a recent book Walter Jost advances the assertion that "Newman's intellectual stance is thoroughly and persistently rhetorical" (x). He is rhetorical not merely because of his successful and famous apologetic or polemical works. Rather, if Aristotle is correct in saying that rhetoric is "a faculty of observing in any given case the available means of persuasion" (1355b25), then rhetoric possesses an immediate and essential connection to Newman's exploration of real assents, conviction, and even the illative sense itself. In fact, it seems that Aristotle alludes even to the illative sense when he says, "it may also be noted that men have a sufficient natural instinct for what is true, and usually do arrive at the truth" (1355a15-18). Language and rhetoric can assist in man's integration, for a rhetorical exercise is expressly intended to produce real assents, or as Newman would say, make things "real" to an audience. It is no coincidence that Newman had a great faculty for doing just that, nor is my use of "integration" or "reintegration" merely coincidental with Newman's own proclivity for the word "integrity." The connection here between the work of rhetoric and our reintegration with reality suggests that rhetoric has a very wide and even necessary field of operation open to it in the work of redemption itself. Its domain exceeds simple exhortatory homiletics and extends so far as to be an aid to the assents of faith necessary for redemption; again, it is rhetoric that can make things real to an audience prone to languish in unreality.

The sermon under consideration treats of man afflicted by unreality, specifically of words and language. Quite properly, as shown, Newman begins by emphasizing the existence and availability of truth—no relativist he. But he quickly notes that we suffer a schism or gap in our grasp of truth, a gap which cannot be closed by pretending it doesn't exist. Typically, Newman dwells on sincerity: "[I]t need scarcely be said, nothing is so rare as honesty and singleness of mind; so much so, that a person who is really honest, is already perfect" (970). The moral emphasis here is not simply the attendant quality of sermon literature; Newman insists that utterances are human acts, they are deeds, and thereby we bear responsibility for them. As products of the human intellect and will, utterances pertain to our moral nature. There exists, then, the potential for false professions, statements of feeling or belief which are either deceptive or unrealized by the speaker. "To make professions is to play with edge tolls, unless we attend to what we are saying. Words have a meaning, whether we mean that meaning or not; and they are imputed to us in their real meaning. . . . [One] cannot frame a language for himself" (972).

Unreality can haunt language in a manner beyond the conventionally understood insincerities of its users; words become unreal when, for whatever reason, the intellect marshalling them is unacquainted with the words' terms or ends. "Of course," Newman amplifies, "it is very common in all matters, not only in religion, to speak in an unreal way; viz., when we speak on a subject with which our minds are not familiar" (972). Using a favorite example, Newman postulates the case of a "dim sighted man" declaiming upon color or visual proportions. "We should feel that he spoke on and from general principles, on fancy, or by deduction and argument, not from a real apprehension of the matters which he discussed. His remarks would be theoretical and unreal" (973). Note that two significant shifts have occurred here. Newman does not say that the remarks would be untrue. He does not insist that speaking "from general principles" or by "deduction" is necessarily false. He merely says it would be unreal, that is, unrealized or not fully grasped by the speaker. He has moved from denouncing overt falsities, false professions, to a notice of distance or removal on the part of a speaker from that which is spoken of, whether true or false. His concern over this distance or removal is obvious. The body of his works is marked by a distinct preference for the apprehension of things rather than deduction. Though—and this is a condition of critical importance—Newman vigorously describes and defends the role of abstract reasoning, his rhetorical sensitivity is to the acts of intellect rooted in thought less abstract, more immediate and, in a sense, more persuasive. However true, inference, induction, and deduction leave much of a man behind. The successful rhetorician is one who works that the audience might see and apprehend a thing fully, much as God has "wrought that we might see" (969). It is, as Aristotle says, a chief means of persuasion. The theologian says, "There is one God of three Divine Persons," but the rhetorician points to a clover and converts an island.

The second shift is away from the directly moral and religious sphere. Newman does not say the blind man sins by speaking of color, nor that the "man without ear" offends God by appraising "musical composition"—potentially making a fool of oneself is one thing, offending God is another. With the psychological sensitivity of a novelist, Newman explores the fallen psyche's travails in a perplexing world rather apart from any moral consideration. Clearly stimulated by his subject, Newman casts example after example of unreality of various sorts. "Another sort of unreality," he tells us, " . . . is instanced in the conduct of those who suddenly come into power or place. They affect a manner such as they think the office requires, but which is beyond them, and therefore unbecoming. They wish to act with dignity, and they cease to be themselves" (974). We are also told of men who "are set upon being eloquent speakers." "They use great words," he says, "and imitate the sentences of others; and they fancy that those whom they imitate had as little meaning as themselves. . ." (974). Reality of expression and sentiment is not achieved summarily. So deep is the mental confusion and limitation of experience consequent upon the fall that sometimes "real words" and feelings are well nigh impossible. In a poignant example, Newman admits that unreal speech is often all we have to offer:

> [M]any men, when they come near persons in distress and wish to show sympathy, often condole in a very unreal way. I am not altogether lying this to their fault; for it is very difficult to know what to do, when on the one hand we cannot realize to ourselves the sorrow, yet withal wish to be kind to those who feel it. A tone of grief seems necessary, yet (if so be) cannot under our circumstances be genuine.
> (974)

Not surprisingly, the unreality plaguing the individual will also plague the society. Corporate or public unreality is evident when bodies of people are asked to look at questions pertaining to specific departments of knowledge with which they are unfamiliar. "They look at them as infants gaze at the objects which meet their eyes, in a vague unapprehensive way, as if not knowing whether a thing is a hundred miles off or close at hand . . . " (973). This is the particular danger of democracies. Newman notes that in his day, all men are required to make judgments upon all matters, political, social, religious, despite the fact that they rarely have "exercised their minds upon the points in question" (973). Common sense can carry one a long way, Newman admits, but it is not all-powerful. Thus the judgments made upon such public matters are heavily dependent on fairly limited, usually rhetorically presented, criteria and information. Lamentably, the rhetorical art is easily abused in the public forum. Cicero warns that "if anyone neglect the study of philosophy and moral conduct, which is the highest and most honorable of pursuits, and devotes his whole energy to the practice of oratory, his civic life is nurtured into something

useless to himself and harmful to his country . . . " (3-5).
Rhetoric, too, can fall, can be debased. Though Aristotle enjoins
the rhetorician to learn how to argue upon both sides of a
question, it is "not in order that we may in practice employ it in
both ways (for we must not make people believe what is wrong),
but . . . that, if another man argues unfairly, we on our part may
be able to confute him" (1355a 30-35). All too often, another
man does argue unfairly, and then rhetoric does not bring the
real to the full apprehension of persons. It is made to dance and
frolic within the very gap between people and the real. It is
utilized to exploit the hollowing out of language and words for
political or ideological gain.[A]s all persons who attempt to gain
the influence of the people on their side know well) their
opinions must be purchased by interesting their prejudices or
fears in their favor;—not by presenting a question in its real or
true substance, but by adroitly coloring it, or selecting out of it
some particular point which may be exaggerated, and dressed
up, and be made the means of working on popular feelings. And
thus government, and the art of government becomes, as much
as popular religion, hollow and unsound (974). It is this use of
rhetoric which gives it a bad name. Huxley, when told he was
a rhetorician, replied that he would never "plaster the fair face
of truth with that pestilent cosmetic, rhetoric."—which, as
Chesterton points out, is as fine a piece of rhetoric as any (26).
But the imprecation is there, and it is now a commonplace that
"rhetoric" is insubstantial fluff, fluff employed to advance covert
designs upon an audience.

The particular motive behind this sermon is, of course,
specifically religious, and Newman's style intensifies as the
unreality of religious talk in Victorian society becomes his
immediate target. He is clearly irritated. The empty talk in
secular matters—sign of our fall and indication of our often
pitiable psychic dislocation—becomes consistently dangerous in
religious matters. The self-deception incurred by lightly tossing

about pious platitudes is difficult to expose and resistant to correction. Newman is famous for upbraiding comfortable Victorian society for its religious complacency, but his attempt to expose unreality of profession was more often than not akin to a voice in the wilderness. "Who, I?" was the overwhelming response of a society told it lacked faith. To assure itself, it merely had to call to mind its regular church attendance, ownership of the prayer book, payment for its pew. It is difficult to penetrate a superficiality which is both habitual and respectable. Likewise dangerous is the use of religious words for thaumaturgy. That is, sincere though the effort be, one does not create an effect or emotion merely by saying one has it. "[W]e ought to have our hearts penetrated with the love of Christ and full of self-renunciation; but that if they be not, professing that they are will not make them so" (975). Members of Victorian society all too frequently "have commonplaces in their mouths . . . they speak to clergymen in a professedly serious way, making remarks true and sound, and in themselves deep, yet unmeaning in their mouths; . . . or in low spirits or sickness they are led to speak in a religious strain as if it was spontaneous" (975). Newman's sense of social propriety was acute to the point of fussiness, but he does not accept "false professions" for propriety. The all-too hastily assumed religiosity of those thrust into the company of clergymen indicates cultural habits and phrases rendered unreal and superficially maintained.

Mere religiosity can pervade entire historical periods as well. Newman suggests that love can wax cold; the truths and expressions formulated in times of passion and zeal can become problematical for entire Churches when the originating zeal passes. Seen in Church discipline and ritual, the expressions and traditions gradually suffer a kind of distancing from those people perpetuating them. In part this is the well-known tendency of repetition to weaken original vigor or intensity—a verbal version of familiarity breeding contempt. But it extends to a deeper psychological level; love can cool, entire historical periods and geographical regions may wax or wane in their lively devotion to God, and when the natural consequences of repetition intersect with a kind of cultural religious malaise, the effect is the evacuation, the emptying out, of religious language. To revert to the original figure, religious language becomes remote, as it were, from those employing it; there is a gap, a kind of linguistic, psychological and spiritual crevasse separating the speaker and what is spoken, the perpetuator of the tradition and the tradition itself. Thus, in Newman's words, "unreality may steal over the Church itself" (977). Newman's considered response to a Church plagued by "unreality" and unreal words was to reanimate the faithful, to re-lnvigorate the Church with spiritual vigor and strength thus striking at the root of the original malaise. His perception of unreality as a kind of evacuating curse resultant from man's fall leads him to place emphasis on reanimation or realization of the tradition and its formulations. The temptation to adjust the language, to scrap the traditions, would be a false solution, a papering over the chasm without addressing its genuine cause. It would be a capitulation to the malaise. Realization of truths, rather than adjustment of their expression to fit our hollowed-out and imprecise conception of them, is just that peculiar strength of rhetoric—a strength to be placed in the service of spiritual reanimation.

Up to this point, Newman has been full of hard sayings. "Unreal words" are on every hand and exacerbate our fallen state. Devotional language seems almost too dangerous to employ for any but the saintly. What if we stand convicted of speaking "more than we feel?" Newman was ever the rhetorician, but as Henry Tristram, Placid Murray and others remind us, he was ever the pastor and priest as well (Murray 4-5). Newman has effectively made his point—he will therefore caution as to extremes, and assuage overly-anxious minds:

> Profession beyond our feelings is only a fault when we might help it;—when either we speak when we need not speak, or do not feel when we might have felt . . . . Persons are culpably unreal in their way of speaking, not when they say more than they feel, but when they say things different from what they feel.
>
> (977)

Or, more to the point, we should make an act of faith. "We even promise things greater than we can master, and we wait on God to enable us to perform them" (977).

But—this is a parochial sermon, not a theoretical disquisition—practical counsels for dealing with this unreality of language must be provided. Because of the practical nature or end of this discourse, that counsel is primarily negative. This too, however, displays a psychological and human perspicacity; a peculiar illness which perpetuates itself in a specific activity must first be confronted by abating, stopping, that activity. In true spiritual fashion which many a monk would recognize, Newman counsels: Hush. "Let us avoid talking, of whatever kind; whether mere empty talking, or censorious talking, or idle profession, or descanting upon Gospel doctrines, or the affectation of philosophy, or the pretence of eloquence" (978-79). Silence is a virtue not merely as it avoids untruth, but often even as regards truth itself. "There are solemn truths which need not be actually spoken, except in the way of creed or of teaching; but which must be laid up in the heart. That a thing is true, is no reason that it should be said, but that it should be done; that it should be acted upon; that it should be made our own inwardly" (978). To make something one's own, inwardly, is to bring the object of thought into a state of apprehension immediate and imaginatively striking. It is to make it real—not in and of itself, of course, for the creation of reality is the sole province of the Creator, but to make it real relative to ourselves.

Paradoxically, this is often effected by less talk, not more. It is telling that, as a shocked young observer reported, the one subject never discussed at the nightly chats in Newman's Oxford rooms was religion. The habit of unreal—specifically religious—speaking is first attacked by not speaking, by breaking that original habit of idle or empty talk and profession. It is not enough that the alcoholic try not to get drunk; he must banish the bottles from his house. When one must speak, Newman says, "aim at things and your words will be right without aiming. There are ten thousand ways of looking at this world, but only one right way. . . . Aim at looking at it in God's way. Aim at looking at this life as God looks at it" (978).

To aim at seeing things the way God sees them is to see them *sub specie aeternitatis*. But "under the aspect of eternity" means much more than simple "detachment" or even Newman's "Time is short, eternity is long" (978). To see as God sees, is to see things preeminently as they are. God, of course, can neither deceive nor be deceived. He suffers no gap or chasm between himself and reality, no disordering of faculties or hollowing out of word. And this brings us back to the fundamental note of this sermon, and indeed, of Newman's life's toil. God sees things as they are. Man is strangely capable of insulation, isolation from things as they are. He is capable of becoming numb to the significance that fills the world about him and is susceptible to the profoundest self-deception. The disorder of his being—the dislocation of intellect, passions, and will—is evidenced even in his use of language and the manner in which language can become an insulating layer of verbiage between the speaker and reality or truth. Unreal words, cliches and suchlike, interpose themselves, anesthetizing the intelligence and rendering it incapable of the nimble sensitivity required for life in a world complex and vibrant. This is the negative, the illness or problem. But the negative presupposes the positive. If God sees things as they are, and men often do not, then either men should despair or they should toil to cooperate with the divine intervention on their behalf. The intervention—supernatural, sacramental—is of primary importance; yet just as the fall resulted in natural defects, so can the natural order do its part in the reintegration of man. Rhetoric, when well used, can facilitate the full integration of man with the whole of reality by resensitizing us to words and language, specifically to the terms or termini of those words. Rhetoric can heal its own crippled components by making human intelligences fully apprehend the significance of utterances and words; it can restore us, in measure, to our language and its fullness. It can help us to reality by restoring to us our terms for dealing with reality.

I am fully aware that the ideas underlying Newman's approach to unreal words are anathema to much of the current world of linguistic thought. Theories which make principles of such things as "difference" and "absence" can only be hostile or contemptuous with regard to an idea of language based upon the dreaded "metaphysical presence." The very slippery surfaces which contemporary theorists codify (if I may be indulged a paradox) as "all we've got" are not, however, unrecognized by Newman. Quite the contrary. Newman's entire effort here is to describe the way in which words become empty and language subtly deceptive. In contrast to the view taken by some contemporary theorists, Newman regards this phenomenon in its broader and more nuanced relation to man's own nature, his intellect, and most particularly, his status as a fallen creature. Seen thus, the problem of the indeterminacy of language is just that—a problem, not a linguistic dead-end. It is susceptible to correction, emendation, reintegration. Unreal words can be made real through the proper exercise of the intellect and imagination. The patient Newman seeks to heal, our contemporaries often seek to bury, the one because he knows the source of the illness, the other because they do not acknowledge the existence of health. The use of language to reintegrate man with reality is neither a small purpose nor a small feat. As Newman indicates, it is a life-long process.   However, a world in which men are increasingly moved away from the invisible world—precisely that part of reality that gives proportion and meaning to the visible—a rhetoric of redemption is mandatory. To use his well-known terms, persons must be brought to assent, real assent, where the reality of utmost importance to them is known to the depths of their being. The knowledge must be realized, that is, not merely conceptual and abstract, but particular and personal, as God is both person and particular. Theological and philosophical demonstration can prove propositions, but it remains to the common language of men, to rhetoric, to bring those truths home. Unreal words are linguistic stumbling blocks, often arising out of intellectual sloth, and a fear of grappling with a reality not under our control. In the natural sphere it falls to rhetoric—in the case of this sermon even an ostensible occasion of rhetoric or oratory—to fortify man for his struggle, to whet his appetite for the real, and even to partially satisfy that appetite in weaving the fabric of life and consciousness into a piece with the created order. As Newman says, we must "Try to learn this language" (978).

WORKS CITED

Aristotle. *Introduction to Aristotle*. Ed. Richard McKeon. 2nd ed. Chicago: U of Chicago P, 1973.

Chesterton, G.K. *The Victorian Age in Literature*. 2nd ed. New York: Oxford UP, 1946.

Cicero. *De Inventione*. Trans. H.M. Hubbell. Loeb Classical Library. Ed. E.H. Warmington. Cambridge: Harvard UP, 1949.

Culler, A. Dwight. *The Imperial Intellect: A Study of Newman's Educational Ideal*. New Haven: Yale UP, 1955.

Murray, Placid. *Newman the Oratorian*. Leominster, Herefordshire, England: Fowler Wright Books Ltd., 1980.

Newman, John Henry. *Parochial and Plain Sermons*. San Francisco: Ignatius Press, 1987.

Percy, Walker. *Lost in the Cosmos*. New York: Farrar, Straus & Giroux, Inc.; New York: Washington Square Press, 1983.

Thomas Aquinas, St. *Summa Theologica*. Trans. Fathers of the English Dominican Province. 2nd ed. 22 vols. London: Burns Oates & Washbourne Ltd. , 1920. Vol. 7.

The Newman Connection:
Notional Assent and Real Assent in the Novels of Flannery O'Connor

Joseph H. Wessling

I

What constitutes religious belief? How is it related to reason? To feeling? Is there faith without good works? Are there good works without faith? Are belief and unbelief mutually exclusive? Such questions have been the subject of much theological discussion, especially during the past few centuries, and the problem of religious belief has been a major concern of literary artists such as Tennyson, Unamuno, Beckett, and Graham Greene. Of all of those creative artists who have explored questions of belief, one of the most complex and intriguing is Flannery O'Connor. Though she had no formal training in theology, O'Connor was an avid reader of a variety of theologians, both Catholic and non-Catholic, as well as of other important intellectuals such as Jacques Maritain and Francois Mauriac. In spite of her reputation for "orthodoxy," she showed more interest in the speculations of a Teilhard de Chardin than in the apologetics of a Chesterton, and she criticized her Church for "the lack of scholarship, the lack of intellectual honesty" (*Habit* 308). Because she is not overtly didactic and because her fictional believers are seldom educated or articulate, her theological themes are rarely explicit and must be inferred from the dramatic action and dialogue. Her letters and non-fiction prose shed valuable light upon these themes; still, much room is left for critical exploration.

It is not surprising, therefore, that much of the commentary on O'Connor is concerned with the theological aspects of her work. Her stories have been related to the thought of Eric Voegelin, Jacques Maritain, William Lynch, and many other religious thinkers, but, strangely, little reference is made by scholars to John Henry Newman, in whose work may be found an important key to the problems of belief and unbelief in O'Connor's fiction. Such recent works as John Desmond's *Risen Sons* (1987) and Marshall Bruce Gentry's *Flannery O'Connor's Religion of the Grotesque* (1986) make no mention of Newman. Nor is Newman mentioned in Marion Montgomery's invaluable *Why Flannery O'Connor Stayed Home* (1981). Kathleen Feeley's pioneering work *The Voice of the Peacock* (1972) only once quotes Newman, by way of Joseph Pieper, to the effect that truth must be approached with homage (74); and in Ralph G. Wood's illuminating *The Comedy of Redemption* (1988) Newman appears in only one sentence: "Like Cardinal Newman, Barth believes that 'mysticism begins in mist and ends in schism'" (74). There is in John May's *The Pruning Word* a mention of Hazel Motes's "notional assent to the limitation of the human condition which he will eventually convert into a real assent" (133), but May does not cite Newman as the source for these terms, nor does he use them to analyze the faith of Hazel or any other O'Connor character.

That O'Connor was familiar with Newman's thought is easily established. Her personal library contains four books by Newman (*The Development of Christian Doctrine, An Essay in Aid of a Grammar of Assent, Apologia pro Vita Sua,* and *Letters of John Henry Newman*) plus two books about Newman (Louis Bouyer's *Newman: His Life and Spirituality* and Sean O'Faolain's *Newman's Way*). Only *An Essay on the Develop-*

ment of Christian Doctrine and O'Faolain's book are devoid of the notations and markings which O'Connor was wont to make in her books (Kinney *passim*). Of four references to Newman in O'Connor's published letters, three are significant. In a letter to her anonymous correspondent "A" (13 July 1956), she writes: "The old man [Baron von Hugel] I think is the most congenial spirit I have found in English Catholic letters, with more to say, to me anyway, than Newman" (*Letters* 165). In view of favorable references elsewhere, this must be taken, not as a disparagement of Newman, but as a relegating of him to second place behind her favorite, von Hugel. In another letter to "A" (3 Oct. 1959), clearly in reference to the *Apologia*, O'Connor writes: "If Newman is a saint, his saintliness didn't destroy his scrupulous intellect or his finickiness and you'll have to accept him as a finicky saint" (*Habit* 352). So far as O'Connor's ideas on religious belief are concerned, the most significant mention of Newman appears in a letter to Alfred Corn (30 May 1962):

> Another [book to cultivate your Christianity] is Newman's *Grammar of Assent*. To find out about faith you have to go to people who have it and you have to go to the most intelligent ones if you are going to stand up intellectually to agnostics and the general run of pagans that you are going to find in the majority of people around you.
> (*Habit* 477)

It is clear from the above that O'Connor not only read Newman with sympathy and profit, but that she attached a particular value to *A Grammar of Assent*, which she knew not only directly but through Martin D'Arcy's *The Nature of Belief*, a revised edition of which she reviewed in January of 1959 (*The Presence of Grace* 67). D'Arcy is greatly indebted to Newman, and his book contains a long summary and detailed critique of *A Grammar of Assent*. This work by Newman provides an important key to belief and unbelief in the characters of Flannery O'Connor.

It must be noted that there is no way of proving that O'Connor was familiar with Newman's ideas on belief from the beginning of her writing career. The earliest reference to Newman in her published letters is August 9, 1955 (*Habit* 94), and the earliest reference to *A Grammar of Assent* is May 30, 1962 (*Habit*, 477). The copy of *A Grammar of Assent* in her personal library is a 1955 Image Book (Kinney 44). Did she know Newman's theory of belief when she was working on *Wise Blood* in 1946-1951? It is certainly possible but admittedly unproven. Nonetheless, the validity of Newman's theory as a key to O'Connor's fiction is not dependent upon her awareness of the theory. Regardless of when that awareness came about, it clearly struck a responsive chord.

A Grammar of Assent is a highly original work, concerned primarily with religious belief, but dealing, as it must, with general questions of epistemology. What is assent? How is it arrived at? How does it differ from inference? from certitude? from opinion? It is not necessary here to summarize the book as a whole, only to focus on the first four chapters, especially on the fourth, "Notional and Real Assent," wherein is to be found an important key to the nature of belief in O'Connor's characters. That she took particular interest in Newman's distinction between notional and real assent is shown by the fact that of the five marginal linings and five underlinings in her copy of the *Grammar*, nine are in this chapter, the tenth occurring in the Introduction by Etienne Gilson. Some propositions, Newman observes, are notional in character:

> Now there are propositions, in which one or both of the terms are common nouns, as standing for what is abstract, general, and non-existing, such as "Man is an animal, some men are learned, an Apostle is a creation of Christianity, a

line is length without breadth, to err is human, to forgive divine." These I shall call notional propositions, and the apprehension with which we infer or assent to them, notional.

(29)

Other propositions are real:

> And there are other propositions which are composed of singular nouns, and of which the terms stand for things external to us, unit and individual, as "Philip was the father of Alexander," "the earth goes round the sun," "the Apostles first preached to the Jews;" and these I shall call real propositions and their apprehension real.
>
> (29)

As notional and real apprehension differ in character, they also differ in forcefulness:

> Of these two modes of apprehending propositions, notional and real, real is the stronger, I mean by stronger more vivid and forcible. It is to be so accounted for the very reason that it is concerned with what is either real or taken for real; for intellectual ideas cannot compete in effectiveness with the experience of concrete facts.
>
> (31)

Just as propositions and their apprehensions may be notional or real, so too will be the assent to those propositions, and real assent is the more forceful.

> In its notional assents as well as in its inferences, the mind contemplates its own creations instead of things; in real, it is directed toward things, represented by the impressions which they have left on the imagination. These images,

> when assented to, have an influence both on the individual
> and on society, which mere notions cannot exert.
> (76)

For Newman, then, notional assents generally do not affect our conduct as real assents tend to do, and it is the latter that create "heroes and saints, great leaders, statesmen, preachers and reformers, the pioneers of discovery in science, visionaries, fanatics, knights-errants [sic], demagogues, and adventurers" (86).

The notional assent, then, is distinct from the real and, as Newman recognizes, can exist without it. John Stuart Mill had made the identical distinction eleven years earlier, though not so systematically and, of course, without Newman's terminology:

> All Christians believe that the blessed are the poor and
> humble, and those who are ill used by the world, that it is
> easier for a camel to pass through the eye of a needle than
> for a rich man to enter the kingdom of heaven; that they
> should judge not, lest they be judged; . . . They are not
> insincere when they say that they believe these things.
> They do believe them, as people believe what they have
> always heard lauded and never discussed. But in the sense
> of that living belief which regulates conduct, they believe
> these doctrines just up to the point to which it is usual to act
> upon them.
>
> (*On Liberty* 40)

Mill thus recognizes that notional assent can coexist with conduct inconsistent with it, because it is real assent ("living belief") which "regulates conduct."

Literature abounds with characters whose notional assents are not accompanied by real assents. Tolstoy's Ivan Ilych receives, upon graduation from law school, a medallion with the inscription *Respice finem* or "Consider death" (*The Death of Ivan*

Ilych 105). He wears it thereafter, indicating his notional assent to his own mortality, but lives with no real assent until he is stricken with terminal cancer. Face to face with death, he sees the falseness of the values he has lived for—power, wealth, status, decorum—and he must come to terms, not only with his impending death, but with a life wrongly lived. Clearly, the notional assent to his mortality had existed without the real.

But can real assent exist without the notional? I suggest that it can and cite two literary works as examples. Mark Twain's Huck Finn must decide whether to allow Jim to be returned as a runaway slave or to help him to freedom. He *knows* (notionally) that returning a slave is the "Christian" course of action, having been taught about the right of private property. But Huck's real assent is to Jim's freedom, and he voices his decision in the words "All right, then, I'll go to hell" (Clemens 168). We recognize Huck as a Christian who believes himself to be an apostate from Christianity. A second example is the village priest of Unamuno's *St. Emmanuel the Good Martyr* who is acclaimed by his parishioners to be a saint and a man of great faith, but whose terrible secret, known only to the narrator Angela Carballino and her atheist brother Lazarus, is that he does not believe in an afterlife. Knowing that for the villagers, only belief in an afterlife makes earthly life bearable, Don Emmanuel nourishes in the villagers a faith he does not share and lives his life in agony on the cross of a divided self. But in Angela's view, Don Emmanuel—and Lazarus too—actually believed while thinking they did not believe (Unamuno 105). The validity of Angela's analysis must be the subject of another study, but, without using Newman's terminology, Angela is saying that real assent existed in the absence of the notional.

II

This paper will focus, not upon notional Christians, which are to be found in O'Connor's stories just as they are found in life, but upon the protagonists of O'Connor's two short novels, *Wise Blood* and *The Violent Bear It Away*—characters whose flights into notionality are futile efforts to shake off their real assents.

Wise Blood, in spite of its grotesque elements, is in many ways a clear, straight-forward novel, its plot line devoid of the kind of ambiguity that characterizes such explorations of sin and guilt as Hawthorne's "Young Goodman Brown." The basic narrative structure is a two-fold pattern of exile and return. Hazel Motes (known as Haze), grandson of a circuit preacher "with Jesus hid in his head like a stinger" (9-10), is given a sense of guilt and a fear of the Lord by his stick-wielding mother in his spiritual home of Eastrod, Tennessee. "East" suggests birth or rebirth, and, in a religious context, resurrection; "rod" suggests a sceptre (hence a place where spiritual values rule), but it also suggests *rood*, meaning 'cross.' Thus Eastrod designates the city of God and constitutes one pole in what Northrop Frye would call the dialectic of two cities. Haze's first exile into the city of bondage (of enslavement to false gods) is a four-year stint in the army, where he clings doggedly to his chastity, safeguarding a soul which his scornful, brothel-bound companions tell him he does not have. Haze wants to believe them and, having time to study the matter, manages to convert himself "to nothing instead of to evil" (12). Upon discharge from the army, this self-convert to nothingness ironically finds nothingness back in Eastrod. The family home is only a shell of a house and has been looted of all except his mother's chifforobe, in each drawer of which Haze leaves a note threatening death to anyone who takes it.

The second city of bondage is Taulkinham in which Haze intends to "do some things I never done before" (5) and to preach his new Church Without Christ. His gospel is a logical series of denials:

> I'm going to preach that there was no Fall because there was nothing to fall from and no Redemption because there was no Fall and no Judgment because there wasn't the first two.
> (59)

His nihilism is complete: " there's only one truth and that is that there's no truth" (93). Taulkinham has everything one might look for in a modern Babylon. Mrs. Leora Watts's "friendliest bed in town" is the fitting altar on which Haze sacrifices his virginity. On Thursday night—the secular sabbath—all the stores stay open, and the people, not noticing the stars overhead, direct their worshipful gazes into those secular tabernacles, the store windows, where the sacred objects of a commercialized culture are displayed for adoration. Religion especially is commercialized in Asa Hawks and later in the team of Hoover Shoats and Solace Layfield. Mindless animality is found in Enoch Emery, and "adjustment to the modern world" (61) in Sabbath Lily Hawks who is "pure filth right down to the guts" and likes herself that way (86). That vice is not merely random but institutionalized is reflected in the sadistic behavior of Taulkinham's police, who do wanton violence to Haze's car and later to his person. It might seem that in so depraved a city Haze's preaching (no sin, no guilt, no need for Jesus) would fall on welcoming ears. Instead, his exhortations are ignored by the many, appraised for their marketability by Hoover Shoats, and misunderstood by one insufferable fool (Enoch), who tries to play Sancho Panza to Haze's Don Quixote. Why does Haze not get at least an affirming nod? It is not simply a matter of preaching to the converted—of carrying coals to Newcastle. It is that the lukewarm sinners of Taulkinham, who do not take religious belief seriously, find it incomprehensible or irrelevant that someone would take unbelief seriously.

Eventually, Hazel Motes, disillusioned by experience, blinds himself with lye and quietly spends his few remaining consumptive days with barbed wire around his chest and stones and broken glass in his shoes in order "to pay . . . it don't make any difference for what" (115). What his landlady entertains as an amusing notion is metaphoric truth: he has been "going backward to Bethlehem" (113), or, in the words of Mrs. Hitchcock earlier in the novel "going home" (3, 5).

The events which lead up to this denouement are easily identified, but the paradox of Hazel Motes is not easily understood. O'Connor has called him a "Christian *malgre lui*" a Christian in spite of himself. She does not simply mean that a series of reversals have driven him back to being the Christian he once was. She means that in some sense he never ceased to be a Christian:

> That belief in Christ is to some a matter of life and death has been a stumbling block for readers who would prefer to think it a matter of no great consequence. For them, Hazel Motes' integrity lies in his trying with such vigor to get rid of the ragged figure who moves from tree to tree in the back of his mind. For the author, his integrity lies in his not being able to. Does one's integrity ever lie in what one is not able to do? I think that usually it does, for free will does not mean one will but many wills conflicting in one man.
>
> (*Mystery and Manners* 114-5)

Clearly, O'Connor sees Haze as accepting Christ even while denying Him, and doing so with integrity. Her theory of multiple wills would allow for a vacillation in one's relationship to Christ but hardly an "integrity." How can a Christian identity coexist with a formal and persistent renunciation of Christ?

If we apply Newman's theory to *Wise Blood*, the apparent contradiction in O'Connor's assessment of Hazel Motes is resolvable. Haze responds to and acts upon real apprehensions and real assents. His childhood penance of placing stones in his shoes is rooted in real guilt for having entered the forbidden ground of the side show and looked on a naked woman (32-3). His later excursion into apostasy is not only Christ-haunted; it is Christ-driven. Haze is fleeing from the real Jesus, who would lead him where he fears to tread.

> He knew by the time he was twelve years old that he was going to be a preacher. Later he saw Jesus move from tree to tree in the back of his mind, a wild ragged figure motioning him to turn around and come off into the dark where he was not sure of his footing, where he might be walking on the water and then suddenly know it and drown.
>
> (10)

"From tree to tree" is clearly from cross to cross—the tortuous path of sainthood, and Haze refuses the call. He can avoid Jesus if he has no soul to be saved and no sin to be saved from. So Haze constructs a theology of denial. While in the army, he "had all the time he could want to study his soul and assure himself that it was not there" (12). But his theology remains strictly notional, and religion, Newman declares, must be rooted in realities: "To give a real assent is an act of religion; to give a notional is a theological act" (93). Haze's Church Without Christ has no reality to which he can point. He calls for a "new jesus . . . one that's all man, without blood to waste" (72), but when Hoover Shoats wants to meet the new jesus, Haze acknowledges that "There's no such thing as any new jesus. That ain't anything but a way to say something" (81). The dried-up mummy which Enoch offers as the new jesus is smashed and thrown out by Haze, who has seen it through his mother's glasses—through the eyes of a faith he thinks he no longer has. Haze's heart is never given to nihilism, and, though he moves among people who are in bondage to the false gods of Taulkinham—lust, avarice, sloth, pride, power—his allegiance is to something else: "I don't want nothing but the truth!" (107). In his fanatical devotion to truth, Haze engages not only in habitually rude speech but in some reprehensible physical behavior: hitting Enoch with a rock, contemptuously exposing the fake blind man, slamming his car door on the thumb of a charlatan evangelist, and brutally murdering the charlatan's pathetic associate, telling him "Two things I can't stand, . . . a man that ain't true and one that mocks what is" (115). Though Haze's behavior is chronically un-Jesus-like, he has not completely broken with that Jesus who proclaimed himself to be the Truth and who drove the money-changers from the temple. Haze's integrity, O'Connor has observed, lies "in what he is not able to do" (*Mystery and Manners* 115). He is not able to lie (except to himself), he is not able to commercialize his preaching, and he is not able to embrace the false values of Taulkinham. The one concrete symbol of the Church Without Christ is his broken-down Essex, symbolic of the rootlessness of his new religion and (once in a dream) of death in life, a coffin for the living (91-2). When a police officer pushes his car over an embankment, Haze has his epiphany. The car comes to rest upside-down in a partially burned wasteland, presided over by a death-symbolizing buzzard. Haze in his own bizarre way now heeds the call of "that wild ragged figure motioning him to turn around and come off into the dark where he was not sure of his footing . . . " (11). In his self-blinding and the harsh penances of his last days, he is giving a very real assent to his need to atone for real sins. The wise blood that Enoch only thought he had, and which Haze had succeeded only partially in damming, is now flowing freely. That it flows at all is due to the persistence of that ragged figure. That it overflows into self-mutilation and not into "good works" is due to Haze's flawed humanity. His death, hastened by a gratuitous blow of a policeman's billy, completes his release from a world which had become no more than the stage of his voluntary tribulations.

Not all critics have an optimistic view of the novel's ending. Andre Bleikasten gives *Wise Blood* a Freudian reading and sees Haze's final state as an "identification with the dead mother"—an "unconditional surrender to parental powers." For Bleikasten, his self-blinding and other penitential acts constitute a "frenzy of masochism and self-destruction" (147-50). Francis Kunkel views Haze's final state as one of "ascetic solipsism. . . . There is room for only one Jesus and the historical Jesus must abdicate so that Hazel Motes may become the new jesus for his new Church Without Christ" (147).

Such pessimistic interpretations are difficult (perhaps impossible) to refute, for, though it is easy enough to show that such readings are alien to O'Connor's intent and to her theological vision, the reader is under no obligation to make her understanding of the story the reader's own. One problem is the very limited point of view from which we witness Haze's sightless last days. We have the musings of Haze's landlady, Mrs. Flood, who is so locked into a cold, calculating materialism that she finds the unworldly Haze a complete enigma. We have Haze's behavior (as noted by Mrs. Flood), and we have the few words that the landlady is able to get out of him. This problem is compounded by the fact that Haze is not truly articulate (he talks *at* people rather than converses with them) and he has a notably limited capacity for self-understanding. Frederick Asals has noted rightly that O'Connor's characters generally are "among the least introspective in modern fiction" ("The Double in Flannery O'Connor's Stories" 49). Nonetheless, these few words spoken by the blinded Haze should be enough for us.

> "Mr. Motes," she said that day, when he was in her kitchen
> eating his dinner, "what do you walk on rocks for?"
> "To pay," he said in a harsh voice.
> "Pay for what?"
> "It don't make any difference for what," he said. "I'm
> paying."
>
> (125)

Haze's penance and his limited explanation of it recall for the
reader his boyhood act of walking with stones in his shoes for a
mile and thinklng "that ought to satisfy Him" (36). To one who
subscribes to the theological concept of atonement, Haze's
behavior may be extreme but hardly senseless and it even
constitutes a "good work." The interpretation most consistent
with the text is not that Haze has made "an unconditional
surrender to parental powers," or that he has made himself the
new jesus, but that he has made an unconditional surrender to
the Jesus of his spiritual heritage—to that "wild ragged figure
motioning to him to turn around and come off into the dark
where he was not sure of his footing" (11). Whatever the
reader's religious or non-religious orientation may be, that Jesus
is a reality to Haze, whose surrender is an act of real assent,
and real assent, says Newman, produces among other things
saints and fanatics (GA 86). "Saints" and "fanatics"—the terms
are not mutually exclusive. Joyce Carol Oates provides an apt
metaphor: "[O'Connor's] perverted saints are Kierkegaardian
knights of the 'absurd' for whom ordinary behavior is impossible"
(53). Hazel Motes is a striking example of such a knight, as is
Francis Marion Tarwater, to whom we now turn our attention.

O'Connor's second and last novel, *The Violent Bear It Away*,
published in 1960, eight years after *Wise Blood* and four years
before her death, shows a consistency of vision with the earlier
work. In the backwoods of Georgia, old Mason Tarwater, great
uncle of Francis Marion Tarwater, has raised the boy, now age

fourteen, to carry on the work of the Lord in his stead—to be an Elisha to his Elijah. Young Tarwater has been entrusted with two specific assignments: to give old Mason a proper Christian burial when the time comes and to baptize his idiot cousin Bishop, son of the boy's rationalistic, atheistic uncle, Rayber. Mason had made several unsuccessful trips to the city to baptize Bishop; now the baton has been passed to the boy. It is a mission that Tarwater consciously resists, but ultimately fulfills without intending to, becoming a baptizer *malgre lui.* In contrast to Hazel Motes, who turns from Jesus, driven by fear of his own sinfulness and fear of total commitment, Tarwater is driven by pride and by the Rayber within. The boy would welcome an illustrious prophetic career, but he rebels at being a minor prophet's errand boy and at dealing with God through intermediaries.

> The boy doubted very much that his first mission would be to baptize a dim-witted child. "Oh no it won't be," he said. "He don't mean for me to finish up your leavings. He has other things in mind for me." And he thought of Moses who struck water from a rock, of Joshua who made the sun stand still, of Daniel who stared down lions in the pit.
> "It's no part of your job to think for the Lord," his great-uncle said. "Judgment may rack your bones."
> (335)

To his great uncle's repeated reminders regarding Bishop, the boy's response had been constant: "I take my orders from the Lord, . . . not from you" (379).

When Mason Tarwater dies at the breakfast table in his eighty-fifth year, the boy knows from repeated instructions that he is to dig a grave ten feet deep and bury the old man with a cross at his head. That he never completes this task is due in part to the sheer physical difficulty of digging in that stony soil, but also in part to the rationalizing voice of the unseen "stranger," the "friend," who is "digging the grave along with him" (336 ff.). This other voice, which begins as his own voice but "sounded like a stranger's voice" (336) becomes detached and engages in dialogue with young Tarwater. The stranger is clearly a double figure: "Only every now and then it sounded like a stranger's voice to him. He began to feel that he was only just now meeting himself, . . ." (352). The voice has at least a two-fold identity. First it is the Rayber side of Tarwater, the rational side inclined to deny all mystery, suppress all emotion, and dehumanize the individual by reducing his wholeness to accommodate abstract categories. The stranger argues that "any cross set up in 1952 would be rotted out by the time the Day of Judgment comes in" (352), that "the schoolteacher wouldn't consider for a minute that on the last day all bodies marked with crosses will be gathered" (345), and that burning the old man would be a lot easier than all this digging (345). Secondly, the voice is the boy's darker self, his devil within: "Look at the big prophet, the stranger jeered, and watched him from the shade of the speckled tree shadows. Let me hear you prophesy something" (353). "Speckled tree shadows" susgests the serpent in the Garden of Eden, and the jeering tone is commonly associated with the devil, whose existence the stranger denies (354). Young Tarwater's rational (*notional*) self wins out, and after sleeping off a drunk he burns the house, believing the body of his uncle (now buried by the Negro Buford) is still within.

Tarwater sets out for the city home of Rayber and Bishop, proud and defiant, determined not to baptize the child. He is the notional prophet, equating prophecy with heroic status and with a direct call from God: "When the Lord's call came, he wished it to be a voice from out of a clear and empty sky, the trumpet of the Lord God Almighty, untouched by any fleshly hand or breath" (343). Moreover, prophets are not called to such menial tasks as digging a grave or baptizing an idiot child.

Tarwater's trip to the city is an excursion into a world of notionality. He catches a ride with a salesman, Meeks, who "couldn't sell a copper flue to a man [he] didn't love . . . . He said love was the only policy that worked 95% of the time" (362). Meeks confirms Tarwater's rationalization that "You don't owe the dead anything" and expands it: "And that's the way it ought to be in this world—nobody owing nobody nothing" (362). Meeks preaches a morality of expediency: "I'm not going to tell you not to lie . . . don't lie when you don't have to. Else when you have to, nobody'll believe you" (380). Finding Tarwater stubborn and irrational, he concludes that the boy "won't come to no good end" (384).

After the initial shock of seeing Tarwater at his door wears off, Rayber generously admits the boy to his home. The former is a splendid example of notional man—of what Marion Montgomery, following Eric Voegelin, would call a modern (or secular) gnostic (*passim*). Rayber has complete faith in the power of human reason to understand and mold reality. O'Connor presents him much more sympathetically than she does her more self-seeking or cynical rationalists (Julian Chestny, Shepherd, Meeks), and, though he has an affinity to certain Hawthorne characters grown monstrously rational (Ethan Brand, Aylmer), Rayber makes genuine attempts to do good in the world, however unsuccessful the attempts. His efforts on behalf of the father Tarwater never knew were sincere though they led to the father's suicide (392). His efforts to help Tarwater are likewise sincere. But he has deliberately suppressed his emotional side, though with limited success.

> moments would still come when, rushing from some inexplicable part of himself, he would experience a love for [Bishop] so outrageous that he would be left shocked and depressed for days, and trembling for his sanity.
> (401)

Joyce Carol Oates sees in Rayber a "quite justified terror of the Unconscious—he must act out of his thinking, calculating, mechanical ego simply in order to resist the gravity that threatens to carry him out of himself; otherwise, he will become another 'fanatic,' another victim of that love that is hidden in the blood, . . " (44). In the binary opposition of energy and control, Rayber has opted for control—control of self and control of others.

Tarwater, unsophisticated as he is, knows this opposition well from his uncle's indoctrination: "'It was me could act,' the old man said, 'not him [Rayber]'" (379). The boy later echoes his great uncle in his taunting of Rayber, who had confessed to an abortive attempt to drown Bishop: "'I ain't like you. All you can do is think what you would have done if you had done it. Not me. I can do it. I can act'" (451). Tarwater's notion is a simple one; Newman had a deeper insight:

> The heart is commonly reached, not through the reason, but through the imagination, by means of direct impressions, by the testimony of facts and events, by history, by description. Persons influence us, voices melt us, looks subdue us, deeds inflame us. . . . No one, I say, will die for his own calculations: he dies for realities.
>
> (*GA* 89)

Tarwater, already influenced by his uncle's version of facts and events, will find himself melted by the voice of a child preacher (411-16), subdued by the look of Bishop (427), and inflamed by a homosexual rape (468-73). Rayber, even when he realizes that out on the dark lake Tarwater is drowning Bishop, is trapped in his own psychic paralysis.

What Rayber can do is to intellectualize, to deal in abstract categories, and when such intellectualizing becomes the chief mode of engagement with others, it dehumanizes both the knower and the known. Tarwater has heard again and again his great uncle's enraged account of being the subject of a scientific study published by Rayber in "that schoolteacher magazine"—a study which reduced his prophetic calling to a fixation (341). "He felt he was tied hand and foot inside the schoolteacher's head, a space as bare and neat as the cell of the asylum, and was shrinking, drying up to fit it" (378). It is the fate from which he is proud to have saved young Tarwater. But the boy is a doubter, and on the way to the city he tells Meeks, "My great-uncle learnt me everything but first I have to find out how much of it is true" (380). The boy learns very quickly that one thing the old man was right about was Rayber, who sees Tarwater as raw material to be molded into a pattern that Rayber "held fully developed in his mind" (388). He also views the boy as an object for scientific study: "Rayber had intended to keep notes on him and write up his most important observations . . ." (399). The uncle's self-image—"sympathetic, knowing, uniquely able to understand" (423)—and his mechanistic view that everyone's conduct is determined by certain laws (452) lead him to make arrogant, counterproductive statements to his nephew—"I can read you like a book!" (438)—and yet be confident of success, thinking that the boy "could not escape knowing that there was someone who knew exactly what went on inside him . . ." (446). Rayber, who has no respect for the mystery of the universe, will not allow that each human person is an unfathomable mystery, not to be gotten inside anyone's head, not to be reduced to mechanical laws. Tarwater is as enraged at this dehumanization as was his great uncle, and a contest of wills develops, which culminates in Tarwater's deliberately drowning Bishop, thereby showing that he can *act*, in contrast to Rayber whose nerve failed in his own attempt to drown the child. But Tarwater, even in the act of murder, reveals a Hazel Motes-like integrity shown in what he is not able to do: he is not able to refuse his prophetic assignment. Involuntarily, he pronounces the words of baptism over the drowning Bishop. At this point, Tarwater has the second of four key epiphanies. The first had occurred when, upon arrival at Rayber's home, he caught sight of Bishop: "Then the revelation came, . . . He knew that he was called to be a prophet and that the ways of his prophecy would not be remarkable . . . . He tried to shout, 'NO!' but it was like trying to shout in his sleep" (388-9). Though he cannot deny the call, he manages for a time to ignore it. His drowning-baptizing of Bishop brings on the second epiphany: "He knew with an instinct as sure as the dull mechanical beat of his heart, . . . that he was headed for everything the old man had prepared him for, . . . " (456). But, though the boy has defeated his uncle Rayber, he has not overcome his shadow self, the Rayber within. He hitches a ride with a truck driver to whom he confesses the baptism-drowning, but rationalizes: "The words just come out of themselves but it don't mean nothing. You can't be born again. . . . I had to prove I wasn't no prophet and I've proved it" (458). When he is put out of the truck, he continues his journey homeward—to "where he could begin to live his life as he had elected it" (463). When he is drugged and raped by a man in a lavender and cream car, he is aroused to prophetic fury even though he is still resisting the call. He sets fire to the scene of his pollution—an act of ritual purification—and makes his way to the forked tree through which he can see the charred ruins beside which his great uncle's chimneys "stood like grieving figures" (474). When his "friend" (the "stranger," his double) whispers "Go down and take it, . . . it's ours" (475), the double's presence becomes "as pervasive as an odor, . . . a violet shadow hanging around his shoulders" (475). His shadow self merges with the lavender-and-cream rapist, and Tarwater, recognizing that shadow for the first time, begins building a wall of fire between himself and his grinning double. It is his third epiphany, and it prepares him for the fourth. Descending to the clearing, which had been his home, he finds that the corn the old man had planted has been freshly plowed. He finds also his uncle's grave with a cross at its head. Buford is there with a rebuke and an explanation: "It's owing to me he's resting there. I buried him while you were laid out drunk. It's owing to me his corn has been plowed. It's owing to me the sign of the Saviour is over his head" (477). Buford has finished Tarwater's leavings. Both commands of the prophet have been fulfilled, the one by Tarwater involuntarily, the second by Buford in his stead. The shock triggers a vision: the boy sees a multitude being fed from one basket, and old Mason Tarwater is among them, hungry for the Bread of Life. The boy suddenly realizes that it is his hunger too. His gaze turns to the treeline which is now blazing with the fire he had set.

> He knew that this was the fire that had encircled Daniel, that had raised Elijah from the earth, that had spoken to Moses and would in an instant speak to him. He threw himself to the ground and with his face against the dirt of the grave, he heard the command. GO WARN THE CHILDREN OF GOD OF THE TERRIBLE SPEED OF GOD'S MERCY. The words were as silent as seeds opening one at a time in his blood.
>
> (478)

The silent opening of seeds is a far cry from the trumpet call Tarwater had demanded, but he heeds the call: "His singed eyes, black in their deep sockets, seemed already to envision the fate that awaited him but he moved steadily on, his face set toward the dark city, where the children of God lay sleeping" (479).

The boy who returns to the city is a much humbled prophet. Gone is the illusion of grandeur. Gone is the demand for a fanfare of trumpets. He has been brought low to the earth of his great-uncle's grave by devastating visitations of God's mercy. He can now speak about that mercy with authority to the children of God. Will they turn from their evil ways as did the people of Nineveh? We have no reason to expect it. O'Connor did not expect it: "The children of God I daresay will dispatch him pretty quick" (*Habit* 342). Tarwater does not expect it. He knows, no doubt, that more prophets died in the lions' dens than survived them and he "envisions the fate" that awaits him. But, however his mission turns out, Tarwater's assent to his Christian calling is real, his flight into notional denial at an end. Was this real assent always present, even when it was being denied? The involuntary baptism of Bishop sugsests that it was. So too do certain passages in the text.

> Although Tarwater claimed to believe nothing the old man had taught him, Rayber could see clearly that there was still a *backdrag of belief* [italics mine] and fear in him keeping his responses locked.
>
> (402)

> [said Rayber,] "Children are cursed with believing."
> The boy recognized the sentence. "Some ain't," he said.
> The schoolteacher smiled thinly. "And some who think they aren't are," he said.
>
> (436)

Tarwater, like Hazel Motes, emerges in the novel as a Christian *malgre lui*. He had submerged his real assent as forcefully as he had submerged Bishop, but it rose up to overwhelm him.

III

This paper has focused upon just two of O'Connor's stories and upon Newman's distinction between notional assent and real assent as a key to the nature of belief and unbelief in certain characters. Other characters in other stories invite a similar analysis. (Mrs. May in "Greenleaf" is an obvious

candidate.) Moreover, it should be noted that the distinction
between notional assent and real assent is not relevant only to
religious belief. In "Everything That Rises Must Converge," the
dispute between Mrs. Chestny and Julian over whether true
culture is in the heart or in the head (489) is an opposition of
the real and the notional, though the issue is not one of religious
belief specifically. One great irony of the story is that Mrs.
Chestny does not realize how much her culture is rooted in the
notional and Julian does not realize that his conduct is less
governed by reason than he thinks it is.

In short, Newman's distinction between notional assent and
real assent has much further relevance to the fiction of Flannery
O'Connor and to that of others than has been touched upon in
this article, whether those others be familiar with Newman's
thought or not. Just as a Freudian interpretation does not
depend upon the creative writer's knowledge of Freud, so too
Newman's theory of assent can illuminate the work of writers
unfamiliar with it. His theory is a key to a better understanding of many fictional characters and hence to a better self-understanding for anyone able to recognize in himself/herself a little
of Francis Marion Tarwater, perhaps even a little of Hazel
Motes.

Works Cited

Asals, Frederick. "The Double in Flannery O'Connor's Stories." *The Flannery O'Connor Bulletin* 9 (1980): 49-86.

Bleikasten, Andre. "The Heresy of Flannery O'Connor." *Critical Essays on Flannery O'Connor.* Ed. Melvin J. Friedman and Beverly Lyon Clark. Boston: G. K. Hall & Co., 1985. 138-158.

Clemens, Samuel Langhorne. *The Adventures of Huckleberry Finn.* New York: W. W. Norton & Co., Inc., 1962.

D'Arcy, Martin. *The Nature of Belief.* London: Sheed and Ward, 1931.

Desmond, John F. *Risen Sons: Flannery O'Connor's Vision of History.* Athens: U of Georgia P, 1987.

Feeley, Kathleen. *The Voice of the Peacock.* New Brunswick: Rutgers UP, 1972.

Gentry, Marshall Bruce. *Flannery O'Connor's Religion of the Grotesque.* Jackson: UP of Mississippi, 1986.

Hawthorne, Nathaniel. *The Complete Novels and Selected Tales of Nathaniel Hawthorne.* Ed. Norman Holmes Pearson. New York: The Modern Library, 1965.

Kinney, Arthur F. *Flannery O'Connor's Library: Resources of Being.* Athens: U of Georgia P, 1985.

Kunkel, Francis L. *Passion and the Passion: Sex and Religion in Modern Literature.* Philadelphia: The Westminster Press, 1975.

May, John. *The Pruning Word.* Notre Dame: U of Notre Dame P, 1976.

Mill, John Stuart. *On Liberty.* New York: W. W. Norton & Co., Inc., 1975.

Montgomery, Marion. *Why Flannery O'Connor Stayed Home.* LaSalle, IL: Sherwood Sugden & Co., 1981.

Newman, John Henry. *A Grammar of Assent*. New York: Doubleday & Co., Inc., 1955.

Oates, Joyce Carol. "The Visionary Art of Flannery O'Connor." *Flannery O'Connor*. Ed. Harold Bloom. New York: Chelsea House Publishers, 1986.

O'Connor, Flannery. *Collected Works*. New York: The Library of America, 1988. All references to O'Connor's fiction are to this edition.

—. *The Habit of Being*. Ed. Sally Fitzgerald. New York: Farrar, Straus, and Giroux, 1979.

—. *Mystery and Manners*. Ed. Sally and Robert Fitzgerald. New York: Farrar, Straus, and Giroux, 1969.

—. *The Presence of Grace*. Comp. Leo J. Zuber. Ed. Carter W. Martin. Athens: U of Georgia P, 1983.

Tolstoy, Leo. *The Death of Ivan Ilych and Other Stories*. New York: New American Library, 1960.

Unamuno, Miguel de. *Saint Emmanuel the Good Martyr* in *Abel Sanchez and Other Stories*. Trans. Anthony Kerrigan. South Bend: Gateway Editions, Ltd., 1956.

Wood, Ralph C. *The Comedy of Redemption*. Notre Dame: U of Notre Dame P, 1988.

Index

ROMAN CATHOLIC STUDIES

DATE DUE			
			Printed in USA